# Mathew Brady

By the same author

*The Explorer King: Adventure, Science, and the Great Diamond Hoax—*
*Clarence King in the Old West*
*A Certain Somewhere: Writers on the Places They Remember* (editor)

# Mathew Brady

*Portraits of a Nation*

ROBERT WILSON

B L O O M S B U R Y

NEW YORK • LONDON • NEW DELHI • SYDNEY

Published by Bloomsbury USA, New York

All papers used by Bloomsbury USA are natural, recyclable products made from wood grown in well-managed forests. The manufacturing processes conform to the environmental regulations of the country of origin.

LIBRARY OF CONGRESS CATALOGING-IN-PUBLICATION DATA

Wilson, Robert, 1951 February 21–
Mathew Brady : portraits of a nation / Robert Wilson.—First U.S. edition.
pages cm
Includes bibliographical references and index.
ISBN 978-1-62040-203-0 (hardback)
1. Brady, Mathew B., approximately 1823–1896.   2. Photographers—
United States—Biography.   3. United States—History—Civil War,
1861–1865—Photography.   I. Title.
TR140.B7W55 2013
770.92—dc23
[B]
2013016928

First U.S. edition 2013

1 3 5 7 9 10 8 6 4 2

Typeset by Westchester Book Group
Printed and bound in the U.S.A. by Thomson-Shore Inc., Dexter, Michigan

For Martha, Matt, Cole, and Sam

"Mr. B is a capital artist, and deserves every encouragement. His pictures possess a peculiar life-likeness and air of resemblance not often found in works of this sort."

—Walt Whitman, 1846

# *Contents*

# *"Photo by Brady"*

I n the first decades after the invention of photography, the sun was often credited as the author of a photograph. Sunlight was required to expose the metal plates on which images were fixed in daguerre-otype, the first widely used photographic process in the United States, and the sun was necessary in all the processes that followed until artificial light came into wide use in the 1880s. Adequate lighting was so crucial during the early days of photography, given the state of the lenses and chemistry involved, that photographs could not be made on cloudy days, and photographers installed skylights in the roof of their studios to let in more sunlight. In the 1840s, writers on both sides of the Atlantic often seriously argued that American daguerreotypes were better than English ones because "an American sun shines brighter," as one newspaper writer put it.[1]

The names first given to photography—sun drawing, sun pictures, nature's pencil—suggest that a photograph was something created mechanically, scientifically, objectively. Nature, in the form of sunlight, pushed the pencil that drew the image. No artist—indeed, no person— was responsible for the photograph itself, which was a precise representation of what the lens of the camera faced. Even a man as sophisticated as Oliver Wendell Holmes, writing in the early 1860s, titled two influential articles he wrote about photography "Sun-Painting and Sun-Sculpture" and "Doings of the Sunbeam."[2]

This idea of photography's objectivity seems naïve today. The camera itself does not have a point of view, of course; it's only when a person uses the camera to take a picture that it becomes something more than the sunbeam's doing. The question of whether photography is an art form was settled long ago, and yet we often think about the photographers in these first decades of the medium's existence, and the photographs they made, as being if not objective then somehow artless; or, at the very best, we think of their makers as bloodless documentarians.

But consider an 1864 photograph by Mathew B. Brady in which he himself appears to the side of a Union general and his staff. Brady had been in the photography business for twenty years on the warm June day when this photograph was taken, and he had labored so tirelessly to make his work and his name known to the public that he had become the most famous photographer in the land. His specialty was studio photography—often of well-known individuals, ranging from the singer Jenny Lind to President Lincoln, or of interesting groups, such as the first official delegation from Japan to visit the United States— and this is very much a studio photograph taken out of doors. Even the flap of the tent at the left of the image suggests the draperies of the studio. The photograph has been artfully composed. Gen. Robert B. Potter's staff officers are arranged around him roughly by height, each of them wearing a hat and turned toward his boss, while Potter is hatless and staring directly into the lens. Brady has posed himself as what he was, not the subject of the photograph but its presiding intelligence, his gaze not at the lens but bisecting the line between the general, who is in the exact middle of the composition, and the camera. Brady is the maker of this photograph as well as being in it.

One of his operators very likely stood beside the camera and drew out a wooden panel covering the glass negative, permitting the exposure; but an intriguing possibility exists, although experts on cameras of the time doubt it, that Brady is operating the camera himself. In his right hand he holds something—could it be a device and is that a wire or tube running down his right leg, connecting him to the camera, moving a lens cover or a primitive sort of shutter, exposing the glass negative to the upside-down image carried by the light? Probably not. But even if Brady holds only a switch he has broken off a tree, who can view this image without knowing that its author was not the sun but a person, the well-tailored artist standing confidently to the right of the frame, hand on hip, leg jauntily cocked. What we have here is, without question, a photo by Brady.[3]

Union General Robert B. Potter, his staff, and Mathew Brady
(June 1864). *U.S. National Archives*

That phrase "photo by Brady" or "photograph by Brady" appeared regularly in the illustrated papers of the mid-1850s through the 1870s. What it meant was that an image taken by Brady's studio was the basis for an engraving that could be reproduced in the papers, since the direct use of photographs in newspapers did not become common until near the end of the century. Especially during the years of the Civil War, *Frank Leslie's Illustrated Newspaper* and *Harper's Weekly* turned repeatedly to Brady for portraits of those in the news, civilian and military leaders alike, and less often but still regularly for outdoor photographs of preparations for battle or of places where battles had occurred. His fame grew in part because of these credits in the papers, credits that gave the impression that Brady knew everyone and had been everywhere.[4]

He was also, like his onetime neighbor Phineas T. Barnum, a master of getting coverage in the press for himself, his studio, and his work, and like Barnum, he made frequent and creative use of advertising in newspapers and other publications. Brady knew early on that promoting himself and his name was good for business, and so, on his first daguerreotypes and his later elegant salt prints, on his ubiquitous cartes de visite and 3-D stereographs, whether sold directly to his customers or distributed by others, his name or the name of the Brady studio was always affixed. He also understood that proximity to celebrity was as good as celebrity itself, and so, early on, he began to photograph presidents and their wives, statesmen, artists, writers, performers. Anyone in the public eye soon submitted to or sought out the mechanical eye of Brady's camera. Not only did he take and distribute these images, but he also hung them on the walls of his studio—his gallery, as he always called it. Over the half century he owned a gallery, he displayed thousands of photographs in this way, and in all those years, he never once credited the sun with taking even a single image.


Mathew Brady was in and out of public view his whole working life and was often mentioned in the press. He gave several long interviews late in life, and was always quick with a story about the many people he had known and the things he had experienced. Yet Brady is someone we cannot know in whole. He did not keep a journal, write or dictate his memoirs, or maintain more than rudimentary records of his business. We don't know when or where he was born, how many siblings he had, how he was educated (if at all), how he met his wife or when he married her. We know almost nothing about any aspect of his domestic life. Of the thousands of photographs attributed to Brady or his studio, many lack basic documentation about when and where they were taken, and indeed whether they were taken by someone he employed or were the work of others and merely collected by him. With very few exceptions, we can know for sure that Brady was present for the making of a particular photograph only if he is in it.

This hidden-in-plain-sight aspect to Brady's story has contributed to a number of myths or misinterpretations. One has it that he was responsible for nearly every photograph we know of the Civil War years, having gone intrepidly from battle to battle. Another claims that he was not a photographer at all, but that he merely took credit for the work of others, since his own vision was too poor for him to operate a camera himself. A third says that he or his men moved dead soldiers around to make more powerful war photographs.

Enough is known about Brady's life and work, though, not only to expose these myths but to argue that he was the single most important person in nineteenth-century American photography. His Broadway portrait galleries in the 1840s and '50s helped popularize photography in its early days and establish the photograph as a thing of value in itself. He helped make being photographed (at least by him and others with fancy studios) a mark of prestige. His efforts to collect portraits of every important American helped create a unifying sense of one American nation, a goal he pursued up until the very moment the Civil War blew it apart. His photographs of the famous, from the Prince of Wales to General Tom Thumb, helped invent the modern idea of celebrity, and his photograph of the presidential hopeful Abraham Lincoln on the day of his Cooper Union speech helped make Lincoln president.

Brady saw immediately the potential for photography to record first-hand the history of the Civil War and did more than any other person to make a visual historical record of the war happen. He went to its opening battle and likely attempted to take photographs under fire, which made him the first person in history to do so. Almost every important photographer of the Civil War era and a number of the most important photographers of the West after the war worked at some point for Brady. Throughout his career he argued for photography as an art form and, through his own high standards, consistently demonstrated its potential as art. For all of this, he is sometimes credited as the father of American photography or as the father of photojournalism.

No single individual and very few consortiums of photographers have left as large or as varied a record of their time as Brady. Others rivaled him as portraitists or gallery owners, as collectors and distributors of images of the Civil War or of the famous; others pushed the artistic possibilities of the medium further; others also worked as photojournalists, to the extent to which we can use that word for the photography of the 1860s. Had Mathew Brady never lived, we would still have a photographic record of America from the 1840s to the 1890s. But nobody came close to doing as much in as many ways as he did, and without him that record would not have been nearly so rich or so complete.

# CHAPTER I

# "A Craving for Light"

Mathew Brady was born around 1823 to an Irish immigrant named Andrew Brady and his wife, Julia, in Warren County, New York. According to the 1830 census, Andrew and Julia and their six children lived in the county in the town of Johnsburg, west of Lake George, and local history has it that the stone foundations of a log house near the town, at a point where Glen Creek flows into the Hudson River, may have been the Brady homesite. But two brothers who went to work for Brady's studio in the 1850s had grown up in the 1830s on a farm said to abut the Brady family farm, near Dresden, which is *east* of the lake. It's possible that Brady's family moved from one location to the other, but in truth, no solid evidence exists that they lived in either place. Brady himself was never much help on his origins, saying only that his family had lived "in the woods about Lake George."[1]

At the time Mathew was born, Warren County was largely rural and agricultural, with about ten thousand inhabitants, with its largest concentration in the village of Glens Falls. The Native American population had long since been driven away in a series of wars, but the woods still held bears and panthers, and wolves were so plentiful and such a threat to livestock that for fifty years Glens Falls offered a bounty of between five and twenty dollars per head to eradicate them. Rattlesnakes were also ubiquitous—one account reports that "the rocks and ledges along the river were once a continuous den of rattlesnakes," but unfenced foraging hogs eventually brought them under control. Since lumber was the county's chief product, the Bradys might well have sold off the first growth of timber on their acreage, and farmers in this time often made potash out of the ashes from burned hardwood trees or stumps, a rare source of cash. Potash was used to make soap, glass, and gunpowder, and in the 1820s, New York State was the center of potash exports to Great Britain, where it was used in large quantities by the textile industry. Farmers could also earn cash by selling shingles they made from spruce trees in their woods. Families such as the Bradys grew crops of wheat, corn, and cotton, and raised chickens, hogs, sheep, and cattle; they also hunted the plentiful wild game in the nearby woods and fished in the creeks, the river, and the lake. Crops and grain would have fed their families, with a portion used for barter or for sale.[2]

Several tanneries had been in business in the county since long before Mathew was born, and one opened in the late 1830s on Glen Creek, close to a possible site for the Brady farm. The Glen Tannery, which employed many Irish immigrants, got hides from New York City and, after tanning them, sent them back to the city, mostly as soles for shoes and boots. This local connection to the tanning industry could explain why the first business Brady would start in New York City was in leather goods.[3]

Rural schoolhouses dotted the county, but no record exists of Mathew's schooling. He was certainly able to write, however, which suggests he had some formal education. The Irish immigrants who settled in the county at about the time that Andrew Brady did tended to be Methodists. Congregations met in the schoolhouses or in private homes until proper churches were erected in the 1830s.

Sawmills, gristmills, and potash asheries were scattered throughout the county, but Glens Falls, about ten miles due south of Lake George, was the closest place to go for store-bought necessities or professional services. A local newspaper reported in 1831 that the village, with a population of about one thousand people, had four lawyers and three doctors, and that among the merchants were nine mercantile stores, two drugstores, three inns, a printer, a watchmaker, and a bookstore. Other shops included tailors, hatters, shoemakers, harness makers, a baker, and a watchmaker. Among the tradesmen were blacksmiths, wagon makers, carpenters and cabinetmakers, a stonecutter, and a cooper. The village also featured mills, as its name suggests, a cotton factory, a marble factory, and even what was called a medical school.

On Saturdays, farm families crowded the stores and streets of Glens Falls, and Mathew undoubtedly went along with his family on shopping trips. Compared to life in the woods, this thriving village on the Hudson must have impressed him with its energy and excitement.[4]

Young Mathew had persistent problems with his vision, and at one point he developed an "inflammation of the eyes" that made him nearly blind. He persuaded his parents to take him for treatment to Saratoga, farther south along the Hudson. There, Brady remembered, "I met a Dr. Hinckley, who restored my sight, though my eyes were never strong." Thinking back on that time in his life, he mused, "I felt a craving for light, and isn't it remarkable that the light which I craved as a boy should have had the greatest bearing on my future career?" We don't know for certain whether Brady went to the riverside town of Saratoga itself or to nearby Saratoga Springs, which had already become a spa attracting those who could afford its indulgences. Either place was twice as big as Glens Falls.[5]

While having his eye treatments in Saratoga, Brady got his first exposure to a real artist, the portrait painter William Page. Page took an interest in the boy, offering to give him drawing lessons at his studio in Albany, still farther down the Hudson. Albany was not only the state capital but, thanks to the completion of the Erie Canal in 1825, had a population of thirty thousand people, making it the ninth-biggest city in the nation.

Page had been born there in 1811, and his family had moved to New York City when he was nine. In the mid-1820s Page had begun to study art, first with a draftsman named James Herring and then with the established painter Samuel F. B. Morse, who is better known as the inventor of the telegraph. Page soon began to exhibit his work at the National Academy of Design, a New York drawing society that Morse had recently organized. In 1832, Page was living again in Albany, seeking portrait commissions.[6]

Brady remembered that, as part of his training, Page "gave me a bundle of crayons"—meaning drawings in crayon—"to copy." Page's biographer describes the painter as handsome, with "a melodious voice, and fine manners," but like Brady, he had come from humble origins and had had only a limited amount of schooling. Unlike Brady, though, Page was a city person through and through. His relative urbanity, his success as an artist, and the attention he gave to Mathew could only have impressed the young farm boy. By 1836, Page had returned to Manhattan, where he opened a studio in the University Building facing the northeast edge of Washington Square. Morse himself, now a professor at New York University, also had rooms in one tower of the five-story gothic marble building. By the end of the decade, Mathew, like so many thousands of other young people of the era, left the farm for life in the city, following his mentor to Manhattan to find work. He would himself be a city person for the rest of his days.[7]

Brady remembered that he made that first trip to his new life with a friend, traveling on one of the fancy steamboats—"perfect palaces," he called them—that connected Albany with Manhattan. As the two young men walked around the boat, wide-eyed not only at its luxury but also at the views of the landscape slipping past, they found themselves by the door to the dining room, looking in longingly. One of three well-dressed men seated together waved them over to their table, asking, "Have you had your supper, boys?" Brady and his friend, perhaps embarrassed at being noticed, hurried away, but the man told the waiter to "catch that boy—the one with the long hair." The waiter obliged, chasing them around the boat until he did catch Brady, and led him back to the gentlemen's table. They insisted that he join them, and, as Brady put it, "nothing was too good for me."

A few years later, Brady's story went, two of those men happened into his Broadway gallery and recognized him. It turned out that one of them was John Van Buren, an attorney in Albany, and son of the U.S. president Martin Van Buren. He was known as "Prince John" for having danced with Queen Victoria at her 1838 coronation. The other man was William J. Worth, who had fought in the War of 1812, serving as an aide to Gen. Winfield Scott, and would fight in the Mexican-American War, again under Scott, rising to the rank of major general. Worth's last army command was in Texas, where the city of Fort Worth is named for him. Brady photographed both men, and came to count them as friends. Together, he recalled, they often laughed about how they had first met. The two men were Brady's first connections to the presidents and generals who would become a staple of his photographic career.

When he arrived in New York, Brady's story goes, he went to look for William Page in the building on Washington Square, knocking on

Professor Morse's door. Page himself opened it, and introduced his young protégé to his own mentor. Morse, who was nearly fifty at the time, was conducting experiments with daguerreotype, Brady recalled. (Brady's arrival must not have been before the fall of 1839, because Morse's experiments with the new photographic process did not begin until then.) After Morse showed him the first daguerreotype Brady had ever seen, Brady asked the professor if he would give him lessons in the process. Morse agreed, inviting him to join a class with several other boys, "but they all dropped out except one other and myself." The story seems a little too pat to be true, and there are no records that Brady was ever a student of Morse. But Morse did give instruction in daguerreotype, charging anywhere from twenty-five to fifty dollars, and gave public lectures on the process, so it's possible that Brady attended one or more of these.[8]

But he did not go immediately into the photography business. Brady's first job in the city was likely working as a clerk for A. T. Stewart, an immigrant from Ireland born of Scottish parents. In 1823, Stewart had started his first business, specializing in Irish linens and other fabrics, in a tiny storefront on Broadway, just north of City Hall Park. By the time Brady was hired, Stewart had become more and more successful and had expanded his line of merchandise, moving to another space on Broadway that was five stories tall and two storefronts wide, where he offered an array of dry goods. In 1846, Stewart constructed his own building at 280 Broadway, known as the Marble Palace for its size, Italianate design, and marble façade. It was the world's first department store.

Stewart's success came in part from a strategy of appealing to women customers by offering no-haggle prices and deferential service. He also ingratiated himself with them by hiring handsome young male clerks. Brady, with his thick jet-black hair and trim physique, certainly qualified in this regard, and his wire-rimmed glasses gave him a serious look to go with the good manners Stewart required.[9]

Stewart was one of the few New York merchants to thrive during the financial Panic of 1837, which had led to the failure of hundreds of banks and businesses in the city, unemployment of more than 33 percent, and an interest rate above 20 percent. Perhaps Stewart's entrepreneurial gusto inspired Brady to start his own business in the early 1840s, even though the effects of the depression that followed that panic and a smaller one in 1839 lingered.

Brady began to manufacture leather cases, marketing them to customers in New York and as far away as Boston. Among the cases he produced were ones designed to protect and display miniature paintings and the mirror-like metal plates on which daguerreotype images were fixed. A city directory in 1843 described Brady's business as a "jewel case man[ufacturer]" at 164 Fulton Street, just off Broadway. The following year, he moved his business to 187 Broadway, on the second floor, above a tailor shop. He lived on John Street, and later on Barclay Street, always a short walk from where he worked.[10]

One of the few surviving letters written in Brady's own hand comes from about this time, addressed to Albert Sands Southworth, a Boston daguerreotypist who had received instruction from Morse. Southworth was about to go into business with Josiah Hawes; their collaboration would last twenty years and produce some of the finest daguerreotype portraits ever made, including those of many New England intellectuals, from Louisa May Alcott to Emerson to Longfellow. Brady wrote:

New York, June 17, 1843

Mr. Southworth

Sir:

I beg leave of communicating these few lines soliciting your attention, I being informed by L. Champney [a student of Southworth] and several of your frends [*sic*] that you are one of the most successful prof. of daguerreotype and doing the most extensive business in Boston and invariably use a great number of miniature cases. I have been engaged some time past in manafucturing [*sic*] miniature cases for some of the principal operators in this city and recently in business for myself and anxious for engagements. I have got up a new style case with embossed top and extra fine diaframe [*sic*]. This style of case has been admired by all the principal artists in this city. If you feel desirous to see my style of cases if you will favor me with an answer I will send them by Horse Express. If my style of cases should suit you I can supply you on reasonable terms.

Yours,
M B Brady

Champney himself wrote to Southworth a month or so later, saying he had purchased some cases from Brady, paying five dollars for a dozen, and had returned with them to Vermont, where he was then working. There he realized, he told Southworth, that the cases "would not be durable." Still, he added of his customers, "They will never know the difference in the country."

Brady experimented with making cases of pressed paper instead of leather, because the leather cases often cost more than the daguerreotypes themselves. Champney might well have bought this cheaper imitation. For whatever reason—perhaps his customers *could* tell the difference—Champney was soon out of the daguerreotype business.[11]

Whether all or even many of the daguerreotypists in New York had admired Brady's cases or this was simply sales talk, it's clear that he had reason to be in contact with the quickly increasing number of cameramen in the city, many of whom were ranged along lower Broadway. By April of 1844, Brady had joined them, opening as a second business his own daguerreotype establishment at 205 Broadway, with an entrance next door to his original Fulton Street office. He called it the New-York Daguerreian Miniature Gallery.

The depression that had followed the panics of 1837 and 1839 lingered in the country at large until the year before Brady opened his gallery. But New York City, the country's financial and manufacturing center, suffered a longer, deeper depression, leading to downward mobility in all classes. Only when goods began flowing to California with the 1849 gold rush, and the discovered gold began flowing back to New York, did the city return to its former robustness. But you could hardly detect these hard times by walking along Broadway. A massive fire in December 1836 had destroyed or damaged much of lower Manhattan east of Broadway and south of Wall Street, pushing retail establishments farther up the boulevard and turning the area around City Hall Park into a bustling business district.[12]

The writer of an 1837 guidebook to New York City warned tourists that to cross Broadway in this area, "you must look up street and down street, at the self-same moment, to see what carts and carriages are upon you, and then run for your life." Five years later, Charles Dickens commented on a visit to Broadway: "No stint of omnibuses here! Half a dozen have gone by within as many minutes. Plenty of hackney cabs and coaches, too; gigs, phaetons, large-wheeled tilburies, and private carriages." Dickens also noticed the brazen pigs that roamed the streets, feeding on garbage. Despite these hazards, the paving stones of Broadway were "polished with the tread of feet until they shine," Dickens noted.[13]

The sidewalks were also jammed with a constant stream of shoppers, workers, promenaders, and idlers, often dressed in their Sunday best. Sunday evenings were indeed the best time for promenading, but a visit to Broadway was an occasion on any day of the week. Broadway was the place to see and be seen, attracting not only those who lived and worked nearby but also a growing number of tourists, many of them drawn to Barnum's American Museum, which he opened in 1841 within sight of 205 Broadway, where Brady's gallery would be. One of Broadway's many attractions for its strollers was to drop into the luxurious daguerreotype galleries, view the images on display there while enjoying a calm respite from Broadway's tumult, and perhaps even submit to the magical new process.

The principle of the camera—that light passing through a small hole projects an image from the brighter side of the aperture to a surface on the dimmer side—was understood by the Chinese philosopher Mozi in the fifth century B.C.E., and by Aristotle and Euclid a century later. In the fifteenth century, Leonardo da Vinci knew about a device created to take advantage of this principle, which Johannes Kepler, the seventeenth-century German mathematician and astronomer, would name a camera obscura (or darkened chamber). Other Renaissance painters likely used the device to trace a projected image on a piece of paper or canvas, and the eighteenth-century Venetian painter Canaletto definitely employed the camera obscura, by now a box with a lens at

one end for focusing the image, to sketch out his huge landscape paintings of his native city.

The magic, then, was not in capturing images from nature but in
fixing them so that they could be preserved. People had known for cen-
turies that naturally occurring silver salts darken in sunlight, and in the
1720s the German scientist Johann Heinrich Schulze created a dramatic
experiment to prove it. He wrapped stencils with words cut out around
a jar filled with a whitish mixture of silver, nitric acid, and chalk. After
he exposed the jar to sunlight and then removed the stencil, he said,
"The sun's rays, where they hit the glass through the cut-out parts of the
paper, wrote each word or sentence on the chalk precipitate so exactly
and distinctly that many . . . took occasion to attribute the thing to some
sort of trick." The silver turning black in the sun was what made the
words so distinct. A Swedish chemist noticed in the 1770s that silver
chloride that had been darkened by the sun could be kept dark by
ammonia, and almost simultaneously a Swiss botanist discovered that
focusing sunlight through a lens made silver chloride darken more
rapidly. Others, including two famous sons of famous fathers—Thomas
Wedgwood and John Herschel—made important discoveries related
to creating prints, the former in 1802, using silver-nitrate-treated leather
or paper to make "sun prints" that would stay fixed if kept in the dark; the
latter finding in 1839 that hyposulfite of soda could permanently fix an
image on paper.[14]

Not long after Mathew Brady's birth, the gestation process for the
daguerreotype began. In 1826 the Parisian painter Louis-Jacques-
Mandé Daguerre contacted a French inventor named Joseph Nicéphore
Niépce. Each of them had had some success fixing an image taken with
a camera obscura. Both men were getting their lenses from a Paris optician named Charles Chevalier, who suggested to Daguerre that he team
up with Niépce. But it took several years of guarded correspondence
before that came to pass. Daguerre had painted scenes for the Paris
Opéra and other theaters, and in 1822 he opened in the city what he
called the Diorama, a theater without actors where landscape and ar-
chitectural paintings on linen were made to seem lifelike and to change—
for instance, from daylight to moonlight—by the clever manipulation
of the sun's rays. The Diorama, located near the present-day Place de la
République, was so popular that Daguerre opened one in London the
following year, and imitators followed. Daguerre used the camera ob-

scura to get the perspectives right for his scenes, but the effort it took to trace the images led to his interest in finding a way to fix them directly on paper.[15]

In 1822, Niépce had invented a process called heliography, which fixed an image on glass or metal using bitumen (an asphalt-like substance), but the process was intended to reproduce engravings, and had not been adapted to a camera obscura, something Niépce became interested in doing. The two men finally became partners in December of 1829, and worked to refine the process, believing they were on the right track, until Niépce died in 1833. "Overwhelmed by this loss," Daguerre wrote, "I gave up on our work for the time being." But in 1837 he produced his first image, a study of a corner of his studio, and in January 1839 he shared his process confidentially with François Arago, a brilliant French polymath who was secretary of the French Academy of Sciences and director of the Royal Observatory. Arago, who would briefly be head of the French national government in 1848 under the Second Republic, immediately presented the news of the discovery to the academy and proposed that the French government reward Daguerre and in return have the right to make the details of the process public. The chambers of Peers and Deputies agreed, granting Daguerre an annuity of six thousand francs, and Niépce's heirs four thousand francs a year, and on August 19, 1839, Arago presented the details of daguerreotype at a joint meeting of the Academy of Sciences and the Academy of Fine Arts. Daguerre had been expected to reveal the details of his discovery himself, but he had a bad sore throat that day and begged off.

The process Arago described would fix the image on a plate of copper coated with silver. First, he explained, the plate must be polished with nitric acid and then exposed to iodine fumes, which turns it yellow and makes it sensitive to light. After the camera is focused, the plate is inserted and left for seconds or minutes, depending on the strength of the light, the humidity, and other factors. Once the image is imprinted on the plate, it is removed from the camera and exposed to the fumes of mercury heated to 167 degrees Fahrenheit. Then it is fixed in a bath of hyposulfite of soda, and finally washed in distilled water. The image created would not disappear or even fade in the sunlight, Arago said, but because the surface of the plate is sensitive in other ways, it must be protected by glass.

At the end of Arago's presentation, a British newspaper reported, "the most enthusiastic cheers responded from the grave benches even of the Academy," and the Academy of Sciences president "complimented M. Daguerre in the warmest terms." But the process sounded more straightforward than it was. How you rubbed the plate to prepare it, how you exposed it to the mercury fumes, and, most significantly, how long it took the light to properly expose the sensitized plate—all these matters were more the product of skill and experience than of science. Daguerre, anticipating that people would want to know more about the process, had created a pamphlet with detailed instructions and drawings of the equipment needed. It was published in Paris two days after Arago's presentation, and an English translation came out almost immediately. By the end of 1839, thirty editions of the pamphlet, in several languages, had appeared.[16]

Arago had only a year before presenting another world-changing discovery to the Academy of Sciences: Samuel Morse's telegraph. Morse had demonstrated his invention at the Paris Observatory, and Arago then offered to introduce and serve as translator for the academy demonstration, which took place on September 10, 1838. Morse wrote later that "a buzz of admiration and approbation filled the whole hall," and he heard the academy's distinguished members crying out, *"extraordinaire!"* and *"très admirable!"*[17]

Morse remained in Paris, where he and his invention had become the talk of the town, hoping for an audience with the king, Louis-Philippe. That interview never came, but Morse was still in Paris in January when news of Daguerre's discovery first appeared. Morse himself had used a camera obscura in his career as a portrait painter and had also, in the early 1820s, tried without success to fix images on paper treated with silver nitrate. Although—or perhaps because—Daguerre's invention now rivaled his own in the public eye, Morse wanted to meet its creator. He sent Daguerre a note asking if he could see his images, offering in return to demonstrate the telegraph for Daguerre. Daguerre agreed, and Morse visited him on March 7 for two hours in his studio, adjacent to the building housing the Diorama itself. Daguerre's seven-by-five-inch plates astonished Morse, who wrote that the "exquisite minuteness of delineation cannot be conceived." The plates included a street scene with a distant sign, whose letters could be read when magnified, and a spider "not bigger than the head of a large pin," which, when also magnified, "showed a minuteness of organization hitherto not seen to exist." In the first image, he saw telescopic power, and in the second, microscopic, and he said of Daguerre's interior views that they "are Rembrandt perfected."

The next day, Morse recounts, Daguerre visited him at noon, spending an hour examining the telegraph, and was also deeply impressed. But, by terrible coincidence, in the very same hour when Daguerre was visiting Morse, his Diorama caught fire during a show, and although the audience got out with only two injuries, his elaborately painted sets and illusionist devices were destroyed within thirty minutes. Daguerre's studio, where he kept his daguerreotypes, equipment, and papers, also caught fire, but these items were not harmed.[18]

Two weeks later, Morse was on his way back to New York, arriving home with "not even a farthing in my pocket." He had spent nearly a year in Europe, attempting to sell his invention to governments there, but was everywhere rebuffed. He decided to "let the matter rest and watch for an opportunity when times look better." Because his professorship had never involved a salary, and having stayed in touch with Daguerre, he decided to begin to experiment with daguerreotype himself in the hope of earning some money by taking photographs, teaching the process to others, or both. Once the English translation of Daguerre's pamphlet arrived in New York, perhaps as early as September, Morse went to an instrument maker named George Prosch, who quickly built a camera to Daguerre's specifications. Others in New York, and in Philadelphia and Boston, also began immediately to experiment with the process, and it quickly spread elsewhere in America. Morse's first successful daguerreotype was of a Unitarian church, taken from the University Building, but as a painter, he specialized in portraits, and so he also began to experiment with daguerreotypes of people, something Daguerre himself had discouraged, Morse said, because of the time involved in making an exposure. Years later, Morse remembered that he took a number of portraits of his daughter, Susan, and her friends, perhaps as early as September or October of 1839.[19]

The daguerreotype arrived in New York City just before Brady did. Morse, whether a direct mentor or a more distant inspiration, was already applying his painter's sensibility to the photographic portrait, and by the time Brady opened his studio in 1844, the portrait was a well-established and commercially viable mainstay of the photography business. By opening a portrait studio, Brady could combine the retail skills inspired by A. T. Stewart and developed in his own case-making business with whatever artistic yearnings had been inspired in him by William Page and *his* mentor, Morse. The new business thrived because of a third quality: Brady's eagerness not only to learn the technical aspects of the daguerreotype process and the equipment involved, but also to tinker with it, much as he had experimented with those paper substitutes for leather cases. Brady's success in his new business would come quickly.

# CHAPTER 2

# "This Great National Map"

Henry H. Snelling, an early historian of photography, recalled that in the first years of daguerreotype he worked at the Brady studio on experiments using colored glass to improve lighting conditions. Brady had had a skylight built in the roof of his new studio, and one newspaper reported that it was big enough to illuminate a group of twenty people posing for his camera. The effect of this large window to the sky was that the light was generalized, "bringing every figure out clear and distinct, without that heavy shadow on one side of the picture." But as Snelling's memory suggests, Brady was not satisfied, believing that tinting the glass in the skylight could make his images clearer and permit the process to work satisfactorily even when the sun was not shining brightly. Blue was the tint he came to favor, a color he would also use in the lenses of his spectacles.[1]

Brady's gallery occupied the top two floors of a building on the southwest corner of Broadway and Fulton. Just inside the entrance, on Fulton Street, was a sign with a finger pointing up the stairs. On the second floor was the gallery displaying examples of his work, many of them hand-colored. Here a potential sitter could evaluate their quality and, if sufficiently impressed, climb a second flight of stairs to the studio and pose beneath the skylight. By October, Brady began to advertise regularly in the *New-York Daily Tribune*, inviting "a just and intelligent public . . . as well as strangers" (by strangers, he probably meant tourists) to visit his gallery and critique his work, whether they wanted to be photographed or not.[2]

The process of daguerreotype involved several different sorts of skills, and its commercial application at the larger Broadway studios required numbers of workers so that the product could be finished while the customer waited. A typical daguerreotype studio of the time would have a well-appointed gallery and waiting room with a receptionist; elsewhere, young boys would clean and buff the metal plates, preparing them for exposure; the camera or cameras occupied an "operating room" or rooms at the top of the building. There the camera operator would actually take the picture. Still other workers would develop and fix the image on the plate (exposing themselves to deadly mercury fumes); artists might color or gild it; and finally others would mat and frame it, often in the sort of leather case Brady manufactured and sold.[3]

Brady's studio was likely not this elaborate. It's hard to imagine where on those two floors he could have found room for all those boys and artists and operators. His advertisements for the first year he was in business claim only one "competent and practical" person who colored the plates—he or she did so, Brady claimed, "in a most beautiful manner." Brady himself did not usually man the camera, and at first he had only one operator, a fellow named James Sidney Brown. (Brown would open his own studio in 1848.) It was he who would slide in the prepared plate, remove the lens cover, and then replace it after what he judged to be the proper length of time, taking several exposures, perhaps, to adjust for the particular conditions in the studio that day. Operators were paid better for their skills than anyone else in the gallery, but whatever artistry they displayed, they were still considered to be technicians.[4]

But Brady undoubtedly knew how to operate the camera, and since he advertised that daguerreotypes could be made from eight in the morning to five in the afternoon, and "in all kinds of weather," it's likely that he at least occasionally filled in for Brown. Brady's main role, however, was as the face of the gallery. He would greet customers, direct them to the images displayed on the walls of the second floor, accompany them up to the studio, and put them at ease so they looked their best. But he was also, as one historian of photography put it, "the controlling aesthetic intellect in the creation of the portraits." He would decide how his sitters would be posed, how close the camera would come to the subject, even how it would be focused. And long before the sitter entered his studio, he would have created more general aesthetic principles about lighting, background, and, later, the props that might be used. He also made decisions about the studio itself—how it would be decorated, how his daguerreotypes would be displayed—and about the equipment they would use. Two years into his business he told a newspaper reporter that he had just ordered from a German optician a new camera with a lens an inch and a half larger in diameter than any yet made, so that he could take larger images that were "equal to the best English engravings."[5]

This story suggests Brady's determination to continue perfecting the process, even though his own success was almost immediate. In the fall of 1844 he entered a selection of his daguerreotypes at the annual fair of the American Institute of the City of New York, held at Niblo's Garden, up Broadway at Prince Street. By December 10 he was advertising in the *Daily Tribune* that his work had won a "First Premium" at the fair. One thing that distinguished his images was their clarity, attributed not only to the lighting but also to his ability to achieve a high polish in preparing the silvered copper plates. Samuel Morse had early on tinkered with mechanical ways to polish plates, so perhaps Brady learned this from him, or built upon Morse's ideas. A writer for the *New York Herald* attended the 1846 fair, noting "the exquisitely finished specimens presented by Mr. Brady," with their "softness of expression—a naturalness . . . that called forth universal admiration." So it was not just the technical skill that set his work apart, but also an aesthetic sense that favored directness and simplicity in the posing and composition of a portrait. In any case, Brady's work would win first prizes at the next year's fair for best colored and best plain daguerreotypes, another first prize in 1846, a silver medal in 1847, and a gold medal in 1849.[6]

Like Morse, Brady also immediately began offering what his ads called "instructions carefully given in the art." We don't know whether Brady could command the fees of up to fifty dollars that Morse had charged to teach the process five years earlier, but Brady's eagerness to offer lessons shows his confidence that he had mastered the subject. That he took on teaching while running his gallery and his leather case business suggests an abundance of youthful energy, a need for new sources of revenue, or both. But given the number of operators who passed through his gallery over the next three decades and went on to have successful careers of their own, it's safe to say that Brady's ability as a teacher matched his skills as a businessman and photographer.[7]


In 1845 or 1846, Brady took on two new projects, both of which involved making portraits. One would show him a path he did not want to pursue as a photographer, and the other would define the rest of his photographic career. For the first project, he was asked by Eliza Wood Farnham, who would later become a well-known writer and feminist, and was at the time the warden of the female prison at Sing Sing, to make daguerreotypes that would be engraved to illustrate a book she was introducing to the American public. The book, *The Rationale of Crime*, by Marmaduke B. Sampson, had been published in England in 1841. It employed the pseudoscience of phrenology, which supposedly could determine mental characteristics from the shape of the skull, to predict criminal behavior. Throughout much of the nineteenth century, phrenology was widely accepted in Europe and the United States, and even the *Tribune* editor Horace Greeley was a proponent. Farnham, who had gotten her job at Sing Sing through Greeley, believed phrenology proved that certain types of criminal behavior were involuntary, and thus prisoners convicted of such crimes should be treated sympathetically. The pseudoscience also purported to identify those prisoners who could be rehabilitated.

Brady made head-and-shoulders portraits of whites and blacks, women, men, and a number of "lads," and Tudor Horton engraved nineteen of his images for use in the book. Under each engraving was a description of the subject, with phrenological interpretations such as "In her head destructiveness is enormously developed, with large secretiveness and caution, and very defective benevolence and moral organs generally." Farnham thanked Brady in the book for his "indefatigable patience with a class of the most difficult of all sitters." Beyond whatever problems the subjects themselves posed, Brady had to get his equipment up the Hudson to Sing Sing and across the East River to the penitentiary at Blackwell's Island (now Roosevelt Island) and the Long Island Farm School (near Long Island City today), where the boys were kept. Brady's daguerreotypes are lost, but Farnham called them "very accurate," and because the engravings themselves are primitive, hers is the best description of them possible. Still, these engravings are among the earliest existing representations of a Brady portrait.[8]

Some years later Brady would be the subject of an article in a phrenological journal. We don't know whether he took on Farnham's time-consuming assignment because he supported her views or simply for the pay or the exposure from her book. He never again participated in a project of this sort, and except during the Civil War—when his studio often photographed ordinary soldiers, or his operators photographed them in camps or in the field—he did not generally photograph working-class people, much less the downtrodden. In the Bowery there were daguerreotypists who would charge as little as a quarter for a portrait, but Brady and others like him could charge from two to as many as five dollars, a week's salary for many people.

Appealing to those who were well off or who wished to seem so was a strategy that other businesses like Brady's in the neighborhood of City Hall, from hotels to shops to large stores, also employed. Richard L. Bushman writes in *The Refinement of America* that stores such as A. T. Stewart's "exceeded the décor of domestic drawing rooms, even in mansions, and adopted the name 'palace' to suggest the ambience they sought to re-create. Their extravagant architecture and decoration made them the marvels of the city . . . an irresistible magnet for genteel customers." In the same way, Brady's gallery would by 1851 be seen as "the largest and most fashionable [photographic] establishment in the city."[9]

Part of his plan for attracting clients was to collect for the walls of his gallery the portraits of well-known people, so that those among the Broadway strollers drawn up the stairs by the pointing finger could imagine their own images displayed on his walls. Just a block up Broadway, past St. Paul's Chapel, was the tony Astor House hotel, where Brady could troll for celebrities, offering them a free sitting as an inducement. If they agreed to make the short walk to sit under his skylight, he would keep one of the exposures for his gallery. With the exception of the actor Edwin Forrest (whom Page had painted in the early 1830s) and the painter Thomas Cole, we don't know just who these early subjects might have been, but in the next fifteen years or so Brady would photograph many actors, journalists, poets, artists, publishers, lecturers, clergy, public officials—the sorts of people who were all around him on Broadway near City Hall.

Sometime in 1845, Brady began to think of this effort as his Hall of Fame, but soon it became more ambitious than a gathering of local celebrities, however far their reputations went beyond New York. He realized that the medium of portrait photography gave him the opportunity to become a sort of historian—the word *photography* means "writing with light"—someone who could record for posterity the great American faces of his era. His impulse to do this was not an original idea. Morse himself had worked as a painter on a project of this sort even before Brady was born, and another early daguerreotypist and a student of Morse, Edward Anthony, in his National Miniature Gallery on Broadway, featured long lists of "American Statesmen," many of them photographed in Washington in 1842. Late in life, Walt Whitman would recall that he and Brady had "had many a talk together: the point was how much better it would often be, rather than having a lot of contradictory records by witnesses or historians—say of Caesar, Socrates, Epictetus, others—if we could have three or four or half a dozen portraits . . . that would be history—the best history—a history from which there would be no appeal."[10]

Among the first images that Brady collected for the ages was one of the last daguerreotypes, taken in 1845, of a visibly dying Andrew Jackson at the Hermitage, his Tennessee home. Brady claimed later that he had taken the picture, but even if he meant only that he had arranged for someone else to take it, his claim is probably untrue. An 1845 magazine attributed an engraving of Jackson to an Edward Anthony daguerreotype taken at the Hermitage. Other sources say the original daguerreotypes of the former president were taken by a Nashville photographer named Dan Adams or by the Langenheim Brothers, a well-known firm in Philadelphia. Daguerreotypes were one-of-a-kind images, and could at that time be reproduced only if someone took a daguerreotype of them, a skill Brady acquired early on. However it got there, an image of President Jackson would be the first of a president admitted to Brady's Hall of Fame, and would be featured on his wall for many years. More than a dozen other presidents would join Jackson over the next four decades.[11]

In the middle to late 1840s, Brady photographed the naturalist and painter John James Audubon, the historian William H. Prescott, and New York governor Silas Wright. He also began to take an interest in the American officers in the Mexican-American War, photographing in their uniforms the generals Zachary Taylor, Winfield Scott, and William J. Worth—his friend from the Hudson steamboat. So many of the younger officers in Mexico would have important roles in the Civil War that these connections served Brady well later in his career. Among many others were George B. McClellan, Ulysses S. Grant, William T. Sherman, Thomas J. Jackson, P. G. T. Beauregard, Joseph Hooker, James Longstreet, and George G. Meade. Late in life Brady would remember that he had known Robert E. Lee "since the Mexican war when he was upon General Scott's staff." Even if Brady did not photograph most of these younger officers in the 1840s, they would eventually know his images of their commanders and comrades from that earlier war, and many of them would sit before his camera in the 1860s, when they themselves had become the leaders of their respective armies.

Eventually, Brady's ambitious goal would be "to form a gallery which shall eventually contain life-like portraits of every distinguished American now living." Given the course that his career would take, it's apparent that photographing famous people was a passion as well as a business plan. But however alluring were the people represented on his walls, his income depended on those who paid to have their portraits made, and there were other strategies for attracting them. Competition among daguerreotype operators on Broadway was fierce, so Brady used every advantage he could find. Because his gallery was within sight of Barnum's American Museum, just one block up and across Broadway, Brady put a huge sign on 205 Broadway with the words BRADY'S GALLERY OF DAGUERREOTYPES, in letters so large that no tourist could miss it when leaving the American Museum. The museum was becoming the leading attraction in the city, and Barnum would claim that as many as fifteen thousand people a day paid the twenty-five-cent entrance fee.[12]

By this time Brady had expanded his gallery to include the upper floors of both 205 and 207 Broadway, and he had entrances on both Broadway and Fulton. He shared 205 with Edward Anthony, who in addition to taking daguerreotypes had started to make engravings and to specialize in selling what he called "daguerreotype materials" to others in the profession. Anthony's business would later also include making and distributing photographic prints, and throughout Brady's career Anthony, later joined by his brother Henry, would be Brady's most steadfast business associate, often extending him credit when others would not.[13]

Perhaps Brady's acquaintance with Anthony, who had set up his camera in the Capitol building itself in 1842 to get images of Washington legislators and justices, helped to convince him that he also needed to go to Washington if he was going to fill out his own growing gallery with the country's leaders. Sometime in 1848, Brady visited the capital to photograph the much-loved former First Lady Dolley Madison at her home on Lafayette Square, only yards from the White House, which she had so dramatically escaped during the War of 1812. Even a year before her death, Madison looks jaunty in a light-colored cap, with a boldly striped wrap gathered at her waist. Brady would also photograph another woman connected to the country's founding generation, Elizabeth Schuyler Hamilton, Alexander Hamilton's widow. Roger B. Taney, the chief justice of the Supreme Court, also posed during this time.

By early the next year, Brady had decided to open his own studio in Washington, in rooms rented from a watchmaker and jeweler on Pennsylvania Avenue, near 4½ Street Northwest, close to the Capitol, in what had become a photographer's row. His purpose then, according to the city's *Daily National Intelligencer*, was to take "daguerreotype portraits of all the distinguished men who may be present at the approaching Inauguration" of Zachary Taylor on March 4. On February 14, outgoing president James K. Polk wrote in his diary that he had "yielded to the request of an artist named Brady, of New York, by sitting for my daguerreotype likeness today. I sat in the large dining-room" of the White House. Returning to the White House on May 5, Brady photographed the new president, Zachary Taylor, seated and in profile. The lighting, presumably from a window off to the side of the camera, picks out every wrinkle and bulging vein on the side of Taylor's face. At the Capitol in March, Brady photographed the new vice president and next president, Millard Fillmore, seated and gazing straight into the camera, hands folded across his belly, looking relaxed with his legs crossed. The flesh tones of Fillmore's face, hands, and hair were then subtly rendered in color, as was a screen in the background. During this time, Brady also made individual photographs of each of the seven members of Taylor's new cabinet, and Francis D'Avignon and Abram J. Hoffman made a beautiful composite lithograph of them together with the president. D'Avignon would soon go into partnership with Brady in New York.[14]

During his time in Washington, Brady also photographed every member of the Supreme Court and a large number of congressmen, including former vice president and now senator John C. Calhoun, who, according to Brady, visited his studio in March and April accompanied by his daughter. Brady recalled that when viewed through the camera, Calhoun's eyes looked like "two balls of fire" and that "his cheeks were sunken by the consumption that was gnawing away his life." The South Carolinian would be dead a year later.[15]

After some months in Washington, Brady was forced to go to court because the landlord for the rooms where he had his studio wanted to evict him. Brady won an injunction against the landlord, but once the lease was up he was not able to renew it. That, combined with the fierce competition among daguerreotypists in the city, convinced him to give up on Washington and return to New York, which he did sometime in 1850. One result of his time in the capital was meeting his wife-to-be, Juliette R. C. Handy, known as Julia, the same name as Brady's mother. About nineteen at the time, Julia Handy came from Somerset County on the Eastern Shore of Maryland, where her father had been a prominent lawyer. The story went that she had come to Washington as a little girl, when her father worked in the Jackson administration, and that the president had been so taken with her that he joked he wanted to adopt her. No record exists of Brady's marriage to Julia, but an 1850 letter from one member of the Handy family to another mentions that the couple was living on Staten Island.[16]

Brady had continued to operate his New York studio during his Washington sojourn. In June 1849 a second member of the Great Triumvirate, after Calhoun, visited 205 Broadway and sat for five exposures. This was Daniel Webster, who was accompanied to the sitting by his close friend and the proprietor of the Astor House, Charles Stetson, with whom Brady was also friendly. Brady was struck by the theatricality of Webster's manner; the great orator wore an attention-getting blue coat with gleaming gold buttons. But when Webster took his seat under the skylight it was he who set the photographer at ease, saying, "Use me as the potter would the clay, Mr. Brady." Brady later remembered that Webster "had a grave, noble, dignified face, large, luminous dark eyes full of lustre, and a high, broad forehead."[17]

President James K. Polk (February 1849). A later photograph from a
Brady daguerreotype. *Library of Congress*

Brady also photographed the politician and orator Henry Clay in New York, remembering that it happened "during the winter of 1849." Clay spent nearly a week in New York City in late November of 1848, so this could be when the sitting occurred. But a different Brady image of Clay, perhaps, was alluded to in an ad in the summer of 1848, in which Edward Anthony thanks Brady and others for providing daguerreotypes of Clay for a new engraving Anthony had put on sale. Brady said he took five images of Clay, whom he remembered as having a light complexion, "quick, running, laughing eyes," and a grin that went from ear to ear. But nobody was posed grinning, or even slightly smiling, during the daguerreotype era, and all three members of the Great Triumvirate look in Brady's images like the serious statesmen they were, each striking a pose suitable for a statue.[18]

Brady's interest in history had its first serious culmination in a project called the *Gallery of Illustrious Americans*, announced in 1850 for a subscription series of lithographs made by D'Avignon from Brady daguerreotype portraits and accompanied by brief biographies. Among the first twelve subjects offered were two presidents—Zachary Taylor, who died on July 9, and his successor, Millard Fillmore—senators Calhoun, Webster, and Clay; the pathfinder John C. Frémont; General Scott; and Audubon, Prescott, and Wright. A new subject would appear every other week on "imperial folio drawing paper," sixteen inches by twenty-three inches, with care given not only to the reproduction of the lithograph but also to the typography. They cost a dollar apiece, although an ad in July offered the first six for five dollars, including delivery, and the whole series, projected to include twenty-four subjects, was available in advance for twenty dollars. An ad in the fall of 1850 inviting people to see the portraits in Brady's gallery referred to the project as "this great National Map." An article introducing the series, by journalist Charles Edwards Lester, who also wrote the biographical sketches, promoted Brady as someone who "has been many years collecting portraits of a National Gallery" and whose "reputation in his art has been too long established to need commendation." Perhaps more important for Brady's position a decade later, when the Civil War began, Lester describes him as having "experienced the utmost courtesy and encouragement from eminent men."[19]

The advertisement, which appeared in *The Literary World*, was signed Brady, D'Avignon and Co., of 205 Broadway. Despite its claim

General Winfield Scott (1850). Lithograph by
Francis D'Avignon from a Brady daguerreotype.
*National Portrait Gallery, Smithsonian Institution*

that the work "has been received everywhere with admiration and applause," and had "a large and constantly increasing list of good subscribers," the series was apparently not a financial success. Among the upfront expenses was the one hundred dollars Brady spent for each lithographic stone, and after the first dozen numbers were released, the series ended. But the project was successful in other ways. Brady, D'Avignon, and Lester were able to garner an astonishing amount of national publicity for their work, and to sign up agents for the project in nearly half the nation's thirty states, including many in the South, and in England and France. The Brady ad called the work "A National Tribute to our Great Men," and Lester emphasized in his introduction that "there is nothing sectional in the scope of this work" and offered his hope that it would "bind the Union still more firmly together." They cloaked themselves in patriotic idealism, then, and D'Avignon's delicate and detailed engravings imbued Brady's straightforward portraits with dignity and seriousness. No one could doubt that these were Americans who deserved to be admired.[20]

\* \* \*

Despite the proximity of Brady's gallery to Barnum's American Museum, and their later collaborations, Barnum did not draw Brady in to one of his greatest publicity coups, the American tour of the singer Jenny Lind, the "Swedish Nightingale." Lind was often photographed during her wildly successful 1850–1852 American visit, which was conceived, arranged, and promoted by Barnum, and she sat for Brady fairly soon after she arrived in New York, met at dockside by enthusiastic crowds of as many as forty thousand people and a torchlight parade of the city's firefighters. But Brady claimed in an interview late in life that "Barnum was opposed to me, and he did all he could to have her go elsewhere." Brady managed to snag her, though, by contacting an old schoolmate of hers in Sweden who now lived in Chicago but just happened to have worked as an operator for Brady in New York. The story goes that Brady paid for the operator, who had the grand name of Johan Carl Frederic Polycarpus von Schneidau, to travel to New York to make the daguerreotype of Lind. In Chicago in 1854, von Schneidau would take one of the earliest known images of Lincoln. (An 1846 daguerreotype is the only Lincoln picture known to precede it.) He was also one of photography's early martyrs, his 1859 death generally attributed to his exposure to the mercury fumes that were used in the development process. The *New York Herald* covered the Jenny Lind photography session at Brady's on Saturday, September 14, at noon. Like many of Lind's movements during the tour, this one became an event:

> As soon as it was known she was there, a large crowd collected around the place, which continued to increase to such a degree, that it became rather formidable to face it by the time the likeness was completed. A ruse was accordingly resorted to, and she was conducted out of the door in Fulton Street, instead of Broadway; but the crowd were not to be outwitted so easily. The moment they perceived the movement, they made a rush, and one of the hard-fisted actually thrust his hand into the carriage and held it, swearing that he must see Jenny Lind. The carriage was completely surrounded, and the driver whipped the horses, when one or two persons were thrown down, but were not severely hurt.

Lind sat for a second photo at Brady's gallery at the end of her American tour in 1852, when the camera operator was Luther Boswell. His wife later wrote that she was present at the sitting. Lind gave her one of the images made that day, she remembered, and gave both the Boswells tickets to her concert that evening. Mrs. Boswell recalled that Lind sang "Home Sweet Home" at the concert and "there was hardly a dry eye in the audience." Years later Brady would remember that Lind "was not a beautiful woman, but her face was a pleasant one . . . and her eyes were beautiful. She had a glint of gold in her hair under the camera, and she took an excellent picture." The Boswell daguerreotype confirms Brady's memory. After her eyes, what draws our own eye is her elaborately embroidered silk dress.[21]

Brady and others have recorded the details of a few of his many interactions with his famous sitters. More than once late in life, Brady recalled that Edgar Allan Poe had visited his New York studio in 1849 with the poet William Ross Wallace, who paid to have his own portrait made. When Brady asked the disheveled, lugubrious visitor if he would sit as well, Poe only shook his shaggy head no. Realizing that cost might be a factor, Brady said it would be his honor to have so great a poet's image in his gallery. But Poe still demurred. Finally his friend got Poe to agree, and he sat without any attempt at primping. "Poe had no vest on," Brady remembered. "He had a small black mustache, and a small mouth, drawn down at the corners as though he had a bad stomach." When the exposure was finished, Poe left abruptly and without comment. He died a few months later in Baltimore. A photograph of Poe that for a long time was attributed to Brady has since been proven to have been taken in Providence, Rhode Island, and was one of the many that Brady copied from other photographers. Whether a different Brady daguerreotype existed at one time, or Brady's memory played tricks on him, or he was simply telling a fib, the anecdote offers a small insight into how his gallery was built.[22]

Brady also spoke more than once about a session with the novelist James Fenimore Cooper. Late in life Brady would claim that Cooper told him he intended to put him in a novel but didn't live long enough to do so. Before Brady got to him, Cooper had posed for another photographer who brought up the sensitive subject of a quarrel the writer was having with his publisher. According to Brady, "Cooper jumped from his chair and refused to sit. After that daguerreotypers were afraid of him." But Brady was undeterred. Hearing that the novelist was nearby,

> I ventured in at Biggsby's, his hotel, corner of Park place. He came out in his morning gown and asked me to excuse him till he had dismissed a caller. I told him what I had come for. Said he, "How far from here is your gallery?" "Only two blocks." He went right along, stayed two hours, and had half a dozen sittings . . .

A daguerreotype does exist of Cooper, taken at Brady's studio in 1850, although Brady or more likely the reporter got the name of the hotel wrong. It was Bixby's, run by a former publisher and a place favored by literary men such as Cooper and Nathaniel Hawthorne, and by journalists and naval officers. In the daguerreotype, the expression Cooper wears falls somewhere between relaxed and resigned. Brady introduces this story by saying, "I never had an excess of confidence, and perhaps my diffidence helped me out with genuine men." But there was something audacious about Brady's arriving unannounced at the door of a famous and difficult writer whom other photographers feared. It's clear that Cooper did not have to be talked into posing. Either Brady's reputation, combined with that audacity, or his easy manner and practiced charm convinced the writer to sit.[23]

CHAPTER 3

# "In Daguerreotypes . . .
# We Beat the World"

Americans in the 1840s and '50s embraced the new and growing art of photography. The availability of images from the
most distant places on earth made the world a more knowable
place, a revolution in human knowledge comparable to the invention
of movable type or the Internet. But of more immediate personal value
was the possibility of having images of yourself and the people you
loved fixed forever in a form you could possess and pass on. Suddenly
a kind of immortality previously available only to the rich, who could
afford to have their portraits painted, or to those with the means to
commission a miniature from an itinerant painter, was now within the
reach of almost everyone. Even if you could afford a painted portrait,
the result would be another person's impression or interpretation of what
you looked like. This new medium, it was generally agreed, portrayed
you as you really were. At a time when children often did not survive
childhood and might be remembered only by a posthumous photo
taken of them in burial clothes, or when a son who went out west in
search of gold had little hope of communicating with the family he had
left behind, or they with him, or a husband went to sea leaving a wife
and family whose images he might gaze upon and who themselves could
not know when or if he would return, the small daguerreotypes that
people in the 1840s and '50s rushed to have made had a value that we
can only guess at today.

A nineteenth-century photographer from Cleveland, James F.
Ryder, told a story about working in central New York State, where in

one village the whole town flocked to have pictures made, and "All were friendly and genial—save one." This one person happened to be the village blacksmith, a characteristically over-muscled and bad-tempered fellow, who needled Ryder, calling him an idler and a swindler, and threatened to run him out of town. Ryder thought it wise to take the initiative and move to another village a few miles away. Soon the blacksmith showed up in a wagon outside his door. "He had a crazed manner which I did not understand and which filled me with terror," Ryder recalled. The man told the photographer to put his camera in his wagon and go with him. When Ryder asked why, the man "burst into a passion of weeping quite uncontrollable." After he was able to speak again, the blacksmith "grasped my hands . . . and told me his little boy had been drowned in the mill race and I must go and take his likeness."[1]

Photography was also among the first examples (along with the telegraph and the railway) of a phenomenon that has become almost commonplace in our time—an advance in technology that transforms rapidly from a state of inconceivable mystery or even magic to something that everyone could and must have access to. In his 1853 dictionary, Noah Webster ended a brief description of the daguerreotype process with "and then the images appear as by enchantment." Photography was at first as surprising as the possibility of wireless telephone communication seemed to us two decades ago, and then as urgent a necessity as the smartphone is today.

The number of people making daguerreotypes grew as quickly as the demand. Hawthorne, in *The House of the Seven Gables*, chose a daguerreotypist as his protagonist, his career representative of the economic fluidity of the day, when a person of modest background could easily enter the middle class, especially through trade. The materials required for starting a daguerreotype business were relatively inexpensive, and at least at first everyone was a newcomer to the process itself. Thus, a large number of tradesmen unemployed by the recession decided to give photography a try. One early proponent of photography claimed that by 1855 "nearly every village of note" in the country had a photographic establishment. In 1853 the *New York Tribune* estimated that "there cannot be less than three million daguerreotypes taken annually" in the country as a whole. By 1855 more than 400,000 daguerreotypes had been taken in the previous year in the state of

Massachusetts alone, and the 1860 U.S. Census counted 3,154 photographers in the nation.[2]

The explosive growth of photography as a business in its first decades
in America could not have happened without help from the economy
and a near doubling of the population. Even during the depression following the panics of 1837 and 1839, the photography business grew. A
New York writer for a Washington newspaper wrote in 1843 that in
what he called "these Jeremiad times," only two sorts of people were
thriving, "the *beggars* and the *takers of likenesses by daguerreotype*." But
by the end of the 1840s, New York began to thrive again as a port and
a banking center, and as a result of the wealth from these businesses
the city became the country's most important manufacturer of products, from iron to ships to sugar.

At the west end of Fulton Street, a few blocks from Brady's, the
docks were thick with the masts or stacks of sailing or steam-powered
ships from more than 150 distant ports. The streets of Lower Manhattan were clogged with sailors, longshoremen, tradesmen, garment workers, clerks, tourists, and businessmen, and by 1853 the city's omnibuses
carried more than 100,000 passengers each day. Between 1840 and
1860 the population of Manhattan grew from 313,000 to 806,000,
and the country grew from 17 million to more than 31 million. As the
depression eased and the economy grew in these years, Reese V. Jenkins notes in *Images and Enterprise*, the expansion of railroads and ca-
nals into the interior of the continent and the growth of telegraphic
networks made the shipping of photographic equipment and supplies
more feasible and economical, and the business evolved from one supported by individual craftsmen to a nascent manufacturing industry.[3]

Brady's timing was fortunate. He got into the photography trade
early, and when the demand dramatically increased, he was already
well positioned, having learned his craft and won those prizes at the
American Institute fairs in his first years as a photographer. He kept up
with and was sometimes ahead of the rapid technological changes in
the field, and nurtured his image as an elegant and desirable purveyor
of his art. But the early culmination of his growth as an artist would
come in 1851, at the World's Fair, the famous international exhibition
at London's Crystal Palace.

\* \* \*

The London Fair was formally known as the Great Exhibition of the Works of Industry of All Nations, and among its thirteen thousand exhibits were about seven hundred works, including daguerreotypes, by photographers from six nations. By March, Brady had gathered forty-eight uncolored daguerreotypes of well-known Americans to submit for judging at the fair, and had shown them to a writer for Henry Snelling's *Photographic Art-Journal*, who praised them for a "uniformity of tone, sharpness and boldness we have never seen surpassed." He predicted, correctly, that the images would enhance Brady's reputation. Five medals in all were awarded for daguerreotypes, three to Americans, one of whom was Brady. The jury commented that his images were "excellent for beauty of execution. The portraits stand forward in bold relief, upon a plain background." Horace Greeley, who visited the Crystal Palace exhibition when it opened on May 1, wrote to his *Tribune* audience back home, "In Daguerreotypes, it seems to be conceded that we beat the world." The *Illustrated London News* sent its critic to examine the daguerreotypes, and he agreed that the American photographs were the best.[4]

We don't know whether it was this praise that drew Brady to London, but in July he and Julia boarded a ship for England to see the Crystal Palace exhibition for themselves. Also on board was William Page, who was living in Florence with his wife, Sarah; and James Gordon Bennett, the editor of the *New York Herald*, located just two blocks from Brady's gallery. Brady's investment in the *Gallery of Illustrious Americans* had evidently not left him in hard financial straits, because he and Julia would remain in England and Europe until the following May, leaving the gallery in the charge of George S. Cook, who would himself be known for some important Civil War photographs. Once they reached London, Mathew and Julia were presumably as awestruck as everyone else by the Crystal Palace, a building of cast iron and plate glass covering nearly twenty acres in Hyde Park. The structure was so tall, at 135 feet, that it enclosed some of the park's towering elms.[5]

While they were abroad, Brady considered starting a gallery in London, but nothing came of it. He did take photographs while he was in England, including one of the famous British scientist Michael Faraday, posed sitting and staring intently into the camera. When Mathew and Julia crossed to the Continent, he made arrangements to

copy existing daguerreotypes of the emperor Louis Napoleon, the novelist Victor Hugo, and the poet Alphonse de Lamartine, among others.
On that European trip, Brady would later say in an advertisement, he
had also "carefully examined the most celebrated Galleries and Works
of Art, especially in France and Italy, and [had] brought with him all the
improvements and discoveries made in these countries." He arranged for
European photographers to regularly send him copies of their images of
famous people, so that he could build and keep up to date a European
collection alongside his American one. While in Paris, he also picked out
"a large assortment of Gold Lockets, and rich and elegant Cases," which
he would offer for sale in New York. He had hoped while in Europe to
meet Louis Daguerre himself, but the Frenchman died as Brady and
Julia were setting out across the Atlantic. In Italy, the Bradys presumably
visited William Page, who was busily copying the paintings of Titian at
the Pitti Palace and the Uffizi in Florence.[6]

It isn't clear why Brady stayed so long in Europe. Perhaps it was an
extended honeymoon taken by a young newlywed who could afford it.
Articles before and after his trip suggest that his eyesight had gotten
worse in 1851 but had improved by the time he returned. Perhaps,
though, given the breakneck pace at which he had worked through
much of the 1840s, it wasn't only his eyes that needed a rest. Nothing
about how his business in New York was being run in his absence
seemed to cause him any worry. Even when George Cook moved to
Charleston, South Carolina, where he would open a gallery he ran for
more than two decades, Brady was in no hurry to return home.[7]

Only a few months after Brady arrived back in New York in May 1852,
a credit agency reported that he had built up a large business, about
"the best of the sort in the city" and "had no doubt made money." Further evidence of his financial well-being was the decision to plan for an
elaborate new gallery farther up Broadway. The city was moving north,
and the Broadway purveyors of style were moving with it. A. T. Stewart had built his Marble Palace north of City Hall Park in 1848, and
his success brought more retailers to Broadway, locating farther up-
town still, on the five blocks above Canal Street. Brady's new gallery, at
359 Broadway, would be in between Stewart's and his competitors.[8]

The new gallery occupied three floors in an Italianate building over Thompson's Saloon—not the rowdy sort of saloon of Westerns, but a place where Henry James remembered regularly going as a boy for ice cream with his brother, William. After the gallery opened on March 19, 1853, *Humphrey's Journal* paid a visit and described what they saw in detail. The writer encountered samples of Brady's work displayed by the door in rosewood and gilt cases, and up two flights of stairs came to the reception room, at forty by twenty-six feet, the city's largest.

> The floors are carpeted with superior velvet tapestry, highly colored and of a large and appropriate pattern. The walls are covered with satin and gold paper. The ceiling [is] frescoed, and in the center is suspended a six-gilt and enamelled chandelier, with prismatic drops that throw their enlivening colors in abundant profusion. The light through the windows is softened by passing the meshes of the most costly needle worked lace curtains or intercepted, if occasion requires, by shades commensurate with the gayest of palaces, while the golden cornices, and festooned damasks indicate that Art dictated their arrangement.

The walls of the reception room were hung, as they were at 205 Broadway, with daguerreotypes that Brady had made or collected, "of Presidents, Generals, Kings, Queens, Noblemen." Beyond this room was the business office, where samples of frames, cases, and lockets were displayed, and beyond that was a ladies parlor, also elaborately decorated in silks, velvets, and brocades. The building was 150 feet deep, and at the back were tucked two operating rooms, one with a northern exposure and one with a southern. The two floors above were used for preparing, developing, coloring, and mounting the plates, or for creating what Brady called "daguerreotypes on ivory," an innovation of his that involved having an artist copy an image by hand on an ivory surface.[9]

In *The Refinement of America*, Richard Bushman points out that by creating such lavishly designed and decorated spaces, "daguerreotypists hoped to envelop photographic portraits in the refinement attached to paintings." Brady seems to have returned from his tour of the galleries and museums of Europe with an invigorated sense that the daguerreotype held an honorable place among the arts of portraiture. Americans had embraced portrait photography more readily than European photographers, who had generally focused more on places than people in their early efforts—and the recognition of Brady's work at the World's Fair was evidence that Americans had taken portraiture further. The Broadway daguerreotypists with the same sorts of ambitions as Brady had, like him, tried from the first to create spaces that were impressively stylish. But by the early 1850s, as New York became wealthier and more sophisticated, Broadway gallery owners such as Brady—Jeremiah Gurney, Martin M. Lawrence (who had also won a medal at the World's Fair), and others—poured even more money and effort into surroundings that could distinguish them from the hundred or so other daguerreotype operators working in Manhattan and Brooklyn at the time.[10]

Brady's renewed focus on the art of photography was highlighted in an advertisement in the *Tribune* a year after the 359 Broadway gallery opened, and also after he had won yet another medal at the New York Crystal Palace exhibition in 1853: "I wish to vindicate true art," he pronounced, and invited the public to decide for itself whether his devotion to "the Daguerreotype Art" and his "constant labor to perfect and elevate it" were not evident when his work was compared with the cheaper work of his many competitors. He was charging about two dollars for a daguerreotype at his new studio, whereas the twenty-five-cent miniature was still widely available. Confusingly enough, however, Brady soon advertised that he had found a way to make a cheaper daguerreotype of good quality, and offered it for sale for as little as fifty cents at his 205 Broadway studio, which he had briefly closed but then refurbished and reopened.[11]

Early in 1855 the general subject of daguerreotype as art was still on his mind. He wrote a letter to Samuel Morse asking the now-famous inventor to put his name on a statement meant for publication. Its primary point was that the work of daguerreotypists had been of use to "the kindred arts of painting, drawing & engraving." Almost as an aside, the letter stipulated that it "is understood and appreciated" that daguerreotype had also put "the rarest & most subtle of artistic effects . . . within the general reach." None of Brady's claims in the letter were in any way arguable, but there is no evidence that Morse agreed to have his name used in this way, probably with good reason suspecting that Brady was trying to capitalize on his renown.[12]

Like so many things Brady did in his long career, the letter to Morse seems to have been part idealism and part commerce. Even as Brady succeeded in distinguishing himself from all but a few of his competitors in the city, the struggle to remain among those few was constant. The career of the American photographic pioneer John Plumbe must have served as a cautionary tale. Plumbe went into the daguerreotype business in 1840, perhaps as a sideline while he was lobbying Congress to build a transcontinental railroad, a cause that he had been among the first to advocate. By 1845 he owned a chain of fourteen galleries, including one at 251 Broadway in New York; one on Pennsylvania Avenue in Washington; and others in Boston, Baltimore, Philadelphia, Cincinnati, St. Louis, and in places as far flung as Petersburg, Virginia, and Dubuque, Iowa. He had received a patent for a process for making a colored daguerreotype and had created a lithographic process for reproducing daguerreotypes that he sold as Plumbeotypes. He published books and a magazine, but by 1847, due to mismanagement by those who ran his galleries, he had to sell them to pay his debts, and by 1849 he had given up photography and gone to California to pan for gold. After five years of that, he moved to Dubuque, where in 1857 he slit his throat.[13]

No small part of Brady's success was his own personality. An 1853 article in *Frank Leslie's Illustrated Monthly* spoke of Brady's "urbanity of manners" and "untiring attention to the feelings and happiness of those with whom he comes into contact." The writer concluded, "Mr. Brady has the happy faculty of being attentive without being officious, of possessing suavity without obtrusiveness, and is altogether eminently the right man for the right place." Brady knew, in short, not just how to be likable but how to carry himself with a dignity matching that of his most famous sitters. He worked with hundreds of such subjects, but little is known about his interactions with them beyond what is revealed in the photographs themselves.[14]

For those whose portraits were being made, the novelty and mystery of the daguerreotype process compounded the nervousness and self-consciousness that most of us feel even today when being photographed by a professional. Brady's calm confidence must have gone a long way toward relaxing his sitters, as would the beauty, orderliness, and relative quiet of his surroundings. Each image took many long seconds and even minutes of stillness, with the sitter's head stabilized by what was sometimes indelicately called a vise, as the subject and camera operator waited for the right exposure. Henry James later recalled that an affecting Brady portrait of him with his father, taken at the age of eleven, the standing boy's hand resting on the sitting father's shoulder, required an "interminably long" holding of the pose. In spite of this, Brady managed to take a pleasingly intimate photograph, one in which the affection of father and son is expressed in their physical comfort with each other.[15]

In 1858 the *American Phrenological Journal* offered both a character assessment of Mathew Brady and a biographical sketch. The sketch concludes:

> Few men among us who have attained great eminence and success in business pursuits are more deservedly popular than Mr. Brady, from claims purely personal; for none can be more distinguished for urbanity and geniality of manners, and an untiring attention to the feelings and happiness of those with whom he comes in contact.

Phrenology relied for its credibility on broad generalizations that were hard to dispute, in conjunction with a stab at insight that masked itself as scientific study. In the case of a person as well known as Brady would have been by 1858, the phrenological assessment might be taken as a restatement of his general reputation. The journal concluded that he had a lot of nervous and physical energy; a forceful personality; a deep well of self-esteem; strong likes and dislikes, especially in people; a natural sympathy for others but a quick temper; a good sense of design and style; a first-rate memory; an indifference to religion; and a disinterest in money for its own sake.[16]

Had Brady acquired his suavity and composure on the upstate New York farm of his Irish immigrant parents? It's a mystery, and yet so many people from provincial backgrounds remake themselves overnight into the picture of urban elegance. Perhaps Brady did so when he began to work at A. T. Stewart's. One quality that seemed to be intuitive in him, although he might well have learned it from his neighbor Barnum, was his understanding that it was not enough only to sell his images. He must also sell himself.

# CHAPTER 4

# "Large Copies from Small Originals"

In the middle 1850s, what would be thought of as photography until the digital age—the creation of positive paper prints from negative images (first on glass and decades later on film)—came into wide use, allowing for easy reproduction and even mass production of photographs on paper. As early as 1847, Americans had begun to have success with a process of creating negatives on glass plates, examples of which were displayed at the 1851 World's Fair. Also in 1851, an Englishman named Frederick Scott Archer introduced the use of a sticky material called collodion (from the Greek for "gluey"), made by dissolving guncotton in sulfuric ether, to cover the glass plate with a uniform, light-sensitive film.

John Adams Whipple of Boston was the first photographer to show real mastery of paper prints made from glass negatives (first using an albumen, or egg white, process that also included honey, and then using collodion), and at the 1853 World's Fair in New York his "crystalotypes," as he called them, perhaps to emphasize their clarity, won first prize. He began offering lessons in his process to other photographers, for the reasonable fee of fifty dollars, and by 1854 Brady and his Broadway competitors Jeremiah Gurney and Martin Lawrence had all embraced this advancement in the medium. Brady soon photographed his entire collection of daguerreotypes so that he could easily sell as many prints of each of his images as people wished to buy.[1]

The wet-plate process, as it was called, could also produce what was at first known as a daguerreotype on glass, whereby the exposed collodion glass negative, if darkly varnished on the reverse side, or backed by a piece of black paper or velvet or metal, became a one-of-a-kind positive image most often called an ambrotype (from the Greek for "imperishable"). Introduced in 1854 but reaching the height of their popularity in 1856 and 1857, ambrotypes were generally the same size as daguerreotypes and were presented in the same leather cases. Because they did not have the distracting reflective quality that daguerreotypes did, they were more popular with customers. Since glass cost so much less than silver and copper, the images could be produced much more cheaply than daguerreotypes, and the process did not involve the dangerous mercury vapors that were becoming a concern throughout the nascent profession.[2]

Like the other big portrait studios, Brady's made ambrotypes just as paper printing was coming into wide use, and for a time these studios were simultaneously offering ambrotypes, photographs, and daguerreotypes. In an advertisement in 1856, Brady claimed to have been the first to introduce ambrotypes in New York, and added that they were "finer that any known style of pictures." One inarguably fine ambrotype Brady made in 1856 was of John C. Frémont during his presidential campaign. The pose, with the famous explorer's body turned sideways to the camera and his head facing it, is less statute-like, less like a formal painted portrait, than Brady's daguerreotypes of other great men. Its light background and the light-colored jacket Frémont wears also add to the appealing informality of the image. If it is not varnished on the back, but only placed on a dark background, an ambrotype can be viewed from one direction as a negative image and from the reverse side as a positive, Brady invented an ingenious case for displaying the Frémont ambrotype from the back or the front.[3]

But all the big studios soon began to turn more of their attention to printing on paper, which could easily be colored or even altered with paint, India ink, or pencil. Brady advertised in 1855 in *The Crayon,* an art magazine, that his studio was now making photographs as well as daguerreotypes, and could offer "Large copies produced from small originals. Daguerreotypes from Life, Old Pictures, Paintings, and Statuary as usual."[4]

The shift from daguerreotypes to ambrotypes to paper prints happened with surprising speed. In 1853, daguerreotypes still dominated the market, especially in portraits. By 1856, a new publication called

*Frank Leslie's Illustrated Newspaper* used in its first year 123 illustrations copied from photographs. Of these, 100 were ambrotypes, 13 were daguerreotypes, and 10 were from photos on paper—"a good measure," the historian of photography Robert Taft writes, "of the popularity that the ambrotype was enjoying in 1856." He also counted 97 of the 123 as having been made by Brady, "which shows that Brady was the fashionable photographer of the day." By 1857, of 128 photographs in *Leslie's* that year, just over half were ambrotypes, 60 were from photos on paper, and 2 were daguerreotypes. By 1858 virtually all the photographic sources for illustration in the newspaper were paper prints.[5]

One innovation that helped hasten the demise of the ambrotype can be attributed in part to the Brady studio. In 1856 a Scottish photographer named Alexander Gardner left Glasgow with his family and sailed to America, intending to join a cooperative community in Iowa. Gardner had helped found the community, called Clydesdale, six years earlier, basing it on the ideas of Robert Owen, the Welsh socialist who had begun New Harmony, Indiana. Clydesdale had been dedicated to "a more simple useful and rational mode of life," but now it was having serious financial difficulties. When his ship reached Newfoundland, Gardner learned that many members of the community had come down with "galloping consumption"—tuberculosis.

Not wanting to expose his family to the fatal disease, Gardner sent his wife and two children, his mother, and his brother to New York and went on to Iowa alone to do what he could to settle the community's affairs. Gardner, who was thirty-five years old, had been a jeweler's apprentice in Glasgow, then a loan broker, then the owner and publisher of a Glasgow weekly newspaper, and had worked only briefly as a portrait photographer. His specialty had been the calotype, produced by a process invented by the Englishman William Henry Fox Talbot at about the same time daguerreotype had been made public. The process, which involved creating a negative on paper from which a paper print could then be made, had never been popular in the United States, where, thanks in part to Samuel Morse, daguerreotype became entrenched early and held on.

Gardner's interest in photography might have been sparked by the 1851 London World's Fair, which he visited soon after it opened, and about which he editorialized for his newspaper. Gardner would likely have seen Brady's work on display there and been aware that Brady had won one of the fair's top prizes. When Gardner met up with his family in New York after going to Iowa, he contacted Brady. Gardner's portrait business, which he had begun the year before in the town of Dumbarton, near Glasgow, had not been a success. Still, he was able to convince Brady to take him on. Hiring Gardner was a good business decision, because beyond Gardner's ability or potential ability as a photographer, he also offered Brady his experience as a publisher and businessman.[6]

One practical skill Gardner brought with him was his knowledge of the enlargement process that paper prints made possible. Although larger prints were something Brady's studio had already begun to offer, enlarging was at first a difficult skill to master. It usually involved a special camera, which cast the original image through an aperture onto sensitized paper. The farther the paper was from the aperture, the larger the new image. The most popular device at the time was known as a solar camera, which used the sun as a light source and could take hours or even days to produce an enlargement, depending on the strength of the sunlight. Although Brady, like most serious portrait photographers, had long valued the daguerreotype for its clarity and detail, he was enthusiastic about enlargements on paper, seeing that they also had artistic potential.[7]

Wet-plate photography also encouraged the production of larger images printed directly from larger negatives. Glass plates were not only cheaper, but because they did not require the buffing that daguerreotype plates did, they were easier to prepare at larger sizes. Within a few months of Gardner's arrival in his studio, Brady was offering the public what he called "Brady Imperials," *imperial* being a term that had long been used for a standard size (twenty-two by thirty inches) of paper. Brady had in the early 1850s offered engravings of what he called imperial size. These new Brady prints varied in size from as small as eleven by fifteen to as big as twenty by twenty-four. The prints were made on rag paper treated with a solution of ordinary table salt, and because nothing else was done to make the surface glossy, they retained a soft or matte surface. The prints were treated with sel d'or, or gold toning, a solution that was also used on daguerreotype plates, and that gave the prints a rich brown color. Because of the large size of the negatives, the portraits

were generally either full length or three-quarters length, giving them
a grandness not before known in photographic portraits. They could
also be enlarged without losing as much detail as an image beginning
as a small daguerreotype would. Gardner's hands-on experience with
paper printing undoubtedly contributed to the success of Brady's Imperials and what were called life-size enlargements.[8]

Paper prints could rival painted portraits once they were enhanced
by artists, who could color them with oils, crayons, or watercolors, and
could improve the look of the sitter by subtly redrawing a jawline or
covering up an imperfection. These doctored photographs thus both
imbued photography with the portrait painter's prerogative of flatter-
ing his patron and anticipated today's use of Photoshop. By October
1857, *Harper's Weekly* wrote of Brady's life-size, oil-enhanced photographs, "The vocation of the portrait painter is not gone, but modified.
Portrait painting by the old methods is as completely defunct as is navi-
gation by the stars." Depending on how elaborate the enhancement was
and how skillful the artist, Brady could charge as much as $750 for an
Imperial, which was almost certainly another reason for his enthusiasm
for them. Smaller, rougher, unenhanced, and thus less expensive, prints
also grew popular, as the Brady Imperials became, in the words of one
historian, "the prized acquisition of the élite."[9]

Nathaniel Parker Willis, a flamboyant poet, journalist, author,
and the founder and editor for three decades of the magazine *Home
Journal*, knew Brady and wrote about him from time to time. On one
March morning in 1857 he found himself "loitering past Brady's door"
at 359 Broadway, where he admired an Imperial print on display and
climbed the stairs to wait among "quite a crowd of ladies, as usual," to
have his own portrait made. His experience resulted in musings on the
state of the photographic art:

> For the improvement of mechanism, by which *so much larger
> a likeness* can now be taken, Mr. Brady, I believe, is to have
> the credit; though I think the other secret of the matter—
> the knowing how sunbeam, pose and pencil, should be
> *Brady'd* together—shows more the perseverance of the man.
> He has employed thirty or forty artists to experiment upon
> this. The photograph, as you understand, is first taken by
> the machine, with artistic directions as to the choice of look

and posture. A sitting of fifteen minutes is then given to an accomplished crayonist, who thus makes his memoranda for *stippling* the otherwise imperfect picture—supplying, with the pencil, that is to say, the life or expression left wanting by the photograph's soul-omitting fidelity to mere matter, and removing the mechanical blemishes, such as the deep black with which the photograph copies light eyebrows, and similar defects in shading, which are easily corrected. To do this judiciously—to add life to the dead photograph without altering its type and truth—requires, of course, practical skill and the best judgment.[10]

In the photograph of Willis taken that day he is every inch the dandy, and even more dramatically so in a Brady image taken several years later, his hand tucked over his heart inside a flowing silk coat with kimono-like sleeves. A review surveying the Fair of the American Institute for 1857, where Brady would win a small gold medal for best plain and retouched photographs, said his life-size photographs were by far the best in the show. The writer praises a composite of three such photographs on five-by-seven-foot paper, as "remarkable for its excellence in color, tone and detail," and marvels at the difficulty of handling such huge prints, commenting that he could find only one minor tear. In an advertisement in September 1857, Brady announced a display of his five-by-seven photographs, calling them "the largest in the world."[11]

Edward T. Whitney, an important early daguerreotypist and photographer from Rochester, New York, remembered later that Brady and Jeremiah Gurney, one of Brady's fiercest competitors, had been vying to make the best large print at that same fair. Whitney happened to visit both studios while each was working on his entry, promising not to reveal to either man what the other was up to. "Brady prepared his paper for a life-size group of three," Whitney recalled in 1892. "He floated his paper in an immense tank of gutta percha, 7 feet long and 5 feet wide, on a 'silver wave' that cost $100.00. Gurney spread his silver on the paper with wads of cotton. His subject was a life-size figure of a lady. Brady's group took the prize."[12]

However hard preparing large sheets of paper must have been, the process of enlargement had no theoretical limit, and people built huge

Magazine editor and journalist Nathaniel Parker Willis
(circa 1857). *Library of Congress*

cameras to make bigger and bigger negatives. One camera in Paris had a box a dozen feet long and a three-foot-long lens that was more than a foot in diameter. The studio installed rails on the floor on which the camera could move.[13]

Brady might well have created the biggest print of anyone of his time, when in celebration of the completion of the Atlantic Cable, which created the first (though brief) telegraphic connection between the Old World and the New, he made an image on transparent cloth fifty feet by twenty-five feet and hung it from the front of his Broadway gallery, using six hundred candles to backlight it. Across the top of the display was the printed slogan SCIENCE, LABOR AND ART—UNION CABLE. The celebration was one in a long line of so-called Festivals of Connection in the city, beginning with an event honoring the creation of the United States, and including later celebrations upon the completion of the Erie Canal, the Croton Aqueduct, and the Brooklyn Bridge. For this festival, all the establishments along Broadway tried to outshine one another with the impressiveness of their displays. Brady's grouped Benjamin Franklin (clearly a copy of a painted portrait); Morse, the telegraph's inventor; and Cyrus Field, the driving force behind the Atlantic Cable (and another former shop boy at A. T. Stewart's).[14]

On the first of September, Field led a torchlit parade up Broadway from the Battery to New York's own Crystal Palace, in what is now Bryant Park, riding in the mayor's carriage. But the celebration was not as dramatic as one that had occurred immediately after the first transmission on the Atlantic Cable, which went in Morse code from Queen Victoria to President Buchanan on August 16. Fireworks that night had ignited and destroyed the clock tower and cupola of City Hall, and had very nearly taken down the whole building. Brady's six hundred candles for the later celebration would seem to have endangered his own gallery, but there are no reports that any fire companies were called to the scene.


Business was good in the months after Alexander Gardner first joined Brady in New York. In September 1856, Brady took out a long advertisement on the front page of the *Daily Tribune* lightheartedly headed "Orphic Sayings," a list of fourteen reasons, more spirited than witty, why a reader should have a portrait made at what the ad called "Brady's

Ambrotype Galleries." The final reason warned, on a heavy note, "you cannot tell how soon it may be too late." A year later Brady bought an even longer ad in the same newspaper, running the entire length of a column at the center of the front page. One of the first points it made was that there could be an embarrassing crush of would-be sitters at his gallery at the noon hour, and that potential customers should remember that even as the days were growing shorter—the ad ran in November— he could take sitters until four p.m. The ad also claimed that Brady's had made nearly thirty thousand portraits in the last year. He still oper- ated two Broadway galleries at this time, referring in the ad to the one at 205 as "Brady's Lower Gallery" ("convenient [to] those occupied down town who desire portraits"), but even with this in mind and including daguerreotypes he had copied in ambrotype or on paper, thirty thou- sand seems extraordinarily high.[15]

The staff for Brady's 359 gallery now numbered around twenty-five people, and the ad offered, in addition to portraits by the three photo- graphic methods in use, ones done up in oils, crayon, or watercolor, and on ivory or medallions. Brady listed more than thirty of several hun- dred Imperials on display at 359, including portraits of the current president, James Buchanan, and four of his predecessors: Van Buren, Tyler, Fillmore, and Pierce. His gallery was crowded with gawkers and customers. Not only were his images of the famous available directly from him, but they were used more and more by the illustrated maga- zines. The first woodcut from a Brady image had appeared in 1854, in *Graham's Magazine*; his relationship with *Frank Leslie's Illustrated Newspaper* had begun in 1855; and the first image in a long and active relationship with *Harper's Weekly* appeared on May 2, 1857, made from a photograph of a portrait of Samuel Morse. Brady images would be the basis for fourteen woodcuts in *Harper's* that year.[16]

Given his background in finance and publishing, Gardner is cred- ited with introducing Brady to good business practices, insisting, for instance, that he hire a bookkeeper. But even with Gardner's help and the robust business in his Broadway galleries, credit reports from R. G. Dun & Company throughout the 1850s show a general weakening of credit. According to a report in 1852, Brady "likes to live pretty fast life & spends his money freely, but is [very] prompt and punctual, puts by sufficient funds every year for his bus[iness] Engagements." As the decade wore on, Brady became less punctual in paying his debts, but he was generally considered to be honest, a word that recurs in the reports. In 1856 he was considered "a fair risk for mod[est] amts [of credit] on short time." But by July 2, 1861, days before the First Battle of Bull Run and five years after Gardner had gone to work for him, Dun reported that Brady's "gen'l credit is weak." Nonetheless, Brady's growing confidence in Gardner apparently encouraged him to make another go at a studio in Washington, with the Scot in charge.[17]

The psychology of the two men suggests another possible explanation for Gardner's being sent to Washington. Brady had been in business of one sort or another for about fifteen years when Gardner appeared at his door. His business model, and very likely his ego, involved promoting his own name and himself over the many talented people he would employ during his long career: the man and his studio were one and the same. This practice was common among his fellow photographic gallery owners and businesses of all sorts, from A. T. Stewart's department store to Harper and Brothers publishers. Gardner had not achieved the sort of success or fame that his new boss had won almost from the first moment of his photographic career, but Gardner had owned and run a newspaper and had helped establish and fund the idealist community in Iowa. He was both ambitious and used to being in charge. If his experience had not translated into success in his own portrait business in Scotland, that experience nonetheless made him more than just another of the many camera operators Brady would employ. And given the skill as a photographer Gardner exhibited after going to Washington, he would have had as strong a set of ideas as Brady about the process and the aesthetics of portrait making. Two such oversize personalities were not likely to do well together in the confines of a single gallery.

# CHAPTER 5

# "Startling Likenesses of the Great"

Brady opened his second Washington business on Pennsylvania Avenue, in photographers row, near where his first had been a decade earlier. The new studio was in the middle of a wide but shallow block between Sixth and Seventh streets, and filled the upper stories of two adjoining buildings, the one to the east dating to the 1830s or '40s and the other built to match in 1854. Brick and Italianate, their stucco facades overlooked "the Avenue," the unfinished Capitol looming to the east and the White House, looking out on the unfinished Washington Monument, ten blocks to the west.

Brady erected a sign running across the front of the second story of the two buildings, reading BRADY'S NATIONAL PHOTOGRAPHIC ART GALLERY. Gilman's Drug Store occupied the first floor at 352 Pennsylvania, and the bankers Sweeney, Rittenhouse and Fant were at 350. One door to the east was Galt's Jeweler; Galt's son Norman would be the first husband of Edith Galt, who later married President Woodrow Wilson. Because daguerreotypists had been using the upper floors of 350 since about 1850, it was already fitted out with glass skylights. After Brady got there in 1858 he had a "window wall" built on the north side of the fourth floor. (He would rent these rooms until 1881, after which they would remain empty for more than a century, as the eastern end of Pennsylvania Avenue fell on hard times. Today only the window wall gives any evidence that Brady was ever there.)[1]

Washington was a natural place for Brady to locate to at such a time in the nation's history: the question of admitting Kansas to the

Union and other fundamental, deeply divisive issues were being argued in the capital in an increasingly feverish way. Only seventy years earlier, the city had been carved out of Maryland and Virginia, two slave states that still gave Washington a distinctly southern aspect. Yet the District of Columbia was *the* federal city, dedicated to the union of the states, home of the government, headquarters of the military, and the place to be if you wanted your portion of the wealth and power of the nation. When Congress was in session, the population of some seventy-five thousand (eleven thousand of whom were free blacks, three thousand more of whom were slaves) swelled not only with the people's representatives and their staffs, but also with lobbyists and importuners of every sort, and with those who housed and fed them—and offered them every sort of pleasure, from the tearoom and the theater to the barroom and the whorehouse. From Georgetown to Capitol Hill, it featured both a robust social life, often led by wealthy southern hostesses, and ample opportunities to be swindled, robbed, and assaulted. Washington was an odd combination of being both half built and worn out, and its few grand buildings were insufficient to attract any sort of tourist trade. If the city bustled less than Lower Manhattan, it had the allure of high stakes, high emotions, and ultimate power.[2]

Brady had never lost touch with Washington, undoubtedly in part because of Julia's connection to it, and in 1857 he had photographed the new president, James Buchanan, and had contributed photographs to an exhibition of the Washington Art Association, of which he was a member. The city had not changed greatly since he opened his first gallery there. Henry Adams only slightly overstated his case when he wrote of Washington, "As in 1800 and 1850, so in 1860, the same rude colony was camped in the same forest, with the same unfinished Greek temples for workrooms, and sloughs for roads."[3]

Like his galleries in New York, Brady's in Washington was located in the thick of things. The nicer restaurants, shops, bars, and hotels were also located on the north side of the Avenue. Steps away were two of Washington's most popular hotels, facing each other across Sixth Street. The National and Brown's Marble Hotel (formerly the Indian Queen) were both frequented by congressmen and the many hangers-on that their presence attracted. Across the Avenue's broad expanse, dusty or muddy depending on the weather, and always treacherous in spite of being one of the few cobbled streets in the city, were ramshackle buildings, bordering what was known as Murder Bay, an area of slums frequented by criminals and prostitutes. Also across the Avenue, a few steps to the west, began the city's tumultuous Center Market, which stretched from Seventh to Ninth Streets, offering in season all manner of fruits, vegetables, seafood, and meat, plus a remarkable crop of flies or, also in season, mosquitoes from the open canal and sewer that ran behind it along what is now Constitution Avenue.

Up Seventh Street was the city's main business district. On the left, on Seventh at F Street, the General Post Office and the nearly finished Patent Office, both built of marble in the Greek Revival style, faced each other. On D Street between Fifth and Fourth was Judiciary Square, and City Hall, from which slaves had sometimes been sold before the practice was abolished in the District in 1850. But slaves belonging to southern congressmen, who mostly congregated at the National Hotel, waited for their masters outside on the brick sidewalks of the Avenue, otherwise used as Washington's version of the Broadway promenade. When visiting the gallery in Washington, Brady often stayed at the National or at Brown's, signing in as "Brady of New York."[4]

On January 26, 1858, an advertisement ran in the *Washington Daily National Intelligencer* announcing the opening of Brady's "Gallery of Photographic Art," and promising that "he is prepared to execute commissions for the Imperial Photograph, hitherto made only at his well-known establishment in New York." He also offered the Washington public "a variety of unique and rare photographic specimens" and many of the same famous faces that graced the walls of his Broadway galleries. In April 1858 the *Photographic and Fine Art Journal* reported that Brady's Washington studio was "splendid" and had already "received the highest praise from the papers of that city." In June, the *National Intelligencer* wrote that "this collection of exquisite portraits, this photographic exhibition of fair women and grave and reverent seignors [*sic*] may be legitimately classed in the domain of fine art," and encouraged the public to "while away an hour in scanning this array of beauty, diplomacy, living senatorial and clerical celebrity, besides the speaking, almost startling likenesses of the great ones who have passed from the earth."[5]

Alexander Gardner did not move to Washington until February of 1858, presumably having run Brady's 359 Broadway gallery while his boss was setting up the new one in the District. Gardner's brother,

James, who had accompanied the family from Scotland, had already settled in Washington, and would work with his brother at the new studio.

In Washington, Alexander Gardner soon became acquainted with Amos Kendall, who had been the U.S. postmaster general under Presidents Jackson and Van Buren. Kendall had recently helped set up a school for the deaf, dumb, and blind, and Gardner arranged for his mother, who was deaf, to attend. The school eventually became Gallaudet University, the grounds of which encompass what was Kendall's eighty-acre farm about two miles northeast of downtown. Gardner and his family lived near Kendall, in Kendall Green, also now part of the Gallaudet campus.[6]

Kendall had been hired by Samuel Morse in 1845 to help him find investors in what would become the Magnetic Telegraph Company, and he had been associated with the inventor ever since. Gardner's growing friendship with Kendall led to an interest in electricity, and eventually Gardner would develop a means of electrically lighting the Washington studio for photography. But a newspaper article at the time typically gives credit for the invention to Brady himself. After visiting the gallery, the reporter writes:

> The most curious arrangement to us was Mr. Brady's machine for producing the electric light so necessary for the completion of the photographs, and which, as he playfully observed, allows him to create his own sun-light or moon-light at pleasure.[7]

No other mention is made of this device, even when Gardner opened his own studio a few years later, so it was probably more of a curiosity than a useful enhancement, and photographers continued to rely on natural light until Thomas Edison came along.

In its early years Brady's Washington gallery apparently displayed only photographs, which, according to a letter by one visitor, were "almost all of large size and some coloured . . . the plain ones are touched in india ink, some very elaborately. The coloring must have cost much." The letter writer's overall impression was that Brady's "pictures are certainly very fine indeed. The tone and whites excellent. The positions are not amiss but very monotonous"—by which he apparently meant the poses, which still required the subject to sit or stand very still, braced, because of the exposure time required.[8]

Eventually Brady began to incorporate some of the paintings from his collection in New York into his Washington gallery. Among the most impressive were those of Clay, Webster, and Calhoun, all three of whom had died early in the decade. At least two of the paintings were copied or directly inspired by Brady daguerreotypes. All of them were made by copying on glass and enlarging to life size on canvas Brady's original daguerreotype of each man (or, perhaps in the case of Clay, a daguerreotype by Southworth and Hawes of Boston copied on glass by Brady), and were then finished by oil painters. Henry F. Darby, who had shared studio space with Brady on Broadway in 1855 and later moved to the same block on Pennsylvania Avenue as Brady's new Washington studio, painted the portraits of Clay and Calhoun. The third, of Webster, was likely the work of an Irish painter named Richard Francis Nagle, also known for portraits of Generals Winfield Scott and Ulysses S. Grant, both Brady subjects. The paintings of the three statesmen were displayed together in heavy frames in New York and then, for many years, in Washington. Oil portraits of James Fenimore Cooper and Washington Irving would also migrate from the Broadway studio to the one on the Avenue.[9]

Gardner began to take and add to the collection imperial-size portraits of Washingtonians such as his new friend Amos Kendall and the immensely wealthy banker and philanthropist William Wilson Corcoran, famous for his art collection and his parties at his H Street mansion. His Southern sympathies would cause him to leave Washington for Paris during the Civil War. As the nation lurched toward that war, the Washington gallery would make images of leaders on both sides. Massachusetts senator Charles Sumner, who had been caned nearly to death on the floor of the U.S. Senate for his abolitionist views, sat at Brady's after he returned to Washington from his more than three years of rehabilitation from his injuries. A senator from the opposite end of the Union, holding distinctly secessionist views, Mississippian Jefferson Davis, also sat at Brady's, as did his wife, Varina. Smaller photographs of Washingtonians were displayed in a case by the back entrance to the Brady studio, on C Street, to encourage passersby to stop in.[10]

In the second-floor reception room, in addition to the portraits hung

U.S. senator from Massachusetts Charles Sumner (early 1860s).
*Library of Congress*

regularly along the walls, was a box stereoscope for displaying three-dimensional-seeming stereoscopic photos of Niagara Falls and places of interest in Europe. Taken with a special stereoscope camera that made two images simultaneously from a slightly different perspective (the two lenses often separated by the same distance as the human eyes), stereoscopes were a curiosity fast becoming the rage.

Those who came to the gallery to have their own images made were taken up two more flights, passing the floor where the developed and printed photographs were inked or painted, then mounted, matted, and framed, and arriving at the fourth floor, where operators would take the photograph. The operating room had two cameras, posing chairs, headrests, backgrounds, reflectors, and a stove for warmth. Also on this floor were a dressing room for those about to be photographed and the business office for the studio, where Gardner's bookkeeper would work. These rooms were in 350 Pennsylvania, and the darkroom and printing room were on the fourth floor of 352, leading to the roof. On the roof were racks where the negatives were developed in the sun.

Brady had been criticized as early as 1851 at the Crystal Palace exhibition for not paying more attention to the backgrounds in his daguerreotypes, but with the large-format Imperials, he used not only draperies for backgrounds, but also a small number of recurring props. Portraits made at the Washington studio often show the posing chairs, one of which was elaborately carved of oak, and was appropriated from the House of Representatives, although rumor had it that the chair had belonged to Lincoln. It was sometimes called the "Lincoln chair," if only because Lincoln had posed in it, but also the "Brady chair," because so many other famous people had been photographed sitting in it at his Washington gallery. Among other props was a four-foot-tall column that was Corinthian on one side and Ionic on the other. Subjects striking a standing pose could steady themselves on this, or the column could be elevated on a pedestal to frame one side of the composition, as many of the Imperials taken in the Broadway studio were framed.

Some photographs featured an ornate gold clock, always stopped at eleven fifty-two, or a variety of books, including one volume of the *Annals of Congress*, a project undertaken between 1834 and 1856 to re-create the "debates and proceedings" of the First to the Eighteenth Congresses, which met in the years from 1789 to 1824. Presumably this leather-bound volume would wreathe the many congressmen who sat for Brady in the glory of their esteemed predecessors. For the Imperials taken in both studios, a variety of other props were introduced for specific reasons, such as a telegraph device for a portrait of Samuel

Morse or a globe for a portrait of Cyrus Field, because of his connection to the Atlantic Cable.

The long-standing competition between Brady and Jeremiah Gurney had the positive effect of spurring each man's ambitions. Gurney had opened a New York gallery in 1840 and had been another protégé of Samuel Morse. When the stereoscope was introduced at the 1851 World's Fair in London, it struck the fancy of Queen Victoria, which created a worldwide interest in the device, and it was introduced into the United States the next year. Both Brady and Gurney offered stereoscope viewers three or four weeks later, although stereoscopes did not really catch on till near the end of the decade.[11]

Like Brady, Gurney regularly won medals for his work. The *Photographic and Fine Art Journal*, in an 1858 article surveying "New York Photographic Galleries," wrote that "Mr. G. has taken the premium for his beautiful pictures on many occasions, and deservedly so too for he has had the best operators, and the very best artists and has paid the highest prices for everything"—words that undoubtedly got Brady's goat, since the journal's writer had visited Brady's gallery just before Gurney's. The writer did point out that Brady had twenty-six people working for him at 359 Broadway, and Gurney had one fewer, and also reported that he had found Brady "up to his ears in business." The same article reports that Charles D. Fredricks, who had worked with Gurney until starting his own Broadway gallery in 1856, now had "the largest and most spacious rooms in New York," and that "his monthly receipts are $7,000."[12]

That article appeared in January of 1858. By fall, Gurney had moved his gallery up Broadway, to 707, to what the *American Journal of Photography* called a "photographic palace." By the following fall, Brady had closed both his Broadway galleries, the old one at 205 and the later one at 359, and opened a new gallery, over a barbershop at 643 Broadway, at the corner of Bleecker Street. Even as he moved in at 643, Brady might well have had his sights fixed on a location still farther up Broadway than Gurney's. For one thing, his new neighborhood was so crowded, as one newspaper would describe it, that his gallery was "hidden there in a chaos of hair-dressers, glove-dealers, and miscellaneous men of bazaars," so that New Yorkers knew Brady "rather by faith than by sight."[13]

Brady could stand to be obscured for only so long, and by the fall of 1860 he had leapfrogged over Gurney to 785 Broadway, where he opened his most elaborate and impressive gallery yet, his last one in New York. Located on the northwest corner of Broadway and Tenth Street, it was across from the Gothic Revival Grace Church, designed by James Renwick Jr., who also designed the fashionable St. Denis Hotel at Broadway and Eleventh, where Mathew and Julia had been living since 1857. After a special press preview, the *Herald* wrote, "the new gallery . . . not only far surpasses his former one, but every similar establishment in the world." It went on to say that its "grand entrance on Broadway is as fine as anything of the kind on that great thorough-fare; . . . The interior accommodations are perfect." The *New York Times* called the new Brady gallery, in the excitable prose typical of the era, "a Broadway Valhalla."[14]

# CHAPTER 6

# "Wonderful Strangers"

The year 1860 took Brady to the height of his fame as a photographer of celebrities. In February he made his most influential photograph on what was probably the most important day of his subject's life up to that time. Abraham Lincoln had come to New York two days earlier to prepare for a speech he would give in Manhattan on February 27. Like other presidential candidates, he had been asked to speak at the renowned Reverend Henry Ward Beecher's Plymouth Church in Brooklyn, but he learned soon after he checked in at the Astor House on February 25 that the site of the speech had been moved to the Cooper Union (or Cooper Institute, as it was also often called in those days). On the day of the speech, Richard C. McCormick, a journalist and a member of the committee organizing the event at Cooper Union, met Lincoln with other members of the committee at the Astor House. McCormick later wrote about the experience in the *New York Evening Post*, where he soon would become the editor:

> We found him in a suit of black, much wrinkled from its careless packing in a small valise. He received us cordially, apologizing for the awkward and uncomfortable appearance he made in his new suit . . . His form and manner were indeed odd, and we thought him the most unprepossessing public man we had ever met.[1]

The committee members strolled up Broadway with Lincoln, showing him the sights, and eventually stopped at Brady's gallery, where the historian and statesman George Bancroft either happened or had managed to be. Bancroft greeted Lincoln and welcomed him to New York, McCormick writes. McCormick noticed a "most striking" contrast in the appearance of the two men, the tiny historian "courtly and precise" and the six-feet-four-inch Springfield lawyer "bluff and awkward." (In spite of their political differences—Bancroft was a Democrat—the historian would grow to admire Lincoln the president. Bancroft would ask him for a copy of his Gettysburg Address, and when Lincoln was assassinated, only five years after the meeting at Brady's, Bancroft would be asked by Congress to give the official eulogy for the fallen president.)

This day at Brady's, Lincoln's sly, self-deprecatory humor was on display. "'I am on my way to New Hampshire,' he said to Mr. Bancroft, 'where I have a son at school, who, if report be true, already knows much more than his father.' "[2]

Brady later said that he had had to pull up the collars of Lincoln's shirt and coat for the photograph, presumably to cover Lincoln's long neck. But in the resulting photograph the shirt does not seem to fit very well at the neck or the wrists, so perhaps tailoring was the problem. In any case, the photograph seems to have been posed to accentuate Lincoln's length rather than to regularize his proportions, and there wasn't much Brady could do about that wrinkled suit, at least not until his artists got hold of the print.[3]

A few weeks later Lincoln received in the mail a request for a photograph. He responded to it himself, writing that, "While I was [in New York] I was taken to one of the places where they get up such things, and I suppose they got my shaddow [sic] and can multiply copies indefinitely."[4]

That they would do. The image was the basis for a woodcut engraving on the cover of the May 26, 1860, issue of *Harper's Weekly*, a few days after Lincoln's presidential nomination, and again on the front page a few days after his November election, tiny buffalo in the background emphasizing Lincoln's frontier roots. It was also used for a slew of other Lincoln images and cartoons, favorable and not, that appeared in newspapers and illustrated weeklies throughout the nation in the months before the election. The lithographers Currier and Ives, who advertised their business as "The Grand Central Depot for Cheap and Popular Pictures," offered bulk discounts for Lincoln prints. Another engraver in Manhattan, J. C. Buttre, offered an engraving on a card in an envelope, suggesting in an advertisement that "Every member of the LINCOLN CLUBS throughout the United States should possess a copy of this little gem." The image, either taken directly from the Brady photograph or from the Currier and Ives lithograph, was also used for as many as seventy-six different tintype campaign badges during the 1860 campaign. And Brady's studios in New York and Washington could churn out prints. So there were ample opportunities for every American to see the Cooper Union image.[5]

On the evening of the day Brady photographed Lincoln, more than thirteen hundred men and women, "the pick and flower of New York culture," paid twenty-five cents to sit in red leather armchairs in the Great Hall of the Cooper Union to hear the ungainly westerner speak. The speech was widely reprinted and praised in newspapers, enhancing Lincoln's stature as a presidential aspirant and transforming him from an Illinois favorite son to a national candidate. It was crucial to securing the Republican Party's nomination. Brady clearly thought the photograph was just as crucial to Lincoln's election. He said more than once that, after Lincoln became president, his old law partner, Ward Hill Lamon, whom Lincoln had named U.S. marshal of the District of Columbia and who considered himself to be Lincoln's personal bodyguard, had tried to introduce Brady to the president as if they had not met before. "Mr. Lincoln answered in his ready way," Brady said, "'Brady and the Cooper Institute made me President.'" If Lincoln actually said this, he likely offered it only as a bit of harmless flattery when he saw Brady again on May 16, 1861, about two months after his March 4 inauguration.[6]

One artist who worked with Brady also credited the photograph with influencing the election. In his book *The Inner Life of Abraham Lincoln: Six Months at the White House*, a memoir of his time preparing his heroic 1864 painting *First Reading of the Emancipation Proclamation of President Lincoln*, Francis Bicknell Carpenter writes that

> my friend Brady, the photographer, insisted that his photo-
> graph of Mr. Lincoln . . . —much the best portrait, by the
> way, in circulation of him during the campaign,—was the

Abraham Lincoln on the day of his Cooper Union speech
(February 1860). *Library of Congress*

means of his election. That it helped largely to this end I do not doubt. The effect of such influences, though silent, is powerful.[7]

A day or so after arriving in Washington as president-elect, Lincoln went to Brady's studio in the company of Lamon. On February 24, 1861, Alexander Gardner took five photographs of Lincoln seated in the Brady chair. One of the rare letters in Brady's own handwriting is a note to Gardner written on February 22, 1861, reading, "President Elect Lincoln will visit the gallery on the 24th. Please ready equipment."

George Henry Story, an artist who shared offices with the Washington studio, recalled that he had been asked by Gardner to help him with the Lincoln photo on the twenty-fourth. Story told an interviewer that

> Gardner knew nothing about art, and used to pose his patrons all one way. If there were a Senator, he would have him standing erect with his hand in the breast of his frock-coat, and the other hand resting on a pillar, or a table. It was laughable. I used to say, "Gardner, why don't you change your pose?" But he would say, "Oh, it's good enough. They don't know the difference."

But Gardner would ask Story to help pose important subjects, and on this particular day, he said, "Lincoln's here. Come and pose him."

> When I went in he was carelessly seated at a table waiting to be posed. He did not utter a word and seemed utterly unconscious of what was going on about him . . . "Pose him!" I exclaimed. "No, bring the camera at once." I did not pose him. It was so characteristic of him, I said, "Take him as he is."[8]

Almost a year before Lincoln's inauguration, the first official delegation from Japan to the United States visited Washington. Japan had been closed to the West for 250 years before another Brady subject, Commodore Matthew Perry, persuaded the country under threat of force to open a few of its ports in 1854. Brady was chosen to be the official photographer for the occasion of the delegation's May 1860 visit to Washington, undertaken in part to ratify a more comprehensive treaty growing out of Perry's original one.

As the *New York Herald* correspondent covering the delegation put it, "Owing to the facilities afforded him by the authorities, [Brady] has been enabled to reproduce every remarkable scene in which they have figured, from the moment of their arrival." The delegation of seventy-two people traveled with eighty tons of baggage, "a large amount of treasure, and fifteen large boxes of presents for the President of the United States," according to the *New York Times*. Included in the boxes were "several very handsome rifles [that] are an ingenious improvement upon the Sharp rifle."[9]

One of Brady's assignments was to take photos of the "wonderful strangers" in large and small groups, sometimes wearing Western dress and sometimes in traditional Japanese Samurai garb, bearing swords. He was also expected to photograph their gifts for President Buchanan so that the public at large could see them. An engraving in *Frank Leslie's Illustrated Newspaper* in 1860 shows the gifts being unpacked in a reception room of Willard's Hotel, near the White House, while Brady's operators set up a large box camera and prepare the lighting, and as the artist who made the sketch for the engraving itself looks on. The *Herald* also reported Brady's "intention to make a Japanese gallery, to form a prominent feature in the splendid new establishment which he is about to open."

The clothing, the manners, the expressions, the eating habits—indeed, everything about the Japanese embassy, as the group was called, stirred intense interest in the United States, beginning when they visited San Francisco before sailing to the East Coast, crossing the Isthmus of Panama by train. They visited Philadelphia and New York after their stay in Washington. New York let out all the stops, even scrubbing and repainting City Hall, giving it "a clean and wholesome appearance," the *Times* reported, and gave them a concert and a parade, complete with local militia units that would soon be performing graver duties.[10]

In the middle of 1860, two innovations in photography began to catch on in the United States almost simultaneously. These were the carte de

Three men in traditional samurai dress from the 1860 Japanese embassy to the United States (May 1860). *U.S. National Archives*

visite—the calling-card-size (2.5 by 4 inches) photographic portrait print—and the tintype, a form of ambrotype, which like it and the daguerreotype was a one-of-a-kind picture that could not be reproduced directly but was exposed onto a thin sheet of treated iron or other metal (instead of glass for an ambrotype).

The idea for the calling-card-size portrait arose in several places with the advent of wet-plate photography, but the first patent for cartes de visite was made by André-Adolphe-Eugène Disdéri in Paris in November 1854, a year after he opened a large, chic photography gallery in the city. In defending his patent application, Disdéri wrote, "To make printing photographs practical commercially, the cost must be greatly reduced, which my process would do." His idea was to expose ten (later eight) images on a single photographic negative, both by using more than one lens at once and by having a device called a holder that could move the plate to expose different parts of it. Special cameras for taking cartes de visite would eventually have four tubes, each with its own lens, so that four images could be made on a photographic plate at once. However the images were made, the printing would be much more efficient, and the resulting prints could be cut up by hand to provide multiple copies at a modest price to the sitter.[11]

The small cards did not begin to catch on until several years after Disdéri's patent was granted. Perhaps in the same way that Queen Victoria's interest in stereoscopes created widespread interest in them, when Disdéri photographed Napoleon III and his wife, Eugénie, for cartes de visite in about 1857, the small images began to grow in popularity. The fad spread from Paris to London and later crossed the Atlantic, where a Broadway photographer named S. A. Holmes was the first to advertise them in America, on January 7, 1860: "The London Style / Your Photograph on a Visiting Card / 25 copies for One Dollar." But Jeremiah Gurney's old partner Charles D. Fredricks and a photographer named George Rockwood were both offering them before that date, and Rockwood later claimed, "The first *carte de visite* made in this country was of Baron Rothschild by myself." Within a year, a faddish interest in the carte de visite had spread across the whole country.[12]

The tintype's popularity can be traced to the 1860 presidential campaign, though its inventor, Hamilton L. Smith, a professor of natural science at Kenyon College in Ohio, began to tinker with the process in 1853 and acquired a U.S. patent in 1856. In the summer of

1860, very small tintypes of the main presidential candidates—Lincoln, John C. Breckinridge, John Bell, and Stephen A. Douglas—and of their running mates, were incorporated into medals that supporters could wear. The medals themselves, also known as portrait badges or shell badges, were generally made of brass and would often have the image of the presidential candidate on one side and his running mate on the other. Some also came in what were called "jugates," which featured both candidates on one side of the badge and a pin or buttonhole on the other side. Some also hung from ribbons like military medals.[13]

The September issue of *Humphrey's Journal* reported that so many people wanted tintype images of their candidates, "in the shape of brooches, pins, studs, etc.," that "an unprecedented demand has arisen" for tintype materials, which suppliers were having trouble meeting. Because tintypes were cheap to make and durable, they were perfect for this purpose, but once the November election was over, *Humphrey's* reported in early December, the demand for tintypes was "all played out."[14]

Cartes de visite became so popular so fast that, as the photographic historian Robert Taft puts it, at first those "left by visitors were placed on a card tray; then as the number increased, a basket was employed, but still the number grew. From the necessity, thus created, of finding a place to put the 'cards,' came the family album." Albums had pockets in which to slip several of the cards per page, so that hundreds of cards could be organized and displayed in a single volume. The large number of pockets to fill undoubtedly increased the demand, so that people collected images not just of relatives and friends but also of those they admired, from statesmen to poets to singers and actresses. Oliver Wendell Holmes, in one of his influential articles about photography, observed in the July 1863 issue of the *Atlantic Monthly* that what he called "*card-portraits*" had become "the social currency, the sentimental 'green-backs' of civilization, within a very recent period."[15]

Gardner acquired carte de visite cameras for the Pennsylvania Avenue gallery in expectation of the wave of soldiers that would come to Washington as the threat of war grew. Often for the cost of a single daguerreotype, these soldiers could have enough copies made to send one to family members, friends, and perhaps a sweetheart back home. By the time carte de visite prints came along, printing paper was being treated with albumen, taken from egg whites, which, as Taft puts it, "added a pleasing gloss to the finished print." As Holmes suggested, it also kept a lot of hens employed.[16]

On October 7, 1860, Brady, having closed his other Broadway studio, celebrated the opening of the new gallery on Broadway and Tenth Street with a reception. A week later, on October 13, he welcomed there a man of infinitely greater social prestige, if less ultimate historical importance, than Abraham Lincoln. Albert Edward, the prince of Wales and heir to the British throne, was the first future British king to visit New York since his great-uncle, eventually crowned William IV, was there as a naval midshipman during the Revolutionary War. Albert Edward, who would wait another forty-one years before succeeding his mother, Queen Victoria, as Edward VII, visited New York as part of a much-publicized and altogether successful four-month tour of Canada and the United States. Perhaps because he had been studying at the University of Edinburgh a year before the trip, the nearly nineteen-year-old prince traveled under one of his Scottish titles, the Baron of Renfrew. The trip featured stop after triumphal stop throughout Canada, where he laid the cornerstone for Parliament Hill in Ottawa, and in the five weeks he spent in the United States, he visited a number of American cities, beginning with Detroit and ending with Boston. In all, the *New York Times* published more than two hundred articles about the prince's tour of North America, and the press followed his every move. Although General Washington had approved a plan to kidnap his great-uncle during the Revolution (it was never attempted), one of the stops Edward made was at Mount Vernon, where he paid his respects at Washington's grave in the company of President Buchanan.[17]

When Edward arrived in New York with his retinue on October 11, Mayor Fernando Wood greeted him, and a cheering crowd watched as the prince made his way up Broadway, eventually crossing over to Fifth Avenue and stopping at his lodgings at the Fifth Avenue Hotel, located between Twenty-Third and Twenty-Fourth Streets on Madison Square. A six-story structure that had opened the year before, the hotel was described by a correspondent covering the prince's trip for the *Times* of London as "a larger and more handsome building than Buckingham Palace."[18]

The following night, a committee of four hundred prominent New Yorkers threw the prince an opulent ball at the Academy of Music on Fourteenth Street and Irving Place (the largest opera house in the world when it opened in 1854), inviting so many thousands of people that parts of the dance floor collapsed. Carpenters were brought in, hammering away for two hours while the prince cooled his heels on an upper floor of the academy. At midnight, the repairs done, the dancing began in earnest.

The next day, the prince emerged from his hotel at twelve thirty P.M., greeted again by the cheering crowds that were ubiquitous while he was in New York. His carriage and those of his party headed down Fifth, followed by carriages full of young ladies. They made a right on Tenth Street and soon arrived at Brady's new studio. The proprietor, who had closed his business to other visitors that day, having been notified that the royal party was planning to visit, waited with his wife, Julia, in the second-floor reception room to greet the young prince. This was a huge room, 150 feet long, its walls lined with life-size portraits, hung as many as four high, of the famous or the merely wealthy. Long upholstered benches in the center of the room provided a place from which to focus on a particular portrait among the sea of images. The prince and his party took their time looking at the faces Brady had been gathering for some fifteen years. As *Harper's Weekly* reported,

> It was remarked that most of the suite evinced familiarity with the names of those eminent in American literature, while the portraits of our distinguished statesmen were comparatively unknown. Washington Irving, Bryant, and Prescott attracted far more attention than Webster, Clay, and Calhoun.

After spending time in the richly carpeted gallery, the prince and his party went up one more flight to sit for Brady's operators. The *New York Times* wrote that "three imperial photographs of the whole party, arranged in as many different groups, were taken in the first place; then an imperial full-length photograph of the Prince alone, and similar representations of each of his suite." Then cartes de visite were made of the prince and members of his party. *Harper's* wrote that the prince "quite astonished Mr. Brady's veteran operators by evincing an intelligent familiarity with all the details of the process," and added that he had definite ideas about "backgrounds, posing, and grouping." Not wishing to cave in entirely to the unrepublican worship to which the prince was treated while in New York (an Irish regiment of the New York militia did refuse to participate in the welcoming ceremonies), the writer goes on to say that "The princely theories on these and kindred subjects may have been unsound, but they were pungently expressed."

One incident happened at the end of the visit that could warm even the most fervent republican heart. An older man named Stevens, an Englishman employed in Brady's studio as a gilder and framer, had told Brady that morning that he had been working in Buckingham Palace on the day nearly nineteen years before when Albert Edward was born. His boss had come to Stevens and the other workers that day to announce the birth and had given them money to go out and raise a glass to the new heir to the throne. Before the prince left Brady's, as he was standing at the top of the staircase leading from the second-floor gallery down to the street and the waiting carriages, Brady introduced him to Stevens and told the prince his story. According to *Frank Leslie's Illustrated Newspaper*, "The Prince addressed [Stevens] in the most kindly terms, and seemed touched by the circumstance." The *Times* wrote that the prince even shook Stevens's hand. *Harper's* added, with patriotic fervor, "the venerable old man thus enjoyed an opportunity of meeting face to face the son of his sovereign, which in England would have been denied him."[19]

The articles about the visit report that the royal party stayed at Brady's for two or three hours and ordered a number of prints, not only of themselves but also group portraits of the president and his cabinet, members of the Senate and the House, and of the two candidates for president. The prince signed "Albert Edward" in Brady's visitors' book; ten other members of the royal party also left their names there, including the Duke of Newcastle. *Leslie's* wrote that, "On leaving[,] his Royal Highness extended his hand cordially to Mr. Brady, and expressed the great gratification he had derived from his inspection of his collection." When he walked out into the street the prince encountered "an immense crowd which had been waiting patiently all that time to get a glimpse." Later in the afternoon, Brady received a note of congratulations from a member of the retinue, saying how well his portraits of the prince had turned out. Brady would remember that he received a cane and a ring from the prince, and that Julia also received a present, but none of the reporters who had been rounded up for the visit made mention of these gifts, which might have been delivered later.

While they were still at Brady's, someone in the royal party sent a messenger to Barnum's saying that the prince would like to go there next. Barnum himself had invited Edward to visit his museum two days earlier, but had heard nothing back, so he was not there that afternoon, but at his Barnumesque estate in Bridgeport, Connecticut. The prince asked to be driven through the Bowery before arriving at Barnum's, where the day's regular patrons "kept at a respectful distance from the Prince," the *New York Times* reported, "and he had ample opportunity to see every thing." That would include Barnum's giants and midgets and Siamese twins and albinos and the showman's infamous "What Is It?" exhibit, featuring a black man it claimed to be the missing link between humans and apes. (Darwin's *On the Origin of Species* had only recently been published.) The prince listened attentively to the "What Is It?" spiel, and then moved on. All in all, according to the newspaper, Edward was greatly amused.

Late in the afternoon, after returning to the hotel, the party set off again down Fifth Avenue to visit Gen. Winfield Scott at home. Because nobody had warned the general that they were coming, a servant told the captain who rang the bell on behalf of the royal party that General Scott was having dinner and could not be disturbed. When it was pointed out that the future British monarch was sitting outside in a barouche, the party was quickly invited up, and the beefy old general offered them all a glass of wine and showed off his Newfoundland dog.

That evening, the prince appeared on a balcony outside his hotel suite with the mayor of New York to watch a torchlit parade of nearly six thousand firemen from the city and surrounding jurisdictions. More than half a million New Yorkers turned out for the event, and it must have seemed as if most of them were right there in Madison Square. As the *Times* writer put it, "Of all the jams that the Prince's presence has yet created, that in front of the Hotel last Saturday evening was the jammedest." Edward raised his hat as each of the firemen's units passed, and the firemen responded by shooting off Roman candles that occasionally "flew in at the windows, and caused a great commotion among the dames and damsels." Still, the evening was a success, with the firemen marching through the crowded streets for many hours after the

Albert Edward, the Prince of Wales, who would be Edward VII (October 1860). *National Portrait Gallery, Smithsonian Institution*

last brigade passed by the hotel at eleven P.M. and the prince returned to his rooms.

The whole day was a triumph for New York and for Brady. Although the royal party also visited a fine store called Ball, Black and Co., which offered artwork, jewelry, and silver objects, spending more than ten thousand dollars on presents for the queen and others back home, no photography studio but Brady's made the agenda, and the visit to Brady's was written up in detail on the front page of the *Times* and in other publications. Brady later remembered asking the Duke of Newcastle why the prince had chosen his gallery among all the others in the city. " 'Are you not the Mr. Brady,' he said, 'who earned the prize nine years ago in London? You owe it to yourself. We had your place of business down in our note-books before we started.' "[20]

As *Leslie's* wrote some weeks later, "It need hardly be said that the *éclat* of so distinguished an honor brought the fame of Mr. Brady freshly and prominently before the country, into every section of which accounts of the visit penetrated, or that Brady's Gallery became the 'lion' of fashion and its followers in all parts of the United States." *Harper's* wrote about three weeks after the princely visit that Brady's had been unpleasantly crowded ever since, which undoubtedly had its pleasant aspects for Brady himself.

Only two things might have marred Brady's delight in the whole event. The *Times* article had found it necessary to say that Brady's collection "contains more well-delineated likenesses of men of mark than any other gallery in the City, except Mr. GURNEY'S." More disturbing, probably, was an article that appeared after the prince had sailed for home. It reported that a letter from the British consul to New York to Gurney, written on October 15, noted that the prince, "having been unable to visit your gallery on Saturday, has directed me to say to you that if you will go on to Boston he will sit [for] you for his photograph." The article reports that Gurney and his workers hustled up to Boston the very next day, "fitted up a sumptuous operating room, immediately under the Prince's apartments at the Revere House, and His Royal Highness did them the favor of sitting no less than four times." The prince was so pleased with the images from the first three sittings that he ordered eight hundred copies of them sent to Buckingham Palace. The last sitting occurred as his carriage was waiting to take him to his ship, and the prince was apparently so anxious to have one more likeness taken that he sat in a drizzle under an open skylight so that there was enough light for a successful exposure.[21]

Brady was not, however, entirely outmaneuvered by this visit of Gurney's to Boston. The *New York Herald* of October 19, reporting on the prince's visit to Boston, notes that at a fancy ball intended to rival the one in New York, "One meets many New York faces. Among them that of Brady, the photographer, who received, as an especial favor and mark of esteem, a special ticket from the Prince himself, who, hearing Mr. Brady had no ticket, sent for one and presented it to him." The occasion for the *Times* article about Gurney was an announcement that the photographer would put his own copies of the prince's portraits on public display at his gallery. So Brady was not the only one, not by a long shot, to capitalize on the princely visit long after the prince had returned home.

The story of Brady's "venerable old" employee Stevens meeting the young heir to the British throne caught the attention of the press, and rightly so. It was a lovely coincidence and a touching moment, certainly one that those crowds of ordinary New Yorkers lining the city's streets during the royal visit, and the other ordinary Americans who read about it, could well appreciate. Brady understood the publicity appeal that the meeting with Stevens would have for the press, as did the prince's retinue. But from this distance, the meeting seems like a spontaneous gesture on Brady's part, something he was willing to undertake only at the end of a visit that had gone extremely well. It was a meeting that might further amuse and even flatter the prince, yes, but it's hard not to see it as an act of kindness on Brady's part toward one of his many workers.

This is of interest in part because so few examples exist of how Brady interacted with his employees. It also matters because the prince's visit, coming almost exactly six months before Fort Sumter and the beginning of the Civil War, marks not only a high point but also a turning point in Brady's career. Much of what comes later, especially in the first half of the war, has to do with Brady's relationships with Alexander Gardner and the camera operators who would photograph the war under Brady's aegis. Brady is sometimes portrayed unflatteringly in these dealings, as a man who takes all the credit for himself, exploiting those who do the actual work. But these relationships were more complicated than that. It's worth remembering his act of kindness toward old Stevens when considering this new phase of Brady's life.

# CHAPTER 7

# "Last Place . . . to See the Nation Whole"

Every American's life would change during the year 1861. Compared with those who went to war, who left their jobs or businesses, or who seriously risked or even lost their lives, Brady faced changes that could be said to be fairly minor. But in the context of his whole career as a photographic entrepreneur, 1861 was the hinge between Brady the purveyor of artistic portraits and Brady the distributor of war photography, the two principal ways in which he is remembered today. He would remain a studio portraitist for the rest of his life, but he also left the studio in 1861 and ventured out into the bright light of the open air. Or it might be more accurate to say he moved his studio out of doors, because the technology of the camera continued to require stillness, resulting most often in studio-like poses or scenes that did not feature much in the way of activity.

Early on, the war provided a windfall for Brady and for photographers at almost every level of the profession. By the time the Civil War began, Americans who had any income at all could afford and were familiar with both cartes de visite and tintypes. The day after the surrender of Fort Sumter, on April 15, 1861, President Lincoln called for seventy-five thousand Union troops, and such was the fervor in the North that northern governors mustered even more militiamen than that.[1] The Southern states had called for recruits the month before Fort Sumter, and although they had a far smaller pool of eligible men to draw from, the initial response was also enthusiastic. Many of these troops sat for cartes de visite before leaving for war. Their loved ones also went to be photographed, so that soldiers and their families could keep images of one another during their separation.

After a soldier arrived in camp, he would find "the tintype operator waiting for him to record his appearance from week to week as his whiskers gradually grew longer." The relative indestructibility of tintypes, compared to paper prints or glass ambrotypes, made them popular with soldiers and camp photographers alike. As *Humphrey's Journal* reported in February of 1862:

> The photographer accompanies the army wherever it goes and a very large number of soldiers get their pictures taken and send them to their friends. Friends at home, in return, send their portraits to the soldiers, and in this way an immense transportation business has been done by the Post Office. Not infrequently a number of bags go out from the Washington office entirely filled with sun pictures, enclosed in light but bulky cases.
>
> Most of these pictures are taken on the [tintype] plate for the reason that it is light, durable, and easily sent in a letter.[2]

These camp-following tintypists were more like the itinerant daguerreotypists of the 1840s and '50s than the studio operators in cities and towns. Because tintype images were one of a kind, they had no commercial value beyond their immediate sale to the soldier or a member of his family, so the business was all about volume. One *New York Tribune* writer reported in August of 1862 that "quite a company" of camp photographers was following Gen. Ambrose Burnside's army at Fredericksburg, and that "their tents are thronged from morning until night." He wrote that a pair of brothers from Pennsylvania had in a single day taken 160 photographs, charging a dollar for each. The business of these camp photographers was in almost every way the opposite end of the scale from what Brady did and what his gallery represented.[3]

Even before Fort Sumter, concern for the safety of Washington City ran high. When Virginia seceded soon after Lincoln's call for troops, the threat to the capital was just across the Potomac bridges, and although Maryland did not secede, Lincoln had had to sneak through Baltimore in disguise on the way to his inauguration, out of fear for his safety. On April 19, a week after the shelling of Fort Sumter began, troops from the Sixth Massachusetts had to fight their way through Baltimore to get to the nation's capital. The city's mayor and the governor of Maryland warned President Lincoln not to send more troops through the state and, to prevent this, burned the bridges on rail lines leading to the north. Soon the Potomac River bridges upriver from Washington were also destroyed, and the telegraph lines to the north cut. As more regiments from Massachusetts and also from Rhode Island and New York slowly made their way by other routes to the lightly armed national capital, Lincoln famously asked, "Why don't they come? Why don't they come?"[4]

But no attack from the South came, either; nor did the many Southern sympathizers within Washington itself revolt, although some of them practiced military drills within the city's boundaries. After a few days that must have seemed like weeks or months, the regiments from Massachusetts, Rhode Island, and New York did arrive. As other troops turned up—from Minnesota, from Pennsylvania—and paraded along the Avenue, some marching to the music of their own bands, secessionists within the government and the military began to leave town. The most prominent officer to defect was Robert E. Lee, who resigned from the U.S. Army on April 20 and soon left his home at Arlington Plantation, which overlooked the city of Washington from what is now Arlington Cemetery, and took command of Virginia's forces. So many Union troops were camped in Washington that feeding them and keeping them out of mischief became a serious problem. But all this proved to be a boon for Brady's Washington and New York studios, where soldiers and officers alike hurried to have photographs made to send home before they put themselves at risk. So many Union soldiers wished to be photographed at the Washington gallery that the wait was sometimes hours long.[5]

Among those who had to wait in line were the colorfully garbed troops of Col. Elmer Ellsworth, who commanded the Eleventh New York Volunteer Infantry Regiment, or Fire Zouaves, made up of New York City firemen. Ellsworth had been born not far from Brady, in Saratoga County, New York. When his dream of going to West Point to become a soldier did not come true, he moved to Illinois, where he

President Lincoln in the Brady Washington gallery (May 1861).
*Library of Congress*

eventually read law in Lincoln's Springfield law office and was part of the group that accompanied the president-elect from Springfield to his inauguration in Washington. Earlier, he trained a troop of Illinois cadet militiamen in the acrobatic drills of the bright-plumed French Zouaves in Algeria. His troop toured nationally and internationally to perform, including a display on the grounds of President Buchanan's White House. After arriving in Washington with Lincoln in February, Ellsworth realized that he was unlikely to get the job in the War Department that the president-elect had hoped to create for him, so he went back to New York, where he helped muster from the brigades of daring New York City firefighters the Fire Zouaves that he would lead.[6]

While he was in New York, Ellsworth went to the Brady gallery on Tenth Street and posed for at least two full-length carte de visite portraits, in both of which he bears a sword and drapes his dark coat romantically over his shoulders. In one he is sporting at a jaunty angle a gold-braided red kepi, looking every inch the hero he was about to become.

Once in Washington, Ellsworth's firemen soldiers were soon widely regarded as being among the most rambunctious if not obnoxious of all those encamped there. As Margaret Leech puts it in *Reveille in Washington*, "they were as wild as wharf rats." Upon their arrival on May 1, they bivouacked in the Capitol itself, and amused themselves by dangling by ropes from the inner dome of the Rotunda, and performing other stunts. One of their favorite tricks was to liberate a local fire engine and pull it all around the town; another was to charge up meals and merchandise either to President Lincoln or President Jefferson Davis. But after they had been in Washington for just over a week, they endeared themselves to the local citizenry when they put out a fire at a tailor's shop next door to Willard's Hotel, the nexus of political Washington, creating vertical bucket brigades to get water to the upper floors, and preventing the fire from spreading to the hotel itself.[7]

As Northern militias filled Washington, and the secessionists left town, the fear of an attack from Virginia lessened, and Maryland itself calmed down sufficiently so that Northern troops could again pass through Baltimore unmolested. But Virginia's Potomac shore, especially the ridge that overlooked it in Arlington, presented a danger to the capital from artillery, and the visibly close port of Alexandria, with its train depot, also posed a strategic threat. On May 23 the citizens of Virginia formally voted to secede. Hours later, soon after midnight, federal troops began to move across the Potomac bridges to secure them and the nearby heights, including Lee's mansion at Arlington Plantation. At the same time, Ellsworth's Zouaves boarded two steamboats at the mouth of the Anacostia River and traveled the short distance down the Potomac to Alexandria, where they anchored offshore and waited for first light. Ellsworth had passed part of his weeks in Washington at the White House, a welcome guest of Lincoln and his family. He knew from a telescope in the executive mansion that a huge Confederate flag—the newly adopted "Stars and Bars"—was visible flying over Alexandria, an irritant and, to Ellsworth, a challenge. The flag, eight by fourteen feet, had been erected on a tall staff above the four-story Marshall House, a small brick hotel at the corner of King and Pitt Streets.[8]

Under a truce flag at dawn, a Union officer met with the commander of the Confederates in Alexandria, who agreed, in the face of thousands of Union troops converging by land and river, to withdraw his five hundred soldiers in order to keep the women and children in the city out of harm's way. They quick-marched up Duke Street and boarded a train stopped half a mile beyond the depot and headed west, deeper into Virginia. As the Zouaves and other units that had crossed Long Bridge secured the city of Alexandria, Ellsworth took it upon himself to capture the Confederate flag on the Marshall House, as a trophy for Mrs. Lincoln. The man who had raised the flag, James W. Jackson, an ardent secessionist, had recently leased the building and opened his business after several years of running the (for him) inappropriately named Union Hotel at Fairfax Court House. Jackson had made and begun to display the flag in April, when a special convention in Virginia first voted for secession. In the weeks since, he had prophetically said more than once that if anyone tried to lower the flag, "there would be two dead men about."[9]

Ellsworth, with a few of his Zouaves, the regiment's chaplain, and a reporter for the *New York Tribune*, burst into the Marshall House that morning and climbed the stairs to the attic, where Ellsworth went out a dormer window and up a ladder to the peak of the roof. He tore down the Rebel banner and clutched it in his arms as he descended the stairs. On the steps leading to the second-floor landing, the group came face to face with Jackson. Legend has it that Ellsworth called out, "I have the first prize," and Jackson responded, "And I the second." Jackson then fired one barrel of his shotgun into Ellsworth's chest, where the force drove a gold medal the colonel wore into his heart, killing him instantly. One of his Zouaves then shot a Minié ball into Jackson's head as the second barrel of Jackson's gun discharged into a doorframe. Thus did Jackson's vow come true, and each side have its first martyr of the war. The Zouaves wrapped Ellsworth's body in a red blanket, tore a door of the hotel from its frame, and, using their muskets to support the door, carried their colonel down to the dock at Alexandria, where he was transported to the Washington Navy Yard.[10]

There his body went on display as streams of people came to pay their respects, and the next day it lay in state in the East Room of the White House. After a funeral service there, a hearse drawn by four white horses carried Ellsworth's remains down Pennsylvania Avenue, past Brady's studio, to the Baltimore & Ohio station south of the Capitol, where it was loaded on a train to New York, and there again lay in state at City Hall. The deeply bereaved president rode in the funeral procession, and the people who lined the streets were somber. Margaret Leech captures the scene and its meaning with elegant economy:

> On the Avenue, the pendant flags were tied with crape. The crowds were out, but there were no cheers, only silence and tolling bells. From the capital, sorrow spread in a wave over the Union. It was as if the people of the republic, so inexperienced in war, had closed their eyes to the purpose for which their young men had been sent to Washington; as if Ellsworth's death had for a moment undeceived them, and a premonition passed, like a shudder, over all their hearts.[11]

Nothing we know about Mathew Brady suggests that he was an ardent Unionist, much less any sort of abolitionist. He was born and had always lived in the North, with only short forays in Europe and Washington. But New York City had strong economic ties to the slave South, and its business class, of which Brady was a part, was not eager to punish the states that had seceded. His wife, Julia, was from a plantation family on Maryland's Eastern Shore that was likely to have owned slaves. But in the years leading up to the outbreak of war, years filled with real animosity (Senator Sumner's caning was only the most violent of the bitter disputes in Congress), Brady's studios were carefully neutral. He continued as he had for more than a decade to seek out every figure in American life that could be of interest to history, and the demand for Brady photographs as the basis for illustrations in the press gave economic reinforcement to this impulse. For example, in June of 1860 he made a five-by-six-feet photographic compilation of nearly every member of the House of Representatives. Within a year, most of its Southern members would have decamped to their seceded states, but here they were all together for one last time, nearly 250 of them, in a single picture. Brady reduced the image to twenty by twenty-four inches and sold reproductions for five dollars each. As the *New York Times* reported on June 29, Brady had "caught the House of Representatives by the power of his wonderful art, and holds them still in continuous, and what is more surprising, in respectable and harmonious session." Brady made a similar composite photograph of the entire U.S. Senate. As Mary Panzer writes in *Mathew Brady and the Image of History*:

> The truly national character of Brady's gallery here comes clear, for he provided images of every figure, from every party and every state. Brady's collection and gallery became the last place in which it was possible to see the nation whole.[12]

It says something about Brady's reputation for neutrality, even as his operators documented the war from the Union side, that soon after Appomattox, General Lee sat for Brady amid the ruins of Richmond. Still, the death of Ellsworth must have affected him. Besides photographing the young colonel at least once—a color engraving of Ellsworth in full Zouave regalia, thought to be based on a Brady photo, suggests a wholly different sitting—he also photographed Private Francis Brownell, the Zouave who killed Ellsworth's killer (for which he would, years later, receive the Congressional Medal of Honor). Brownell posed in uniform with a boot on the bloodstained Stars and Bars flag for which Ellsworth had died and bearing the musket with which he had shot Jackson, on which was fixed the bayonet with which he had then stabbed him.

Whatever Brady's own emotions, his cartes de visite of Ellsworth and Brownell were in demand throughout the Union. No records exist of how many of these images were sold, but cartes de visite of Maj. Robert Anderson were being printed at the rate of a thousand a day during the weeks when he was holding out at Fort Sumter before his surrender on April 14. Given the emotional outpouring after Ellsworth's death—three towns in the Upper Midwest were named for him, and the Forty-fourth New York Infantry dubbed itself Ellsworth's Avengers—it's likely the sales of his image far outstripped those of Anderson. Even large galleries such as Brady's could not print cards in the quantities that the carte de visite craze was now demanding, so in March of 1861, Brady and Gardner had made a deal to have them made from Brady negatives by his old friend Edward Anthony. Anthony and Company, which had become the nation's leading photographic supply house, had recently created a card-making factory. Indeed, it was Anthony who was cranking out the image of Robert Anderson, which had been taken in Charleston by Brady's former office manager George Cook. Some experts believe that in the early 1860s the Brady galleries sold tens of thousands of cartes de visite through Anthony.[13]

# CHAPTER 8

# *"Illustrations of Camp Life"*

By the time the Civil War began, photography was an established fact of American life. In the 1840s the daguerreotype had introduced the necessity for a likeness that was both permanent and somehow objective, a step beyond the portraits of silhouette makers, sketchers, miniaturists, and formal portrait painters. The 1850s had introduced a variety of both one-of-a-kind and reproducible options for photographic portraiture and, increasingly, for views of nature or places of cultural or historical interest. Publications with engravings from photographs made such images deeply familiar, and created a greater need in the public to see what they were reading about, whether the source was a photograph or the work of a sketch artist. The beginning of the 1860s brought an explosive demand for tintypes and cartes de visite, but also for stereographic views of foreign as well as familiar scenes. War, with its many faces and places, then, was a natural subject for photography.

Brady and Gardner would each claim credit for the decision to aggressively photograph the war, but it was an obvious idea. In June of 1861 a meeting of the American Photographical Society in New York proposed something similar and appointed a committee to suggest it to the War Department. Covering the war in a systematic way was also a natural outgrowth of the photographic work Brady and Gardner were doing in both studios. By the spring of 1861, when they were photographing generals, officers, and soldiers in both Washington and New York, and turning a handsome profit while doing so, it wasn't much of a leap to send operators to photograph them where they were, in encampments in and around the capital, and to picture them not just as individuals but as military units. People back home wanted to see where their men were living and whom they were living among and might soon be fighting alongside. Because of the growing interest in stereographs, Brady's operators often took more than one camera along, capturing the same images in stereo and for cartes de visite. Anthony offered prints in both formats, and soldiers could buy prints directly from the Brady galleries.[1]

Brady was not the first entrepreneur to realize that war could be good for business. Still, there was nothing exploitative about what he was doing. The demand for images generated by those who were going to war and by their families is more than understandable, considering both the dread of separation and the fear of injury or death—even given the widespread optimism in the land that the war would be short and painless. Brady was merely satisfying this demand, especially at prices that were kept reasonable by the competition coming from both established and itinerant photographers. A second part of Brady's war business, encouraged by the enthusiastic market for the Major Anderson and Colonel Ellsworth cards, was to provide Anthony and Company with collectible images of military figures ranging from General Scott, general-in-chief of the U.S. Army, at least until he stepped down in the fall of 1861; to generals and commanders in the field; to members of Lincoln's Cabinet, such as war secretary Simon Cameron or navy secretary Gideon Welles. A third part of the war business was related to the second, to provide these same images for the pictorial weeklies and monthlies. At the very least these last two parts of the business fueled a civic interest in the great events shaping the divided nation and could be expected to help ignite patriotic support for the Union.

There were plenty of places for Brady and Gardner to send their cameramen. As Geoffrey C. Ward writes in *The Civil War*, "Union camps encircled the District. Washington would soon become the most heavily fortified city on earth, ringed by 22 batteries and 74 forts." Brady operators photographed the Twelfth New York Infantry Regiment at Camp Anderson in the District and the First Rhode Island Volunteer Regiment at Camp Sprague, out North Capitol Street on Bladensburg Road, near where Gardner and his family lived at Kendall Green.

In May, two photographers working for Gardner at Brady's Washington gallery went to Georgetown to photograph soldiers from the Seventh New York Infantry Regiment at what was called Camp Cameron, which one soldier later called "a nursery for brigadier-generals." There, George N. Barnard and C. O. Bostwick took a number of images of soldiers in front of the neat rows of their tents, or performing Zouave-like stunts such as creating human pyramids. Soldiers from the same regiment also went to the Washington gallery to have photos made individually and in small groups. Casually posed pictures of soldiers at their encampments appeared for sale in a card series with the words "Illustrations of Camp Life" printed under the image, and "Brady," and "Washington" under that. Once Union forces took Arlington and Alexandria in late May, Brady's operators also ventured across the Potomac, to photograph the engineers of the Eighth New York Infantry Regiment in Arlington in June, and Brig. Gen. Irvin McDowell with his staff on the steps of Lee's mansion, Arlington House, where Lee had lived with his wife, Mary Custis, George Washington's step great-granddaughter.[2]

The medium had still not matured to the point of being able to capture the action of battle, in spite of the introduction as early as the daguerreotype era of so-called "instantaneous" photography, which could take place only in strong natural light and involved quickly removing and replacing a lens cap, sometimes in a fraction of a second. Why no more than a very few images of battle were taken is not entirely clear. Without a doubt, the equipment required was burdensome, the glass negatives were fragile, and the preparation and development of them was a delicate and deliberate process. Unless the lighting was optimal and the haze of smoke from cannons and muskets was minimal, capturing an image would take longer than that of an instantaneous exposure, which would make any sort of movement problematical. The topography or the presence of woods could obscure the fighting, making it hard to find a suitable vantage point. And battle scenes were chaotic, confusing, and, of course, dangerous.[3]

As the sketch artist Edwin Forbes, who covered much of the war for *Leslie's*, wrote in a book called *Thirty Years After: An Artist's Memoir of the Civil War*,

It may be believed, therefore, how difficult it is at times to witness a battle, and how, even when one is favorably placed— but without responsibility—excitement and confusion put to flight a realizing sense of events. Soldiers engaged in the thickest of a fight do not know what is taking place within a few hundred feet of them, and learn of results in a general way only after the fury has subsided.[4]

Forbes also admits that in his first experience of battle, at Cross Keys, Virginia, in June 1862, he was determined to see an infantry charge, but the vantage he found was within the range of Confederate artillery, and once he began to see wounded men carried past him from the front, "my ideas of witnessing a battle underwent great change."[5]

But given the numbers of photographers following the course of the war—by one estimate, "more than 300 civilian photographers covered the actions of the Army of the Potomac alone"—and given the efforts of Brady and others to construct portable darkrooms on wagons and dozens of fixed darkrooms in encampments, it seems that even happenstance would have produced more images of battle than exist. But perhaps that would be true only if there were a greater demand for battle scenes from the public, or a greater value put on them by the photographers themselves. The historian of photography William Stapp points out that "of the hundreds of illustrations deriving from photographs that were published in the illustrated press during the Civil War, only about two dozen were from views taken in the field; the remainder were almost all studio portraits."[6]

The experience of Edwin Forbes is again illustrative of how photographers of the war might have conceived of their roles. Forbes was not burdened by photographic equipment or by the processes required to obtain a photograph; he needed only a pencil and a sketchpad to do his work. But the evidence of a large percentage of the more than three hundred illustrations in *Thirty Years After* suggests a distinct preference for scenes featuring soldiers doing almost anything else but fighting: marching, patrolling, cooking, washing their clothes, building bridges and fortifications, and just plain waiting for something to happen. His interest was more sociological than journalistic.

Admittedly, as the historian William J. Cooper Jr. writes of Forbes, "His employer liked the action coverage best, and because of that prefer-

ence fewer than half of Forbes's wartime sketches ended up being reproduced in *Frank Leslie's Illustrated Newspaper.*" Still, that means scores and
scores of sketches unrelated to battle *were* published in the newspaper,
despite the aggressively competitive nature of the New York papers of the
era, which would presumably have put a premium on action photos.[7]

Studio photographers such as Brady, Gardner, and their men went
to war, then, taking the sorts of photographs they were used to taking:
of posed individuals and groups or of scenes that were as static as the
drapes and columns and fine carpets in the studio photographs. Not
only were the subjects similar to those in the studio, but the composi-
tions themselves were also studio-like, a situation in which the sitters
themselves were complicit, as Mary Panzer points out in her book
about Mathew Brady. She highlights a famous photograph of Ulysses
S. Grant that Brady was present for in June of 1864 at Cold Harbor,
where Grant steadies himself against a loblolly pine as he might have
leaned against a column in Brady's studio. "In the field," Panzer writes,

> Brady's operators and their sitters brought along a set of con-
> ventions that had become synonymous with the art of por-
> traiture itself. They welcomed conditions that would mimic
> the empty, placeless setting of the studio, with its dreamy,
> constant light. Sitters assumed the heroic postures they had
> learned to hold with the help of iron posing stands and ta-
> bles, though now they supported themselves against trees,
> camp furniture, and tent poles. Though they are no longer
> confined by the studio walls or the reach of a skylight,
> groups are posed and organized in the same rhythmic, sym-
> metrical clusters that studios required.[8]

A pine tree also supports the subject of another well-known Brady
photograph, from 1861, although the pose cannot be called heroic. It
shows a soldier from the Fourth Michigan dressed in a very civilian-
looking checked shirt, right shoulder leaning on the tree, left hand on
hip, and right leg crossed over his left, the pose as casual as the shirt.
Photos such as this one were undoubtedly intended to reassure the
folks back home.

\*   \*   \*

No evidence exists that Brady's decision to photograph the war came at any single moment. Years later he would say that "A spirit in my feet said 'Go,' and I went." But more likely the plan simply evolved. Between Fort Sumter in April and Bull Run in July, a number of small military actions led to an escalating sense that there would be a decisive battle. But most people in the north believed that the war would be over before its first recruits, members of state militia who had been loaned to the federal government for just ninety days, were mustered out. No one could have predicted how long the war would last or in how many different places it would be fought.[9]

Late in life, Brady would tell an interviewer that he "had men in all parts of the army, like a rich newspaper" and that "I spent over $100,000 in my war enterprises." Because he did not keep comprehensive business records, and few records he did keep survive, it's hard to know for certain how Brady's finances stood at the beginning of the war. R. G. Dun & Company began reporting on Brady's credit worthiness in 1852 (and continued until 1874). Writing before the Dun reports came to light, the authors of *Mathew Brady and His World* conclude that at the start of 1861, "Brady was at the pinnacle of his career, a wealthy man with a thriving business, owner of real estate in New York, an investor in oil wells and silver mines, world-renowned . . . an enterprising, persuasive, self-assured success."[10]

But the Dun reports suggest a somewhat more complicated story of a steady decline in Brady's creditworthiness. By 1861 only Anthony and Company, from which Brady purchased most of his supplies, would do business with him, and at that time only on a cash basis. But increasingly the two businesses were becoming intertwined. The sketchiness of the Dun reports, however, makes it hard to draw reliable conclusions about Brady's financial situation. One scholar surely looks only at the dark clouds when she concludes that Brady was in financial trouble well before 1861 and that his "motivations for covering the war may have been partly an effort to recover what he had lost in earlier ventures."[11]

Whatever the truth was about Brady's finances before the war, he was solvent enough to be generous with his most important clients. About Gen. Winfield Scott, whom he photographed many times, Brady remembers that "I had long known Gen. Scott, and in the days before the war it was the considerate thing to buy wild ducks at the steamboat crossing of the Susquehanna and take them to your choice friends, and I often took Scott, in New York, his favorite ducks."

Lincoln's call for troops in Washington led to what one Brady biographer calls "a landoffice business" in the gallery on Pennsylvania Avenue, and the deal with Anthony to print and distribute cartes de visite, along with the growing interest in images of military leaders— all of this suggests that Brady could be confident about his income, with still brighter prospects to come. That he had grown careless about paying his bills might mean less about his overall financial health than the Dun reporter and the subsequent interpreters of those reports suggest.[12]

As Brady spent more and more time in Washington in 1860 and 1861, he continued to run his business in New York in an engaged and even energetic way. In March of 1860, he unveiled an oil portrait of Washington Irving created from an obscure daguerreotype of the writer taken a decade earlier by an unknown photographer. Brady had gone to some trouble to track down the daguerreotype in Europe and, after finding it, to convince its owner to allow him to copy it. Irving had died the previous November and, because he had not liked having his picture taken, had left no good photographic portrait behind, it was thought. Once Brady managed to find the elusive image and have it copied, he enlarged it and had his artists go to work on a life-size portrait on canvas. The result, according to the *New York Herald*, to whom Brady fed the particulars of the story, was "so perfect . . . in the resemblance that the members of Mr. Irving's family and his most intimate friends have been unable to suggest any alteration which might improve it."[13]

Even with all the upheaval in the nation in 1860 and 1861, as it came closer to war, and the resulting steady demand of the illustrated papers and magazines for images of political and military figures, Brady continued to enlarge his gallery in other spheres. In 1861 in New York, he took a series of photographs of the actor Edwin Forrest, whom he had first daguerreotyped in the early 1840s and again in the mid-1850s. Among the 1861 photographs are eleven of him in costume for various stage roles, including the Shakespeare title characters King Lear, Coriolanus, Richard III, and Macbeth. Macbeth was a famous and infamous role for Forrest, one for which he had been hissed in London in 1845 but was lauded in New York in 1853, when he played the king at the Broadway Theatre for what was then a record run of four weeks. After this success he retired from the stage for seven years, but he went back to acting in 1860, playing Hamlet to enthusiastic reviews at Niblo's Garden in New York. These costume photographs by Brady were undoubtedly intended by both men to build on that acclaim.[14]

Brady's long acquaintance with Forrest complicates the image of the photographer as a man from the lower middle class who catered to the rich and famous. Forrest was considered the greatest Shakespearean actor in America, but his most serious claim on history had to do with one of New York City's ugliest outbursts of class warfare, in which Forrest represented the "lower twenty," from which Brady came, against the "upper ten," or the elites. Forrest had a running feud with the greatest English actor of Shakespeare, William Charles Macready. In 1849, Macready was touring America, and Forrest shadowed him, often playing the same part in rival theaters. Forrest was a hero of the working class, having performed often in the Bowery, employing the sort of loud, stagy acting style that was popular there. Macready, in contrast, had a quiet, refined style, English and aristocratic.[15]

At a May 7 opening-night performance of *Macbeth* at the new, Parthenon-like Astor Opera House (where the dress code required kid gloves), Macready was greeted from the presumably gloveless ticket holders in the upper balcony with rotten eggs and shouts of "Down with the codfish aristocracy." When the frenzy built to a point where the red plush seats were being hurled at the stage, Macready walked out of the theater and announced that he was returning to England. A group of upper-crust New Yorkers, including Washington Irving, urged Macready to change his mind, and he did. Forrest also played Macbeth on May 7, at the nearby Broadway Theatre, where, when he spoke Macbeth's line "what purgative drug will scour these English hence?" the audience gave him a long standing ovation.

At Macready's next performance, on May 10, a crowd of some ten thousand working-class people seething with Anglophobia marched on the opera house, where they were met by two hundred militiamen from the Seventh Regiment, and eventually by bullets. Twenty-two people were killed, among them seven Irish laborers. Tempers cooled in the eleven years between what became known as the Astor Place Riot and the appearance of the English crown prince in 1860, but when Brady took a second daguerreotype of Forrest in 1855, the actor likely still represented something that resonated with Brady's own heritage.

Brady had one other connection to the actor. In 1850, Forrest went through an ugly, tabloid-style divorce from his English wife, during which he falsely accused Brady's friend Nathaniel Parker Willis of seducing her. When the burly Forrest came upon the neurasthenic Willis in Washington Square one evening in June, he knocked Willis down with his fist and gave him a beating with a gutta-percha whip. Willis sued for assault and was awarded twenty-five hundred dollars, later reduced on appeal to a dollar. All this played out in the newspapers for a public increasingly hungry for celebrity gossip. Brady maintained his relationship with both men.[16]

Over the winter of 1860/1861, two photographers who worked for both Brady and Edward Anthony and Company, George N. Barnard and Jacob F. Coonley, labored to re-photograph, at carte de visite size, all the most valuable images Brady had collected throughout his career, ranging from daguerreotypes to Imperials. Brady himself worked on creating composite photographs of the sort the royal party had purchased of the House and Senate. One such photo focused on the members of the Peace Conference that met in Washington on February 4, 1861, a last-ditch attempt, organized by Virginia governor John Letcher, to persuade the states of the upper South not to follow the six states that had already seceded (Texas, the seventh, was in the process of doing so). One hundred and thirty-one delegates, led by former president John Tyler and including nineteen former governors, met in a hall belonging to Willard's Hotel, in an effort that the *Tribune's* hyper-opinionated editor, Horace Greeley, called "the old gentlemen's convention."[17]

Here again was a project that would include men of every stripe from every state in the Union and in the new Confederacy—which also met on February 4 in Montgomery, Alabama, to create a Confederate government. In a sign of the confusion of the times, President Tyler's granddaughter Letitia Tyler raised the first Confederate flag over the Alabama State Capital, in Montgomery, as he opened the Washington conference. The delegates had met with a weeping President Buchanan, who implored them to succeed at their work, and later with President-elect Lincoln on his first morning in Washington before the inauguration. Brady stopped working on the composite once he saw that the Peace Conference was destined to fail.

# CHAPTER 9

# "A Continuous Roll of Musketry"

T he Union Army met almost no resistance as it moved into Arlington and Alexandria in May of 1861, or as it sent patrols deeper into Virginia in the weeks that followed. Maj. Gen. George B. McClellan fared well against Confederate forces in western Virginia in early June and again in early July. Union confidence was high, even though Maj. Gen. Benjamin Butler—a Massachusetts lawyer and politician who had risen through the ranks of the commonwealth's militia without ever getting much in the way of military experience—was repelled by Confederate forces in June as he tried to move up the Peninsula at Big Bethel in southeastern Virginia.

Andrew Carnegie, then only twenty-five and working for the War Department as superintendent of military railways, was building a train trestle to cross the Potomac alongside the Long Bridge, which would link Washington with Alexandria. The most direct route from Washington to Richmond (the path that Interstate 95 follows today) involved negotiating a number of rivers and streams, whose bridges could easily be destroyed, and so was not the best way for armies to move in either direction. A train out of Washington crossing the new railroad bridge and running to Alexandria could follow the Orange & Alexandria line through Fairfax to Manassas and eventually to Gordonsville, near Charlottesville, in central Virginia. At Gordonsville was a junction with the Virginia Central line that ran east directly into Richmond. This was the best overland link between the two capitals, then, and the Orange & Alexandria formed a large section of it, making it crucial to each side both offensively and defensively.[1]

Manassas was strategically important not only because of its location along this route, but also because it was a junction with the Manassas Gap Railroad, which led to "the fertile valley of the Shenandoah, then teeming with live stock and cereal subsistence, as well as with other resources essential to the Confederates." Those are the words of Confederate Brig. Gen. P. G. T. Beauregard, who had forced the surrender of Fort Sumter and now commanded about twenty-two thousand troops in defense of Manassas Junction. His army was near enough to Washington—less than thirty miles—to threaten the capital city. Another Confederate force, of about nine thousand men under the command of Brig. Gen. Joseph E. Johnston, waited in the Shenandoah Valley, supposedly checked by a Union army of sixteen thousand federal troops under Maj. Gen. Robert Patterson.[2]

The Confederate congress was scheduled to meet in Richmond on July 20, and newspapers in the North repeatedly called for the federal army to act before that date. The chorus was led by Greeley's *Tribune*, whose managing editor, Charles A. Dana, headlined its editorial page on June 22 with the words THE NATION'S WAR CRY: *FORWARD TO RICHMOND! FORWARD TO RICHMOND! THE REBEL CONGRESS MUST NOT BE ALLOWED TO MEET THERE.* Dana ran the same headline in the same spot every day for a week. [3]

Washington was now swarming with troops intended for battle, if not necessarily ready to fight. General McDowell had been given command of the Army of Northeastern Virginia on May 14, but even though he was a career army officer, he did not have experience as a commander. Both he and his boss, General Scott, believed the Union army was too inexperienced for a major battle. But after Congress met in a special session called by President Lincoln on July 4, in which the president asked Congress to declare war, and to support the effort with four hundred thousand new troops and four hundred million dollars, it was clear that McDowell would have to attack the nearby Beauregard and push ahead toward the Confederate capital.

On July 16, McDowell's army of some thirty-five thousand soldiers moved out toward Fairfax, Manassas, and eventually, they believed, Richmond. Eleven members of one of the units stationed near McDowell's headquarters at Arlington House, the Eighth New York, posed for a Brady cameraman that very day. In the carte de visite image, they stand before white tents in the gray uniforms that many Northern troops wore early in the war, rifles stacked at the left side of the photo. On the back of the card are the handwritten words "Half an hour before the start at 3 o'clock to Fairfax Courthouse, Virginia."[4]

Like so much else having to do with Mathew Brady, tantalizingly little is known about his own campaign at the battle that everyone knew was coming, starting with when he left Washington. Brady later would say:

> I went to the first battle of Bull Run with two wagons from Washington. My personal companions were Dick McCormick, then a newspaper writer, Ned House, and Al Waud, the sketch artist. We stayed all night at Centreville; we got as far as Blackburn's Ford; we made pictures and expected to be in Richmond next day, but it was not so, and our apparatus was a good deal damaged on the way back to Washington; yet we reached the city.[5]

*New York Times* accounts published on July 23 report that Richard C. McCormick, who had accompanied Lincoln to Brady's studio on the day of the Cooper Union speech, was on a hillside above Blackburn's Ford on July 18, reporting for the *New York Evening Post.* So was Edwin H. (Ned) House, reporting for the *Tribune.* One of the other *Times* dispatches covering the events of July 18 notes that "an artist sketches the conflict coolly," but does not name him. In *Bohemian Brigade,* a book about the correspondents who covered the Civil War, Louis M. Starr writes that the reporters accompanying General McDowell's army on the way to Manassas "advanced en masse. Riding through the Virginia countryside with the singing and banter of the troops in their ears was such a cavalcade as had never been seen." Starr then lists two dozen newspaper correspondents by name, as well as Brady and Alfred R. Waud of the *New York Illustrated News.*[6]

Those who went to Blackburn's Ford, along with several members of Congress—the *Times* reporter refers to them as "Congressional idlers"—were watching the first serious action between the two armies, when a Union brigade tested Blackburn's and Mitchell's Fords, crossings of Bull Run several miles south of Centreville on the most direct route to Manassas Junction. McDowell wanted to see if the Confederates would fall back as they had done ever since the Union army approached Fairfax Court House. General Beauregard had clustered his Confederate forces around each of the major bridges or fords on the small river; hidden in the trees beyond Blackburn's Ford was a Confederate infantry brigade commanded by Brig. Gen. James Longstreet, supported by seven pieces of artillery farther up the hillside to the south of Bull Run.

The Union cannon fired first, shortly after noon, and when there was little response, Union skirmishers, followed by two regiments, hurried toward the stream. As they reached the ford, Longstreet's men opened fire, and a bloody battle broke out: "a continuous roll of musketry was heard, followed by the most excited yells and cries," according to the *Times*. Eventually, the Union regiments retreated back up the hillside overlooking the ford. During the next several hours, hundreds of rounds of artillery flew in both directions. The Skirmish at Blackburn's Ford, as it came to be known, resulted in eighty-three Union casualties and sixty-eight on the Confederate side. Although its seriousness was dwarfed by the fighting that would take place three days later several miles to the west, this "skirmish" was the first time that almost all the participants and reporters had ever seen battle. Col. William Tecumseh Sherman brought his brigade up in support of the regiments that were fighting Longstreet, and wrote in his *Memoirs*, "for the first time in my life I saw cannonballs strike men and crash through the trees and saplings above and around us, and realized the always sickening confusion as one approaches a fight from the rear." The reporters put on a brave face in their dispatches.[7]

A *Tribune* reporter writes in his unsigned article that he returned to Washington after the Blackburn's Ford skirmish in the evening via Long Bridge. So did Charles Carleton Coffin, a correspondent for the Boston *Journal*, who would become one of the most famous of all Civil War reporters. Brady almost certainly did not accompany them, because if he had he would have delivered to the Washington gallery the plates he had exposed along the way and at the skirmish that day. No such images exist. He likely went back to Centreville and spent the nights of the eighteenth and nineteenth there with McDowell's main force and the correspondents who had not returned to Washington.[8]

It was clear from the Confederates' willingness to engage at Blackburn's Ford that a large battle was imminent, but General McDowell dithered for the next two days, giving Beauregard time for Johnston's army to reinforce the Confederate lines. Johnston's men marched across the Blue Ridge Mountains and waited their turn at what is now called Delaplane to board trains on the single-track Manassas Gap Railroad, which took them in batches to Manassas Junction. It was, as Ernest B. Furgurson points out, "the first time in the history of warfare that railroads had been used for strategic mobility." The Union general Patterson had dramatically failed to contain Johnston's smaller force in the Shenandoah Valley.[9]

At two thirty on the morning of the twenty-first, McDowell began to move his men into position. Both commanding generals had had the same basic battle plan: to flank the right side of the other's army. "Strangely," as historian E. B. Long writes, "this could have resulted in both armies going in a circle." Beauregard's intention to move all his troops positioned on his right up toward Centreville and to attack McDowell's left never materialized, especially when part of McDowell's force under Colonel Sherman began to fire heavy guns at Beauregard's middle. From Centreville the main road west was called the Warrenton Turnpike. That road crossed a bridge at a stream called Cub Run and then crossed the Stone Bridge over Bull Run. It was the most obvious way for a large force to get across the river, if not the most direct route to Manassas Junction. McDowell sent part of his troops along this road, and sent a much larger contingent miles upstream to the north and west, to a crossing near Sudley Church, from which they would march south to flank Beauregard's left.[10]

Because of bad planning, this larger movement, which had much farther to march, had to wait for the units in the smaller contingent to cross Cub Run. The larger thrust would take a right turn at a blacksmith's shop beyond Cub Run and proceed on a barely discernible path across fields and then on forest roads to a ford near the church. McDowell set up his command center just off the turnpike, near the blacksmith shop.

One correspondent for the *Tribune*, William A. Croffut, arrived at Centreville on July 20, so he would not have been part of the original group of correspondents with whom Brady traveled. In a memoir published decades later, Croffut wrote that he and Massachusetts senator Henry Wilson, who was chairman of the Senate's military committee, were near the Warrenton Turnpike discussing the reason the troops were heading north—Manassas Junction was five or six miles due south from this spot—when "another civilian came up and joined us . . . and strapped to his shoulders was a box as big as a beehive." Croffut said he asked this man if he was with the commissary, and the man laughed and said, "No; I am a photographer and I'm going to take pictures of the battle." Croffut said the man identified himself as Brady and added that what he was carrying on his back was a camera.[11]

"I saw him afterwards dodging shells on the battlefield," Croffut writes. "He was in motion, but his machine did not seem effective." Croffut adds that later in the day, at about two P.M., "a runaway team of horses came dashing wildly past us, dragging a gun carriage bottom side up," and Croffut suggested to Brady that this would be a good time for him to get out of there. But "I failed to stir him," Croffut writes.

One aspect in particular of Croffut's account is hard to square. Brady himself denied, when asked late in life, that he had carried a camera on his back at Bull Run, saying, "That is not so—I had two wagons to carry my outfit." Other reports say that the wagons contained people who worked for Brady and who would have carried the cameras and taken the photographs, although Brady might well have been on the battlefield directing them.[12]

Although Croffut's account is somewhat confused about where he and Brady first met, it is likeliest that Brady got one of his wagons as close to the Stone Bridge as he could in the heavy traffic on the Warrenton Turnpike, and then perhaps crossed one of the fords with an assistant toting a camera. He might have crossed, for instance, with the New York Sixty-ninth, made up largely of Irish Americans from New York City, a regiment that was part of Sherman's Brigade and that forded the river several hundred yards north of Stone Bridge at about eleven thirty in the morning. Croffut, who had made the long flanking march, would have been in about the same place somewhere north of the turnpike by about noon, and that might well have been where he saw Brady dodging shells and trying to take pictures, and where the incident of the runaway gun-carriage horses might have happened later.[13]

It seems clear from various accounts that Brady later got caught up in the frenzied retreat of Union forces back across Stone Bridge and east on the turnpike toward Centreville. During the day's battle the

Union's ammunition and supply wagons had followed the troops, and as the famous *Times* of London correspondent William Howard Russell described the sight from a hillside in Centreville, the white tops of those wagons marked the course of the road as it rose and fell in the direction of Bull Run. The bridge over Cub Run, which is closer to Centreville than it is to the Stone Bridge, had been a bottleneck in the morning as the Union troops marched toward battle. Now, with the wagons lining the road for miles, all facing in the wrong direction once the retreat began, the route back was clogged. When Rebel artillery scored a hit on wagons on the Cub Run bridge, it was completely blocked. As David Detzer writes in a history of the first Bull Run battle, "For McDowell's army, the jam on the bridge was a disaster. Cub Run was narrow and its water waist high. Men and horses could scramble across, but its banks were too steep to permit vehicles to make it."[14]

At that point the Union army had to abandon anything on wheels, not only its wagons but also some of its cannon, a serious loss. Frightened men, spurred on by Rebel cavalrymen, grabbed horses from the supply and ammunition wagons and headed to Centreville, or simply threw down their weapons, and anything else they carried, and hightailed it.

Russell, who says he had mounted his horse and ridden far beyond Cub Run toward the battlefield before the panic began, was in the thick of it. He wrote in his memoirs:

> The scene on the road had now assumed an aspect which has not a parallel in any description I have ever read. Infantry soldiers on mules and draught horses, with the harness clinging to their heels, as much frightened as their riders; negro servants on their masters' chargers; ambulances crowded with unwounded soldiers; wagons swarming with men who threw out the contents in the road to make room, grinding through a shouting, screaming mass of men on foot, who were literally yelling with rage at every halt.[15]

He adds with some understatement, "This portion of the force was evidently in discord." Sherman himself wrote his wife that "I had read of retreats before—have seen the noise and confusion of crowds of men at fires and Shipwrecks but nothing like this." Even so, in the weeks after the battle, Russell was widely criticized by Union loyalists as having exaggerated in his newspaper account the amount of chaos in the retreat. In fact he was ever after mockingly known as "Bull Run" Russell. But he reports in his defense that Brady told him when he saw him later at the Pennsylvania Avenue gallery that he "could certify that my description fell far short of the disgraceful spectacle and excesses of the flight."[16]

Panic spread to the other side of Cub Run and up the hill into Centreville itself, as the Rebels lobbed shells at the retreating troops and mounted some disorganized and mostly ineffective cavalry and infantry attacks. Members of the retreating federal army feared that Beauregard's whole force would pursue them. Russell writes that even on the Washington side of Centreville, "Once more the dreaded cry, 'The cavalry! Cavalry are coming!' rang through the crowd." He looked back and saw what might have been "taken for horsemen in the act of sabreing the fugitives." Instead, he writes, "they were soldiers and civilians, with, I regret to say, some officers among them, who were whipping and striking their horses with sticks or whatever else they could lay hands on."[17]

There was very little sense of safety in the minds of those who fled, until, hours later, they reached the Long Bridge into Washington itself. But the capital also expected a Confederate attack in the days after the battle.

Wherever Brady took his photographic wagons before or during the battle, those wagons and their contents would have been vulnerable to the riotous crowd, and he lost them. As a result, no images from Brady's whole Bull Run excursion survived. Brady's talented protégé Timothy O'Sullivan, who worked in the Washington studio and might well have occupied one of the Brady wagons, was the unnamed subject of an 1869 article in *Harper's New Monthly Magazine* in which he gave a different explanation: "The battle of Bull Run would have been photographed 'close up' but for the fact that a shell from one of the rebel field-pieces took away the photographer's camera."[18]

Three articles appeared in the month after the Battle of Bull Run that alluded to Brady's presence there, and two of them implied that their authors had seen photographs that Brady brought back from the battle. The *American Journal of Photography* wrote on August 1 that the publication had had word of two unnamed photographic "parties" that accompanied McDowell's army, and that one had "got as far as the smoke of Bull's Run, and was aiming the never-failing tube at friends and foes alike." But when members of this party were caught up in the retreat, they "left their photographic accoutrements on the ground, which the rebels, no doubt, pounced upon as trophies of victory." This was clearly Brady. Bob Zeller, in *The Blue and Gray in Black and White*, says that the other photographer, who is described in the article as having taken a "fine stereo-view of the famed Fairfax Court House," was an Anthony and Company photographer, because such a photograph turned up in their catalogue described as having been taken "just after the Grand Army passed to fight the battle of Bull Run," and that the photographer was quite possibly George Barnard, who worked at times for both Anthony and Brady.[19]

One of the most affecting photographs to come out of the entire war has often been said to have been taken by Brady on his way to Bull Run. It shows the men of the New York Sixty-ninth posed with their Roman Catholic chaplain outside a white tent. The Sixty-ninth was the famous Irish brigade, and the photograph's poignancy comes from the heavy losses the regiment took at Bull Run—nearly two hundred men killed, wounded, or missing. But an article in the Portland (Maine) *Daily Advertiser* on July 20 mentions this image, so it must have been taken not on the Sunday morning of the battle itself, but in the weeks before Bull Run, as were other images of the Sixty-ninth.

The *American Journal of Photography* seems to have gotten the story of Brady at Bull Run just about right. An unsigned piece that appeared two weeks later in *Humphrey's Journal* feels as if Brady himself planted it. Whoever wrote the article imaginatively combines examples of Brady's photographs of Northern militias in their encampments with an account by Brady of what he did at Bull Run, implying strongly that the writer had seen images from the battlefield. "The public is indebted to Brady of Broadway for numerous excellent views of 'grim-visaged war,'" the piece begins. "He has been in Virginia with his camera, and many and spirited are the pictures he has taken. His are the only reliable records at Bull's Run."[20]

When it gets down to describing the photographs, the article asserts that "The groupings of entire regiments and divisions, within the space of a couple of feet square, present some of the most curious effects as yet produced in photography . . . there is nothing to compare with them in their powerful contrasts of light and shade." Since no images of the sort described are known to exist, it seems likely that these were photographs of smaller units of soldiers than regiments and divisions. Brady was well acquainted with newspaper and magazine journalists in New York. This article, which implies much more than it actually says, could well have reflected Brady's own artful retelling.

Two days after the *Humphrey's* article, a *New York Times* report also refers specifically to the scenes of camp life and asserts only that the battlefield photographs were taken. It says Brady went with McDowell's army into Virginia, accompanied by "a full corps of artists and work-men, and embraced every opportunity to add to his collection of illus-trative scenes." It continues, as if having interviewed Brady, "He went upon the field of battle at Bull Run,—accompanied HEINTZEL-MAN'S column into action, and was caught in the whirl and panic which accompanied the retreat of our Army."[21]

Of this *Times* article's eight sentences, one uses the first person, just once, when it interjects that "We saw [Brady] constantly, at every point, before and after the fight, neglecting no opportunity and spar-ing no labor in the pursuit of his professional object." Was this later report written in New York by one of the several *Times* correspondents who had witnessed the battle? But then the *Times* writer continues by saying, "As the result of his arduous and perilous toil, he has brought back a very large collection of pictures which will do more than the most elaborate description to perpetuate the scenes of that brief cam-paign."

Could there have been photographs that survived and then were lost? It does not seem possible. As Bob Zeller points out, Brady never listed any such photograph in a catalogue or advertised them for sale. Given the effort Brady put into collecting his own photographs and the images of others for the Anthony catalogue, he would have placed a high premium on close-up pictures of the first battle of the war—and indeed the first images ever taken anywhere of warfare itself. Roger Fenton is often credited with having done this in his photographs of the Crimean War, but the closest he came to actual battle was a con-troversial image of cannonballs in a road, with no soldiers in sight. Had Brady taken scenes on the battlefield, they would have been of incalculable historical value, which would have been apparent to this very history-minded photographer. Had they existed, they would have exceeded by far the impact of the Lincoln Cooper Union portrait or that of Col. Elmer Ellsworth. Perhaps this is why so many of Brady's contemporaries, and why Brady himself, wanted so keenly for them to exist.[22]

The only known Brady image related to Bull Run is one that Brady had someone take of himself the following day in his Pennsylvania Avenue studio. The intention of this photo is heroic—to show that he was there. The soiled and rumpled look of the linen duster he wears suggests that he has been through something, and indeed Croffut said that Brady was wearing the duster when he saw him on the twenty-first. (Coincidentally, when General McDowell gave reporters permission to travel with his army to Manassas he made the rueful joke that "They should wear a white uniform to indicate the purity of their character."[23])

On the night of the twenty-first and the next day a drizzling rain had fallen, and the condition of the dustcoat and Brady's muddy boots in the photo suggests that Brady might well have had to walk home through the night. This portrait is also noteworthy because the outline of a sword appears distinctly under the dustcoat and extends beneath it for an inch or two. The story goes that a member of the Fire Zouaves gave Brady the sword so that he could protect himself on the way back to Washington. This adds to the drama of the photo, but the chaos of the retreat would have created legitimate fears, making self-protection a serious matter. Russell writes of a soldier who aimed a pistol at him at close range, presumably to steal the horse on which he was mounted, but the gun did not go off.[24]

Brady was a master of promotion, and this photograph, words inked over it in white asserting his presence at the war's first great battle, would contribute mightily to the myth of Brady the Civil War photographer. We cannot tell from the portrait what is in his heart, whether this image shows a man deeply spooked by his experience or not. But we do know that he never knowingly put himself in harm's way again.


To gaze at the photo of Brady returned from Bull Run is to wonder what he could have been thinking when he set off. The white linen duster, the straw hat, the crosstie and white shirt, the gold watch fob hanging below his belt—did he have any idea what war was like? If so,

Photo taken July 22nd 1861

BRADY The Photographer returned from Bull Run

Mathew Brady returned from the First Battle of Bull Run
(July 1861). *Library of Congress*

why did he dress for it like a French landscape painter? Croffut, the *Tribune* reporter, was also wearing a duster at the battle, and people simply dressed more formally while working in those days. If you were someone who had risen in class, as Brady had, you might have been especially careful to look your dapper best, so as not to be confused with your workers.

Beyond that, there was the carefree air of everyone in the North, including the soldiers of McDowell's army themselves, who did not take the South seriously. The notion that they would be in Richmond in a day or two was not only Brady's expectation but widely shared. In an unsigned essay called "The Advantages of Defeat," which appeared in the *Atlantic Monthly* in September 1861, the writer laments about Bull Run, "The troops moved forward with exultation, as if going on a holiday and festive campaign; and the nation that watched them shared in their careless confidence, and prophesied a speedy triumph."[25]

It's safe to say that very few people in the vicinity of Bull Run in July of 1861 had any real idea what they were getting into. That goes for the generals, the raw recruits, and everyone in between, and it goes for most of the journalists on hand, only a few of whom had ever covered a war before. Why shouldn't it also apply to Brady?

But the question of *what* he was thinking as he set off is only part of the larger question of *why*. Why would this urbane and even dandified photographer, Brady of Broadway, decide to leave the safe confines of the studio, when he could so easily have sent the teams of camera operators who had already been photographing soldiers all around Washington? In an 1891 newspaper interview, Brady offers a romantic explanation that is in character with the somewhat whimsical nature of the rest of the interview. But beneath the surface are some darker aspects:

> My wife and my most conservative friends had looked unfavorably upon this departure from commercial business to pictorial war correspondence, and I can only describe the destiny that overruled me by saying that, like Euphorion, I felt that I had to go.[26]

The classical reference to Euphorion is an obscure one today, and would have been obscure even in Brady's own time. How did Brady, with no classical education, and not much education of any sort, know about Euphorion? In his *Faust, Part Two*, published in 1838, Goethe retrieved Euphorion from obscurity as the winged son of Faust and Helen of Troy. In the play, Goethe fashions Euphorion into a tribute to Lord Byron, the poet whose romantic strivings finally destroyed him. Goethe's Euphorion climbs a steep mountain against the wishes of his mother, who keeps urging him to turn back. He climbs higher and higher, with overtones of Icarus flying too near the sun, and like Icarus, he eventually plunges to his death.[27]

But even Goethe's *Faust* would seem to be a referential reach for Brady. The explanation probably has to do with the actor Lewis Morrison, who was a protégé of the famous actors Edwin Forrest, Charlotte Cushman, and Edwin Booth, all of whom Brady photographed. A native of Jamaica who was an officer in the black and Creole Louisiana Native Guard during the Civil War, Morrison became popular in the latter half of the nineteenth century for playing Mephistopheles in a popularized stage version of *Faust*. Given the readiness and the aptness of Brady's use of the Euphorion metaphor, it would seem that he knew the play well, and that he expected the metaphor to make sense to his interviewer and the newspaper's readers. But Brady makes explicit reference to only half of the Euphorion story when he speaks of his going to cover the war against the wishes of his wife and friends, a comparison to Euphorion's compulsion to climb the mountain against his mother's wishes. The other half of the comparison would equate Euphorion's fate with Brady's own plummeting reputation and finances when the war ended, a plunge less lethal than Euphorion's, but almost as steep.[28]

It's possible that Brady went to war, as he said, to follow some inexplicable compulsion. It's also logical that after his years of documenting those who made history, he would want to take advantage of the opportunity to see history being made. Or that, like the tens of thousands of recruits on both sides of the war—and like the lawyers and politicians and businessmen on both sides who formed regiments, sometimes at their own expense—Brady was simply caught up in the spirit of the moment, the *euphoria* of being part of something bigger than himself. Like many children of immigrants, like the many Irish Americans of his day, Brady was a patriotic believer in the better life his parents had come to America to find.

The reason could also have been as mundane as his pals in the press urging him to join them on a summer outing, and his saying why not. His intentions in going were not just historical but journalistic, to see and record for himself. If he failed in the attempt, if he was so rattled by the bloodshed and the chaos that he would never do it again, still, he almost certainly went into the thick of battle. It's possible that Timothy O'Sullivan and George Barnard were there as well, but far less evidence exists of this. Bull Run was the first time in history an attempt was made to take photographs under fire, and Brady was at the very least an important part of it.

# CHAPTER 10

# "More Eloquent Than the Sternest Speech"

However Brady reacted to what he saw at the Battle of Bull Run, his enthusiasm for collecting images connected to the war was undiminished. Soon after the battle, he had one of his employees copy a Mexican War–era daguerreotype of Maj. Thomas J. Jackson, replete with muttonchop sideburns—as they were not yet called; the Union general Ambrose Burnside would soon inspire the term—and offered it to the public as a carte de visite. It's not clear if Brady took the original image, as he did those of other prominent officers from the Mexican-American War once they had returned. Jackson, now a Confederate general, had famously earned his "Stonewall" nickname at Bull Run, and even if Brady had found himself in the line of fire from some of Jackson's men there, he apparently did not hesitate to acknowledge the general's newly heroic status in the South.

On July 22, 1861, the very day that Brady had his own photograph made upon his return from Bull Run, President Lincoln summoned Maj. Gen. George B. McClellan to Washington from western Virginia, where he had been credited for the few bright spots in the Union army's efforts so far. By July 27, McClellan had formally replaced McDowell as commander of the troops in the Division of the Potomac. His first task was to transform the miscellaneous volunteer brigades, which had performed so poorly at Bull Run, into a professional army, using three-year recruits to replace the departing three-month volunteers.

One day in August, General McClellan took time away from these duties to climb the stairs of Brady's Pennsylvania Avenue gallery, his sword jangling, his dark blue uniform fresh, ready to be photographed. Sitting for Brady's camera was becoming an expected ritual for those who rose to the top ranks of military leadership. McClellan was only thirty-four years old, but breathtakingly self-confident and ambitious. Out of context, his poses for Brady or, more likely, for Alexander Gardner seem just slightly ludicrous. In at least two of the images, the "young Napoleon," as he was beginning to be called in the newspapers, slipped one and then several brass buttons of his double-breasted tunic out of their holes and slid his right hand, Napoleon-style, under the dark blue material. But it's fair to note that this pose was not unusual, and was affected by generals from both sides.[1]

McClellan's visit to the Washington studio had consequences for both Brady and Gardner. McClellan soon offered Gardner an official position on his staff, working under Allan Pinkerton's Secret Service operation. Pinkerton had known McClellan since 1857, when he was a private detective in Chicago, where one of his clients was the Illinois Central Railroad, of which McClellan was chief engineer and then vice president. Pinkerton set up a spy service for McClellan in May 1861, when the newly appointed major general was commander of the Department of Ohio. After McClellan assumed command in Washington he again tapped Pinkerton to create an intelligence service. Pinkerton requested Gardner (like him a Scot and about his age) for his operation, and Gardner began working for the military by November, soon after McClellan replaced General Scott as general in chief of the army. (This was in addition to his role as commander of the Army of the Potomac: when Lincoln asked McClellan if he could handle both jobs at once, McClellan's response was, according to Lincoln's secretary, John Hay, "I can do it all.")

Gardner was assigned to the U.S. Army Corps of Topographical Engineers, given the formal title of photographer of the Army of the Potomac, and was known informally as Captain Gardner. In reminiscences decades later, Pinkerton's son William says he spent time with Gardner over the winter of 1861/1862 and knew him for the rest of the war. Gardner worked out of the Secret Service Corps headquarters, "photographing maps and other articles of that kind which were prepared by the secret service," the young Pinkerton wrote, and these reproductions were distributed to McClellan's staff and to field commanders. Gardner soon moved on from copying work to traveling into the field to photograph units of the Army of the Potomac. He also photographed landscapes where future battles might take place or where encampments and hospitals might be situated as the war continued, and he shot bridges, roads, railroads, and other forms of what we now call infrastructure, all of which would justify his placement with the topographical engineers. William Pinkerton recalled, "I used to travel around with Gardner a good deal while he was taking these views and saw many of them made."[2]

Presumably the information flowed both ways between the photographer and the other members of the headquarters staff. No sooner had McClellan taken the reins in Washington than he became convinced there would be an attack by an outsize Confederate force. "I am induced to believe that the enemy has at least 100,000 men in our front," McClellan reported to General Scott, whereas Beauregard's army had only 45,000 men. This pattern of overestimating the enemy, abetted by some gross mistakes by the out-of-his-depth Allan Pinkerton, would continue until Lincoln eventually fired McClellan for his timidity. Gardner surely got wind of these fears of the attack on Washington City that never came, fears that many others had shared since Bull Run, and he got his family out of town. He sent one son to boarding school in Emmitsburg, Maryland, on the Pennsylvania border, which he wrongly presumed would be a safe distance from the war; Emmitsburg is only about ten miles from the Gettysburg battlefield. He sent the rest of his family to McGregor, Iowa, on the west bank of the Mississippi, where the greatest threat would have been the flood-prone river itself.[3]

Gardner seems to have remained connected with the Brady Washington studio even after going to work for the army, and some of his colleagues there, such as Timothy O'Sullivan and Gardner's brother, James, appear to have shared in the work for the topographical engineers and for Allan Pinkerton. Gardner wrote a letter years later saying that O'Sullivan had been "Superintendent of my map and field work," and on a job application with the U.S. Treasury in 1880, O'Sullivan claims that he had held the title of first lieutenant, probably in the same way that Gardner was informally called "captain." Although Pinkerton, as the head of a spy agency, was understandably concerned about secrecy, it's likely that these Brady photographers did dual service during this time, using the access provided by McClellan to the Army of the Potomac to secure photographs of units and of landscapes to be sold as stereoscopes, cartes de visite, or the somewhat larger cabinet cards for Brady and the Anthonys. It was not unusual during the Civil War for photographers to make several exposures of the same subject and use them for different purposes, and Brady often bought or bartered for these duplicates for his growing collection of war images. One early historian of Civil War photography writes that Gardner and his colleagues made more than a thousand images while working for the government.[4]

O'Sullivan would be among the most prolific and accomplished photographers of the Civil War and, after the war, one of the great early photographic chroniclers of the West. Indeed, he was among the most significant artists of the medium's first half century in America. In 1880, Brady would write in a letter of reference for O'Sullivan that he had known the younger man—O'Sullivan was born in Ireland in 1840—since he was a boy. Brady and Julia had moved to Staten Island by 1850, and census data analyzed by the photographic historian William Stapp suggests that O'Sullivan's family moved there between 1855 and 1860. Stapp also quotes a letter from O'Sullivan in which he says he "graduated under M. B. Brady of New York and was afterwards in the employment of Mr. Gardner of Washington," which Stapp interprets as suggesting that O'Sullivan began his working life as "a studio assistant for Brady in New York City while in his teens." O'Sullivan went with Gardner to Washington soon after the new gallery opened there in 1858.[5]

Beginning sometime in the fall of 1861, O'Sullivan worked on the staff of Brig. Gen. Egbert Ludovicus Viele, a civil and military engineer (and a West Point graduate who served before the war under Olmsted and Vaux as engineer for Central Park and Prospect Park) who led a Union expedition on Port Royal, South Carolina, in late fall of 1861 and winter and spring of 1862. The joint army and navy expedition left Hampton Roads in Virginia on October 29 with seventy-seven ships, twelve thousand infantrymen, and six hundred marines, making it the largest maritime military expedition yet undertaken in the United States. After weathering a storm off the North Carolina Outer Banks, the expedition took Port Royal Sound, just north of Hilton Head, South

Carolina, on November 7, a major strategic victory for the North, establishing a federal presence between the important Confederate ports of Charleston and Savannah. The Union constructed a coaling and resupply station on Parris Island in Port Royal Sound, which would support the blockades of other Southern ports.

O'Sullivan took photographs in the towns of Port Royal and nearby Beaufort, and later on Hilton Head, and he accompanied the expedition against other Confederate ports in South Carolina and Georgia, including Fort Pulaski, which controlled access to the Savannah River. It fell after a Union siege in April 1862, and O'Sullivan soon had photographs of the damage Union guns had done to the fort's walls. O'Sullivan would also have been photocopying maps and documents for General Viele's headquarters staff, much as Gardner was doing for General McClellan's. This might explain why there are almost no O'Sullivan photographs for the first half of the campaign. O'Sullivan was also supplying Brady with photographs during this time. There are at least forty-three known images from the expedition, most of them taken in Beaufort, Port Royal, Hilton Head, and Fort Pulaski. The subjects range from the sites of battles to forts and docks to assemblies of Union troops to portraits of generals with their staff or alone—the typical range of photographic subjects throughout the Civil War. There is in addition a series of photographs of local plantations, including several pictures of slaves, photographs that might well have been more politically charged than the images of forts and soldiers. These might well be the first photographs O'Sullivan took beyond the carefully controlled confines of the portrait studio, and there is nothing particularly special about them as photographs.[6]

Oddly, at the same time he was in South Carolina and Georgia, making photographic history as the first successful chronicler of a military campaign and taking the first photographs for which he would later receive credit by name, O'Sullivan was listed in a Washington directory as being a "mes'ger" at "352 Pa. av.," the address for Brady's Washington gallery. Did this reflect his status when he first came to the Washington studio four years earlier, or was it simply an error? Even the famous man who had taught him photography would now have to consider O'Sullivan to be something more than a messenger boy.

\* \* \*

While O'Sullivan was was off on this joint mission for Brady and the Union, the war in Virginia remained quiet, both because of the winter weather and because of the timidity of the generals on both sides. But when the weather began to break in March of 1862, federal troops went on the move, and Brady had men following the two main thrusts. After first being urged and then ordered by his commander in chief, McClellan sent elements of his lumbering Army of the Potomac— 112,000-men strong—toward Manassas Junction on March 7. "McClellan's army made a splendid sight," E. B. Long writes, "as, after long, formal training and a winter's idleness, it paraded out to expected victory."[7]

Jefferson Davis, who had only recently been inaugurated in Richmond as president of the Confederate States of America, knew of the Union movement before it happened, and had written General Johnston, now in command of the forty-eight-thousand-man Confederate Army of Northern Virginia, that he understood the necessity of falling back before the much larger Union force, which Johnston did on the same day that McClellan began to move. And so McClellan's troops, much like McDowell's the summer before, found only the signs of the enemy's recent encampments as they moved deeper into Virginia. When they reached Centreville they discovered that the Rebels had employed a trick that had worked the previous fall—they had painted long logs black and positioned them to suggest that the Confederate troops had more cannon than they actually had. These Quaker guns, as they were called, had fed McClellan's fears of a superior, entrenched Confederate force.

Now the press saw in Centreville what Brady's cameramen would also reveal: the evidence that the North had been "humbugged by the Rebels," as New Yorker George Templeton Strong wrote in his famous diary. But Gardner would write in 1865 in defense of his boss, "as for the 'Quakers,' it was not at all an uncommon thing to place them on deserted positions." Gardner adds that McClellan's army had found multiple tracks of actual cannon being pulled away at Centreville. But the Quaker guns were a public relations setback for McClellan, especially given the widespread feeling that he was afraid to fight or was even in sympathy with the South, a question Lincoln had just raised with him in the White House, drawing a fiery response from the general.[8]

Two photographers from Brady's Washington gallery, George N. Barnard and James F. Gibson, followed the army out to Centreville, Bull Run, and Manassas, where they documented the places that had become familiar as a result of First Bull Run. They took as many as sixty images, their subjects including the Quaker guns and other fortifications around Centreville, Cub Run, the ruined Stone Bridge, Sudley's Ford, the battlefield itself, Beauregard's headquarters, and the fortifications and ruins around Manassas, where the departing Confederates had burned the village, the rail yards, and railroad equipment. Barnard and Gibson must have arrived soon afterward, because the ruins were still smoldering when they photographed them. Gardner wrote of Manassas that "The scene of devastation after the evacuation was terrible. Of the pleasant village only tottering chimneys were left, surrounded by blackened ruins and the *debris* of half-burned [railroad] cars and storehouses." The Civil War historian Bruce Catton quotes a soldier from Georgia as saying that what Johnston's army did on leaving Manassas was "the greatest destruction I ever saw in my life."[9]

With this series of photographs taken by Barnard and Gibson, "The Civil War's first battlefield was," as Bob Zeller puts it, "finally well documented by the camera." He adds that "the images soon appeared for sale in Brady's galleries as stereo views, two different sizes of card photographs, and large format, ready-for-framing folio prints." Brady would advertise the availability of these prints at his Broadway gallery in the September 15 *New York World*, calling them "Consecutive Views of the Leading Scenes and Incidents of the War," and promoting them for their "beauty and fidelity, taken by corps of trained artists, which have accompanied the great Union Armies in several campaigns."[10]

About two dozen of these images would be offered for twenty-five cents each by E. & H. T. Anthony, and listed in its November 1862 *Catalogue of Card Photographs*. Anthony's also sold a number of the stereograph views. Gardner later appropriated some of them for his 1865 *Photographic Sketch Book of the War*, where the negatives were attributed to Barnard and Gibson but the prints were attributed to him. No mention at all is made of Brady in the *Sketch Book*.

Brady did not copyright all the photographs taken for him by Barnard and Gibson. According to the *United States Copyright Book,*

*1861–1868*, Barnard and Gibson themselves copyrighted twenty-eight of their images, both stereographs and large-format plates, on May 5, 1862, noting that the images would appear under the rubric "Brady's Album Gallery." On the same day, Brady copyrighted four other views, including one of Centreville that had clearly been taken by Barnard and Gibson (the other three likely were taken as they followed McClellan's army into northern Virginia), using the same rubric. On May 7, Barnard and Gibson copyrighted twelve more of their images from Bull Run, and Brady copyrighted eleven more images.

D. Mark Katz, in his biography of Alexander Gardner, concludes that "as early as May 5, 1862, all camera operatives in Brady's employ (including Gardner) were free to claim credit for their own work." This is significant because when Gardner left Brady to start his own gallery the following year, and many of Brady's best operators followed, the reason historians have often given for the move is that Brady was reluctant to credit them. But as with so much else related to Brady, and indeed to all the photographers involved—Gardner, O'Sullivan, Barnard, and Gibson among them—very little evidence exists to support this conclusion or any other conclusion about the split. It's true that Brady did not credit individual cameramen in his catalogues of photographs, and that when Gardner made his own catalogues, he did. But as Michael L. Carlebach writes in *The Origins of Photojournalism in America*:

> There was nothing nefarious in the practice of taking credit for all the work produced under [Brady's] auspices; it was an accepted practice in the early days of photography. Camera operators and darkroom personnel were anonymous, and became known only if and when they set up their own operations. As long as they worked for Brady, as long as he supplied the cameras, plates, and photographic supplies, as long as he paid their salaries, he took the credit.[11]

Although Gardner was at least two years older than Brady, he had not gotten into the photography business in its earliest days, as Brady had. In large studios such as Brady's the photographic process itself required a team of people with different skills to make a successful image, but with the advent of the Civil War, these photographers carried their darkrooms and materials with them (as itinerant and other independent operators had been doing for some time). The operator himself could prepare the plate, expose it, and develop it. Photography was becoming the work of an individual, and it made sense that these individuals would receive credit, as they had not when their work represented one step in a complicated process undertaken with others.

It also made sense that Gardner, who was much closer to the act of making photographs than Brady, would see this distinction first. Gardner was a social idealist, whereas Brady the entrepreneur had turned his own name into a commercial powerhouse. But the effect of this difference between them, as Katz and Carlebach both show, has been badly overblown. It's also reasonable to argue that Brady could rightly have been the aggrieved party when Gardner's *Sketch Book* appeared, since although Gardner was scrupulous about giving credit to the photographers, he just as carefully failed to give Brady credit, although the 1862 photographs were clearly taken by people he employed.

The third serious initiative by the Brady gallery to photograph the war in the first half of 1862 followed soon after the Centreville, Bull Run, and Manassas photographs in March, and featured James Gibson as the lead photographer. Gardner would later attribute all the March photographs to George Barnard, but nineteen of them included Gibson's name as well, meaning that Gibson was in an assistant role. But after General McClellan launched the Peninsula Campaign in early April, Gibson soon followed, and his name would appear alone in the credit for at least 120 stereo negatives taken over the next three months, and he would share a credit with John Wood for eight large-format negatives. At least seven other large-format photos were taken with other photographers during this time. The photographs that Gibson (a Scot like Gardner and about thirty-three years old at the time) would take during this campaign would create new standards for war photography, both by enlarging the sheer range of views and by developing an aesthetic sense that went beyond what O'Sullivan had exhibited in his photographs so far.[12]

On March 11, President Lincoln took away McClellan's position as general in chief of the federal armies, but left the position open. By March 17, McClellan had begun to move the Army of the Potomac, which he still commanded after its return from Manassas, on ships two hundred miles down the Potomac and Chesapeake Bay to Fortress Monroe, the federal outpost at the mouth of Hampton Roads, the large protected harbor into which the James and other rivers spill near the mouth of the Chesapeake Bay. When the South's General Johnston fell back from northern Virginia in the face of McClellan's advance, he assembled his troops on the Southern side of the Rappahannock River, about halfway between Washington and Richmond. McClellan would now be far to the south of Richmond and could march or fight his way up the Virginia Peninsula, the land between the James and York Rivers, to the Confederate capital. It took almost four hundred vessels and nearly three weeks to transport the rest of McClellan's army to the foot of the Peninsula. The campaign was for the most part another McClellan exercise in missed opportunities, but there was real fighting before it was over.

The first photographs by Gibson and Wood listed in Gardner's 1863 catalogue are dated May 1, 1862, and because they include images of the headquarters staff and one the next day of the topographical engineers to whom Gardner had been assigned for his copying work the previous fall, it seems likely that this was why Gibson and Wood were there in the first place, so the pictures they took for Brady might well have been ancillary.

A number of the nearly fifty photographs they made in May show an eagerness to find new ways to place the camera in relation to its subject. O'Sullivan had taken some panoramic images while in South Carolina and Georgia—for instance, a distant view of Fort Pulaski showing the damage from federal shelling—but Gibson's panoramic views often have something in the foreground to frame the image or to give it a sense of depth or to help create a point of view. One of his well-known images of McClellan's encampment at Cumberland Landing, taken from the top a nearby hill to show the vastness of the camp, places five figures, four of them soldiers, in the foreground, seated on the hill and seeing what the camera sees. Their backs are to the viewer, in silhouette, so we are looking over their shoulders.

Many of O'Sullivan's images show him struggling as he learns where to place the camera. Often, like new photographers everywhere, he stands too far from his subject, for instance in a picture called "Group on J. J. Smith's Plantation, Beaufort, S.C.," in which the image is mostly foreground and sky, with the group of slaves that are his subject taking up a narrow horizontal strip that covers only a fraction of the vertical surface of the image. In contrast, one of Gibson's photos on May 1, entitled "Comte de Paris, Duc de Chartes, Prince de Joinville, and friends, at Camp Winfield Scott, near Yorktown," almost puts the viewer at the outdoor table where these men informally sit, the camera lens at the same level as their faces, inviting us into the intimate scene.

For another image, O'Sullivan stands well outside the front yard of a South Carolina house where a signal station has been built on the roof, again placing himself too far from his subject. We know from Gibson's photos that his impulse would have been to lug his camera up to the signal station itself, where a man stands on a platform as high as the highest point on the two-story house's roof, and get an image from that vantage point. The difference is crucial. One image makes the viewer a passive observer, and the other, like that of the French royal visitors in McClellan's camp, makes the viewer a participant.

How do we know that Gibson would have climbed up to the signal station? Because in his Peninsula Campaign photographs he does climb up a signal tower to get an aerial view of Camp Winfield Scott, and in one of the May photographs, of Battery No. 4, near Yorktown, he appears to have climbed a ship's mast or webbing. The photograph is taken from above the water, about forty feet out a dock that extends from the shore of the York River. O'Sullivan would certainly learn, through his own experimentation or perhaps from seeing Gibson's photographs, to find unusual vantage points. One of the most interesting photographs of the entire war will come when O'Sullivan goes to the second floor of a church to make several photographs of Grant and his staff arrayed on benches in the churchyard beneath him, consulting maps and conferring about their next move.

Thirty-one of the photographs that Gibson took in the first week of May were copyrighted in Washington, D.C., on May 9. Gibson held the copyright to some of these images, but most were copyrighted later under the designation "Gardner and Gibson" (a brief formal partnership between the two men that would later result in a lawsuit), but all of them were designated as part of "Brady's Album Gallery," and Brady published them immediately.[13]

At the end of May, Gibson made two versions of a photograph that had enough historical significance at the time to appear as an engraving in *Harper's Weekly.* Just before the Battle of Fair Oaks, also called

Seven Pines, a young aide-de-camp to General Johnston was captured while serving as a courier. Strategically, the captured courier's proximity to McClellan's own army warned McClellan that General Johnston (whose army had been ordered south from the Rappahannock to defend Richmond) was nearby, but historically the picture mattered because the young Confederate lieutenant was a great-great-grandnephew of George Washington, James Barroll Washington. The other man in the photograph, also a young lieutenant, and about to become aide-de-camp to General McClellan, was none other than George Armstrong Custer.

As it happened, Custer had been two years behind Washington at West Point, and recognized him when he was captured. After the Battle of Fair Oaks, Custer sought him out and arranged what the Confederate's stepmother would later call in a letter "rather a jollification in one of the headquarters tents," where the two lieutenants and other West Pointers whom Custer had rounded up reminisced about their academy days. One of the photos Gibson took shows Washington, with a piece of white cloth pinned to his tunic that presumably designated him as a prisoner of war, and Custer, his cap removed to show his wavy blond hair, both sitting on logs, a barefoot and bandaged young African American boy at their feet. Washington had called to the young "contraband" in the Union camp to join them, and suggested that the photo be called "Both sides, the cause." Gibson took a second photograph of the two officers, but without the boy. The photograph has more resonance now because of Custer's presence, of course, and it is hard not to detect in the directness with which he views the camera his determination to be someone who would matter. Washington would eventually be returned to duty in a prisoner exchange.[14]

A month later, Gibson took a seminal photograph of the war. McClellan had at last pushed his army close enough to Richmond to hear the city's church bells ringing. Robert E. Lee, who had replaced General Johnston when he was injured in the battle of Fair Oaks, initiated what would be known as the Seven Days, a series of bloody battles that occurred to the east and southeast of the Southern capital, which would push McClellan south to the James River and render his army ineffective for some time. On June 27 one of these battles, at Gaines' Mill, produced a number of Union casualties that were transported south across the Chickahominy River to Savage's Station, where the Union had a supply depot and a field hospital. The next day, Gibson made several photographs, including an affecting one of wounded and sick men resting or sleeping on the ground in the fenced yard of a farmhouse. Some of those pictured wear the straw hats that certain members of the New York "Fighting Sixty-ninth" Irish brigade wore into battle. Their hats are also visible in the photo of them attending Mass with their priest not long before Bull Run.

In its November 1862 number, *Harper's New Monthly Magazine* summarized the impact of this photo:

> This is Savage's Station, with the wounded there after the battle of the 27th June. There is a tree in the middle; a shed and tents; and around the tree, lying thick and close, so that the ground looks like a dull, heavy sea of which bodies are the waves, lie the wounded soldiers. This scene brings the war to those who have not been to it. How patiently and still they lie, these brave men who bleed and are maimed for us! It is a picture which is more eloquent than the sternest speech.[15]

The day after Gibson took his photograph the Confederates attacked a rear guard of McClellan's army intended to protect the hospital at Savage's Station. "The Yankees repulsed this feeble attack," James M. McPherson writes in *Battle Cry of Freedom*, "then withdrew during the night leaving behind 2,500 sick and wounded men (from earlier fighting) and several surgeons who volunteered to share their captivity." Most of these men, presumably including those in Gibson's photograph, became prisoners of war, and would be exposed to the often fatal vagaries of life in a Southern hospital or prison.[16]

More Brady photographers joined Gibson and Wood on the Peninsula Campaign: George Barnard is credited with a photograph at Savage's Station on June 27, the day of the Gaines' Mill battle, and he took other photographs for their historical value, such as one of the house in Yorktown where General Cornwallis surrendered during the Revolutionary War, and some for their value in Brady's "Incidents of the War" series of the Fair Oaks battlefield. In June, a Brady assistant who would remain in Brady's employ throughout the war, David B. Woodbury, was also on the Peninsula, perhaps assisting Barnard. And in late July or early August, Alexander Gardner arrived on the scene for the first time, photographing Union encampments and officers at Berkeley and Westover Plantations on the James River. He might have gone to replace Gibson, who had now been in the field for three and possibly four months, since no photographs of Gibson's have August dates. Nothing suggests that Brady himself ventured south of Washington at any time during this campaign.

O'Sullivan undertook the last major effort by a Brady photographer to cover the war before the battle of Antietam, following Maj. Gen. John Pope through northern and central Virginia in July and August. On June 27, Pope had taken over a new command, the Army of Virginia, which combined all the forces in the state that did not belong to McClellan's Army of the Potomac. Its main job was to protect the nation's capital, but Pope might also be asked to hurry to Richmond to support McClellan in the right situation. After the Seven Days, though, Lincoln decided that the opposite would happen, that General McClellan's army, suffering from illness and facing the worst parts of the summer in the malarial Tidewater, would return to northern Virginia, from which it would support Pope.

O'Sullivan connected with Pope's army at Manassas on the Fourth of July, photographing Blackburn's Ford, and on the next day, he photographed General McDowell's headquarters in the house that his opponent, General Beauregard, had used for the same purpose at Manassas the previous summer. O'Sullivan followed Pope's army south and west to Warrenton and then south to the battle of Cedar Mountain in Culpeper County. Probably the most striking photographs from the weeks with Pope were taken after the August 9 Cedar Mountain battle, where Pope's forces engaged with those of Stonewall Jackson. Although O'Sullivan was in the vicinity on August 9, photographing an artillery battery "fording a tributary of the Rappahannock, on the day of the battle of Cedar Mountain," as a later caption reads, he did not document the battlefield itself until after the hundreds of those killed had been buried. One stereograph shows a few of the newly finished graves and two others show the scattered carcasses of three horses on the ground, taking the photography of war one step further in demonstrating the brutal consequences of battle.[17]

Although O'Sullivan made a few images in the town of Culpeper after the Cedar Mountain battle, there is no evidence that he stayed with Pope's army long enough to witness its major engagement of the summer, the Second Battle of Bull Run, fought on August 29 and 30, with many more casualties than the first battle there, but with a similar result. The North was once again routed.

# "The Terrible Reality and Earnestness of War"

T he victory at Manassas, as the South called the battle, embold-
ened General Lee to cross the Potomac into Maryland in the
early days of September, and to capture the city of Frederick,
which Union troops had abandoned. Lee's Army of Northern Virginia
clearly threatened Washington and, had the people of Maryland joined
the rebellion, as Lee hoped, such cities as Baltimore and Philadelphia.
So great was the concern about the threat that the state of Pennsylvania shipped its archives from Harrisburg to New York for safekeeping.
McClellan, who had typically failed to bestir his army in time to be
much help to General Pope at Second Bull Run, had nonetheless been
put back in charge of all the demoralized armies in Virginia and around
Washington, and Pope was made the scapegoat. But even McClellan
was sufficiently alarmed about the massing of Lee's army at Frederick
to do something, and the Army of the Potomac was on the move on
September 5, 1862. McClellan himself left Washington on the evening
of September 7 to establish a headquarters in Rockville, fifteen miles
to the northwest of Washington.

Gardner followed the army at some point during that week and
was at the general's headquarters on September 9. From there, at eleven
A.M., he sent a telegram to O'Sullivan, who was now back in the Brady
studio on Pennsylvania Avenue, TO COME RIGHT AWAY TO ROCKVILLE
THERE MAKE FOR HEADQUARTERS. BRING CMDR OF TELEGRAPHIC
CORPS ONE HORSE. The telegraph suggests that Gardner and other

Brady employees were still working for McClellan under the arrangement that had begun nearly a year before.[1]

Lee would fall back from Frederick as McClellan's much larger army approached, but once Stonewall Jackson took Harper's Ferry on September 15, Lee decided to make his stand in the village of Sharpsburg, about ten miles due north of Harper's Ferry and about a mile to the east of the Potomac.

When news of Jackson's victory reached newspapers in New York—which at first reported a Union victory, as was often the case with early battle reports—Brady saw an opportunity to promote images that his men, including Jacob Coonley, and he himself had taken at Harper's Ferry and in the vicinity since the start of the war. These were the usual photographs of federal military units and views of the town and surrounding landscape, but what they lacked in actual news value would be outweighed for those who purchased them by their immediate availability.[2]

Brady himself had taken a photo of Col. Dixon S. Miles, the man in charge of Union troops at Harper's Ferry, on the steps of his headquarters there. Miles had been at First Bull Run, but the division he commanded had not been called into that fight, a good thing since he was later convicted of having been drunk during the battle and given an eight-month leave of absence from the army. After that hiatus he was made the commander at Harper's Ferry, where he also comported himself badly, surrendering the town and his twelve thousand troops after his plans for its defense proved useless. Miles managed to avoid further disciplinary action only by getting himself killed at Harper's Ferry in one of the last exchanges of rifle fire before his surrender went into effect.

Brady got prints of his photographs into the hands of editors at the New York *World* and the *Herald*, and both papers reported on September 18 on the photos' availability for sale as part of Brady's "Incidents of the War" series. It was a good public relations move, and demonstrates the continuing value of images of places where battles had occurred, even if the images were not new. But Brady's good press would quickly be overshadowed by what had already happened at Antietam the day before, which was first reported in a famous dispatch by George W. Smalley for the *New York Tribune* on September 20. Smalley had been on the battlefield and over the course of a couple of mostly sleepless days and nights had returned to New York with his six-column account, which was reprinted in many other publications, including the competing *New York Times* and *New York Evening Post.*

On September 14, McClellan's army had engaged Lee in the passes of South Mountain, between Frederick and Sharpsburg. McClellan's uncharacteristically aggressive pursuit was due in part to the discovery in a field near Frederick of a copy of Lee's orders for the Maryland campaign, wrapped around three cigars. It revealed that Lee had divided his army, and one of McClellan's generals later quoted his commander as saying, "Here is a paper with which if I cannot whip 'Bobbie Lee,' I will be willing to go home." Both sides suffered a large number of casualties at South Mountain (including, on the Union side, the future president Rutherford B. Hayes, then a lieutenant colonel, who was shot in the left arm while leading an infantry charge), but it was Lee who dropped back, reuniting his forces and digging in to the west of Antietam Creek.[3]

McClellan massed his army on hillsides overlooking the creek from the east. Two of McClellan's infantry corps established themselves on the Confederate side of the creek late on September 16. At dawn on September 17, these Union troops attacked the Confederate left flank, beginning what would be the bloodiest single day of the war, and indeed in American history. A rough estimate of the casualties is 12,500 of about 75,000 men on the Union side; for the Confederates the casualty numbers range from 10,000 to 14,000 of 40,000 men engaged. Each army lost about 2,000 killed outright, and about one in seven of the wounded would also die.[4]

Nobody knows for sure when Alexander Gardner, accompanied by James F. Gibson, reached Antietam. Since Gardner was with McClellan at Rockville on September 9, wouldn't he have remained with the Union army throughout the tumultuous week that followed, a week in which McClellan intended to crush Lee and presumably end the war? But if so, why are there no images from Frederick or South Mountain? Could Gardner have been engaged with McClellan's Topographic Corps copying maps? But Rockville was close enough to the Brady studio on Pennsylvania Avenue so that it would have been easy for Gardner to return to work and set out again for Antietam after news of the South Mountain battle, for instance, or of the Antietam battle itself.[5]

A later caption on one of Gardner's Antietam photos reads "View of Battle-field of Antietam, on day of battle, Sept. 17, 1862." For many years this was believed to be one of the few photographs from the whole course of the war, and one of the first, to show a battle under way. But in 1963 it was proven that the photograph was taken more than a mile from the battlefield, and that the smoke in the right half of the image was not from rifle or cannon fire but from campfires. Two of the best authorities on Civil War photography, Bob Zeller and William Frassanito, have reached different conclusions about when Gardner's first photos of Antietam were likely taken. Zeller says that "Gardner probably was with other members of the press most of the day of the battle," and watched it from a hill near McClellan's headquarters on the east side of Antietam Creek. He quotes Edwin Forbes, the sketch artist, who wrote that

> the engagement was a spectacle which was not surpassed during the whole war. Thousands of people took advantage of the occasion, as the hills were black with spectators. Soldiers of the reserve, officers and men of the commissary and quartermasters' departments, camp-followers, and hundreds of farmers and their families, watched the desperate struggle. No battle of the war, I think, was witnessed by so many people.[6]

But Frassanito makes a convincing case that the photograph of the "Battle-field" was probably not taken until late afternoon of September 18, and notes that "Gardner was not above stretching the truth in order to increase the historical value of his views." Frassanito's argument is based in part on what is shown in the image itself, but also on the uncontested fact that Gardner did not start photographing the battle-field up close until the morning of September 19.

Why would he have taken that distant battlefield photo (and one other at about the same time and place, of McClellan's headquarters) late in the day on September 17 and then do nothing on the eighteenth? One possible explanation could be that he was working for the army and thus not free to take photographs for Brady until the following day. But it seems likelier that he simply arrived the day after the battle. Interestingly enough, both Frassanito and Zeller ignore a print published in Katz's biography of Gardner titled "Gen. McClellan's Headquarter Guard, 93d Reg. N.Y.S.V." and further identified on the print as being taken "At Antietam, September 16, 1862," and attributed to "Gardner, Photographer" and "M.B. Brady, Publisher." If the date is right, it would certainly suggest that Gardner had been in the company of McClellan's staff the whole time, working mostly for them and not Brady.[7]

Perhaps because of Brady's experience at First Bull Run, none of his photographers had shown any eagerness to be on the scene of a battle when it was taking place. That was true of Gardner, who did not arrive on the Peninsula until the major engagements had been fought and McClellan was beginning to move his army back near Washington, and of Gibson, who had had a number of opportunities during the Peninsula Campaign to witness an engagement but did not. These two were at Antietam, but it also holds true for O'Sullivan, who did not photograph a battle during the coastal campaign earlier in the year and who had been traveling with Pope's army for some weeks but managed to miss both Cedar Mountain, when he was in the vicinity, and Second Bull Run. Of course, with the probable exception of Brady, no other photographer covering the war, or any war that preceded it, had yet thrust himself into a battle, either.

The more than one hundred photographs that Gardner and Gibson took on the Antietam battlefield between September 19 and 22 changed the course of war photography. Brady never visited Sharpsburg, as far as anyone knows, and not until October 28, 1862, more than a month after the battle, did he get as close as about twelve miles to the south of the battlefield, at what is now called Brunswick, Maryland. But Brady's role was crucial to the impact these photos had.

On September 18, the day after the battle, the two armies remained in place, but exhaustion, a misreading of the other side's intentions, and what might have been stunned disbelief at the violence that had occurred ended the battle of Antietam. A few skirmishes took place that day, but no major engagement. During the night of the seventeenth, temporary truces had been negotiated along the facing lines of the two armies so that the wounded and the dead could be retrieved, but many of both remained on the battlefield. Each commander expected the other to attack on the eighteenth, and so there was no general cease-fire in the daytime during which the armies could retrieve the rest of their wounded and bury their dead.

In spite of his losses, General McClellan had more troops at his disposal on the eighteenth than he had had on the day before, and some thirty-five thousand of them were completely fresh, because they had either arrived since the battle or not been committed on the seventeenth. But he held off attacking, believing as he always did that the enemy was far stronger than it was, a decision that led to the end of his military career. McClellan later claimed that he intended to attack on the morning of the nineteenth, but by then General Lee had accepted, at least for the moment, the end of his Maryland campaign, during which the citizens of that state conspicuously had not risen up in his support. Overnight, Lee's army splashed back across the Potomac into Virginia, leaving its dead in the field for the Union to bury.

When Gardner and Gibson began to do their work on the battle-field on September 19, either most of the Union soldiers had been buried or Gardner simply chose to train his camera on the dead of the enemy. Only two of his twenty-five photographs from that day and the next picture unburied Union dead; of these two, only one, showing bodies from the Irish brigade (made up of three regiments from New York and one from Massachusetts), identifies the subjects as Union soldiers. The sights and smells of the dead on that first day on the battle-field must have assaulted Gardner's sensibility as well as his senses, and he might have reckoned that a public that had never seen such images before could tolerate them only if they showed the enemy. Indeed he himself, as an honorary captain under McClellan's forces, might have found it easier to gaze upon enemy bodies than those from his own side.

On that first day, Gardner made only stereoscopic photographs and worked fast, taking bunches of shots within close proximity to one another and to the wagon where the plates would be prepared and later developed, but, with one exception, taking only one image of each scene. The most gruesome shots, and the most famous ones—of dead Confederate artillerymen in front of the Dunker church, of bodies strewn along the Hagerstown Pike and the Sunken Road—were likely taken on the second day. On the third and fourth days the scenes were mostly of the landscape, farmhouses, bridges, and of the village of Sharpsburg itself. On the morning of September 21, Gardner sent a telegram to David Knox at the Pennsylvania Avenue gallery requesting more FOUR BY TEN GLASS, and passing on the news that he had gotten FORTY FIVE NEGATIVES OF BATTLE, meaning the battlefield. Gardner also requested that Jim, the gallery's black teamster, deliver the new plates as quickly as possible.[8]

Each image took ten to fifteen seconds to expose, but the rest of the process was laborious. Presumably Gibson would prepare the plate in the dark and airless heat under a tarp at the back of the photographic wagon—which could take up to ten minutes. Then he would rush it to the camera that Gardner had already aimed, wait while the plate was inserted and the lens cap removed and then replaced, and hurry the exposed plate back to the wagon, where it would either be held in a diluted glycerine solution for later development or immediately developed in the dark, all to the dizzying smell of ether (used in making collodion) and other chemicals. Bob Zeller writes:

> James Gibson's hands would have been black with silver nitrate. He no doubt perspired excessively under the tarp while taking care not to lean his head over the plate, lest drops of sweat fall on the glass . . . Gibson probably had to battle flies as well, which are attracted to the smell of collodion.[9]

Mark Katz quotes a Civil War–era photographer named J. Pitcher Spencer on the difficulty of making photographs in the field: "It took unceasing care to keep every bit of the apparatus, as well as each and every chemical, free from contamination which might affect the picture. Often a breath of wind, no matter how gentle, spoiled the whole affair."[10]

As they were working, did Gardner and Gibson know what they had? Gibson had seen the effects of war close up on the Peninsula, but Gardner had not. Still, each of them had to know that the photographs they were making were unlike anything that had been seen before. William Stapp has suggested that Gardner may have been one of the few photographers in America who had actually seen Roger Fenton's 1855 photos of the Crimean War, which had been made much of as the first sustained effort to photograph soldiers and settings in wartime.

Fenton's narrative about his experience in the Crimea had been excerpted in American publications, but the images themselves had been on display only in Great Britain, where Gardner might well have seen them before setting off for America in 1856. If he did not see the photographs themselves, which traveled widely on exhibit, he would almost certainly have seen the woodblock prints based on them in the *Illustrated London News* in 1855.[11]

But these and all the Civil War photos that had yet been made public, with the exception of Gibson's Savage's Station field hospital photograph in late June and O'Sullivan's images of dead horses and fresh graves at Cedar Mountain in August, were pallid compared to what Gardner and Gibson had seen and recorded. Beyond his role as manager of the Brady gallery in Washington, which required a good sense of what the public wanted to see, Gardner had also been a newspaperman back in Scotland, which would presumably have instilled in him a sense of the news value of the photographs. Whether Gardner and Gibson's motivations were commercial (here were photographs that the public would presumably clamor to see and pay to own), or political (fueled by a revulsion at the slaughter, which they hoped the public would rise up against), or patriotic (an eagerness to show the price of rebellion against the Union), both men had to have been impatient to get back to Washington, and there to start making prints and carrying them up to the rooftop of 352 Pennsylvania Avenue to develop in the sun. Presumably Jim would have taken some of the exposed plates back to Washington in the wagon he used to deliver the glass requested in Gardner's telegram. Perhaps when Gardner and Gibson returned to the gallery the sun had already completed some of the work that they had begun.

Gardner knew that using a stereo camera gave the studio the widest variety of prints to sell, and indeed all the photographs taken at Antietam were stereos, except for a handful of full-plate negatives exposed by Gibson of the Antietam and Burnside Bridges. Zeller explains that

> Each four-by-ten-inch stereo negative produced two four-by-five inch images, which were cut down to three-by-three inch squares for stereo views. Using the stereo negative, they could . . . also make *cartes de visite* and oversized album cards of about twice that size, known as "Imperial Cartes."

Stereo views cost 50 cents each, album cards and *cartes de visite* were 25 cents each.

The stereo photographs would be mounted side by side on a card that was 7.0 by 3.25 inches.[12]

On October 7, Gardner copyrighted eighteen of the Antietam photographs, as Brady's men had been doing for at least six months, but this time the copyright application did not include the explanation that they would be published in "Brady's Album Gallery." But this designation would nonetheless appear on the prints themselves throughout 1862, as they were sold at Brady's galleries and through the Anthonys, which offered nineteen of them in their *Catalogue of Card Photographs*.[13]

"In addition," Zeller writes, "on stereograph cards and albums cards issued by Brady's gallery in 1862, Gardner's name is printed on the front of every card as the photographer who copyrighted the images." Brady also shared credit in this way in his 1862 "Incidents of the War" portfolio, which included seven large prints by Gardner.[14]

The Antietam prints were almost certainly put on display immediately at the Washington gallery (although there is no record that they were) and soon afterward in New York. By October 3 a small notice appeared in the *New York Times* under the headline ANTIETAM REPRODUCED, saying that "battle scenes, procured under circumstances trying to the courage and manhood of his artists," were now available in Brady's gallery to view and buy. A little sign had been posted on the door of 785 Broadway that said, simply, THE DEAD OF ANTIETAM. According to an article in the October 20 *Times*, "crowds of people are constantly going up the stairs" to Brady's second-floor gallery room, where "you find them bending over the photographic views of that fearful battle-field" that Gardner and Gibson had made. They were likely bending over, as we would not normally do when looking at photographs in a gallery today, because they were looking at the stereo images on the sort of box stereograph viewer that Brady also had in his Washington studio. So they saw the images in their full 3-D effect.[15]

The unnamed *Times* reporter writes that "You will see hushed, reverent groups standing around these weird copies of carnage, bending down to lock in the pale faces of the dead, chained by the strange spell that dwells in dead men's eyes." When the reporter himself looked, he was surprised that these lifelike photographs of the dead did not make him want to turn away, "But, on the contrary, there is a terrible fascination about it that draws one near these pictures, and makes him loth to leave them."

Oliver Wendell Holmes took up a similar theme in the *Atlantic Monthly* the following summer when he wrote about the images from Antietam. He suggested that, "Many having seen [this series of photographs] and dreamed of its horrors, would lock it up in some secret drawer, that it might not thrill or revolt those whose soul sickens at such sights." Holmes could write about the Antietam photos with unusual authority, having visited the battlefield four days after the battle, on September 21, the same Sunday that Gardner and Gibson were at work. He apparently did not see the photographers, because he was in the northern part of the battlefield and they were working in the southern part that day, and in his article he gave credit for the images only to "the enterprise of Mr. Brady of New York" (which, depending on what meaning he had in mind for the word *enterprise*, might be an acknowledgment that it was Brady's corps and not Brady himself who actually took the photos). But Holmes noticed some of the same things on his visit that Gardner had already photographed, including what would become an iconic photograph of a dead gray horse that had belonged to a Confederate colonel, which died in a surprisingly lifelike pose, and dead Rebel soldiers in a ditch either on the Hagerstown Turnpike or the Sunken Road.[16]

Holmes was in Antietam while looking for his son, the future Supreme Court justice Oliver Wendell Holmes Jr., who as a captain in the Twentieth Massachusetts Infantry Regiment was injured in the battle. In "My Hunt After 'The Captain,'" an article that appeared in the *Atlantic Monthly* in December 1862, the elder Holmes describes receiving a telegram on the night of the battle reading in part that his son had been WOUNDED SHOT THROUGH THE NECK THOUGHT NOT SERIOUS, and he left by train the next day to find his namesake.[17]

It is on this authority, too, that Holmes can put forth another notion in the October 20 *Times* article about seeing the stereoscope images in the Brady gallery. Holmes writes:

> Let him who wishes to know what war is look at this series
> of illustrations. These wrecks of manhood thrown together
> in careless heaps or ranged in ghastly rows for burial were

A Confederate colonel's horse, killed at Antietam (September 1862).
Photograph by Alexander Gardner. *Library of Congress*

alive but yesterday. How dear to their little circles far away most of them!

The *Times* reporter begins his piece somewhat melodramatically, calling up the list of the dead that "We see . . . in the morning paper at breakfast, but dismiss its recollection with the coffee." But, he reminds his readers, each name "represents a bleeding mangled corpse . . . that will crash into some brain—a dull, dead, remorseless weight that will fall upon some heart, straining it to breaking." The *Times* article goes on to praise Brady for having "done something to bring home to us the terrible reality and earnestness of war. If he has not brought bodies and laid them in our dooryards and along the streets, he has done something very like it." Holmes writes that "the honest sunshine"—meaning the camera itself—"gives us . . . some conception of what a repulsive, brutal, sickening, hideous thing it is, this dashing together of two frantic mobs to which we give the name armies."

Both these writers, then, think first of the personal tragedy each of these bodies represents to the widening circle of relatives and friends who will grieve over each death. Then they turn to the broader social impact of the photographs, the effect they would have on strangers to the dead, whose own loved ones might or might not be at risk of a similar end, but who as citizens bore some of the collective responsibility for what the war did to those who fought it.

The crowds of people visiting the Brady studio on Broadway during the third week in October suggest the impact these photographs had on those who saw them. One advantage of having a gallery located in a good spot along one of the most vibrant avenues in the world was that so many passersby could see the small placard on the door with the electrifying announcement on it, or simply be drawn by those already crowding in. The *Times* writer would have you believe that this is how he himself stumbled upon the story, but Brady was adept at getting stories about his gallery in the New York newspapers. Interest might also have been driven by eight woodcut engravings made from the Antietam photographs that appeared in a two-page spread in the October 18 issue of *Harper's Weekly* over the caption "Scenes on the Battlefield of Antietam.—From Photographs By Mr. M. B. Brady." The attribution strongly suggests that Brady himself placed these images. Five of the eight engravings included the bodies of dead soldiers. The illustrated newspaper was published and circulated in New York, so its readers could easily have gone to the gallery to see the photographs, which in their 3-D format would have had a far greater emotional effect than the woodcuts in the paper.[18]

Every newspaper and magazine in the nation was covering the Antietam battle and its aftermath, but with the exception of the *Times* article (which appeared on page five of the newspaper), the small notice there that preceded it, and the *Harper's Weekly* spread, there was very little coverage of the photographs themselves when they were first presented to the public. If the photographs were shown in the Washington gallery—and it is hard to believe that they would not have been—the Washington press completely ignored them. The Oliver Wendell Holmes article in the *Atlantic Monthly* did not appear until nine months later.

William Stapp writes in *An Enduring Interest*, a catalogue for a Gardner show at the Chrysler Museum in 1991/1992, "While it is, in fact, impossible to estimate how many people actually saw these images, their impact on the audience they did reach must have been exceptionally traumatic." But whatever these hundreds or perhaps thousands of people felt upon seeing the stereos, both in New York and Washington, "Until the end of the war," Stapp writes, "further efforts to document the conflict went virtually unnoticed in the national press and even in the photographic journals." This was the case even though Brady had close connections with many members of the press in both cities, many of whose offices would have been a short walk from one of the Brady galleries.[19]

Gardner and Timothy O'Sullivan would famously take photographs of the dead at Gettysburg, and O'Sullivan would take them again at Spotsylvania. Army captain Andrew J. Russell, who became the official photographer for the military railroads in March of 1863, took well-known photographs of Confederate dead at Marye's Heights, in Fredericksburg, and in that city, too, a year later, Brady photographers took seven photographs of Union casualties awaiting burial. Thomas C. Roche, who worked with Brady until the middle of 1864, might have been one of the two people taking these Fredericksburg photos. On his own at the end of the war, Roche would take twenty-two stereographs of Confederate soldiers, mostly in the trenches where they died, at Fort Mahone, in Petersburg. That was the seventh and final time that a photographer trained his camera on dead soldiers during the Civil War. Lee's surrender came six days later. The series of Roche photographs sold well through the Anthony brothers for several years after the war, and a large number of them still exist.[20]

Historians have attributed the relative rarity of instances in which photographs were made of the dead throughout the war to the difficulty photographers had getting access to the front and the supposition that the bodies were often quickly buried. But Drew Gilpin Faust, in *This Republic of Suffering*, shows how rarely a quick and decent burial followed a large engagement. Part of the problem was a lack of planning for burials on a mass scale. "Burying the dead after a Civil War battle seemed always to be an act of improvisation," Faust writes, "one that called upon the particular resources of the moment and circumstance." She points out that it often took many hours and sometimes many days for all the bodies to be interred. Part of the problem was also that the generals were often of necessity more concerned with their living troops than their dead ones. "Civilians and soldiers alike," Faust writes, "began to understand the meaning and urgency of the phrase [the generals] so often intoned: 'Let the dead bury the dead.' "[21]

Given the number of battles or lesser engagements in which soldiers died, the often careless treatment of the dead during the war, and the number of photographers in the field, it seems surprising that images of dead bodies were taken on so few occasions, especially if they had real commercial value either to the illustrated papers or as prints. The conclusion has to be that, beginning with the Brady photographs by Gardner and Gibson, such images did not really have a great deal of popular or commercial appeal.

When historians talk about the "electrifying" or "stunning" impact of the Antietam photographs at the Brady Broadway gallery, they are talking first, of course, about the impact the photos must have had on those, however few or many, who saw them in person. We know this at the very least by how the images affected the *Times* reporter and Oliver Wendell Holmes, and by their shared supposition about their impact on others. But it is hard to make a case that they had that sort of impact on the public at large, or on the political or military leaders of the time. Nothing suggests that they changed the course of the war in any way. Although Antietam was the bloodiest single day of the war, far bloodier battles followed, including Chancellorsville, Gettysburg, and Chickamauga in 1863 alone.

The most dramatic impact of the photographs was historical. Without a doubt, the Antietam images marked a turning point in the portrayal of war and in the ability of those who did not themselves experience it to both see and imagine its terrible consequences. The grand heroic paintings of battles of the past, and indeed the work of sketch artists during the Civil War, who most often upheld the painterly tradition of romanticizing warfare, could never again be taken seriously as fully realistic portrayals of what war was. But this impact was not immediate. Sketch artists continued to sketch as if the photographs did not exist, and illustrated newspaper editors continued to prefer portraits of generals and empty landscapes to the brutality exhibited in the Gardner and Gibson photographs.

The impact of the photographs grew, and continues to grow, as the impact of media itself grew, and grows. To experience the *Life* magazine photos or newsreel footage of World War II was to have a greater sense of what the Antietam photographs could have meant; to watch network coverage of firefights in Vietnam was to have an even more refined view of how the Antietam photographs ought to have affected those who saw them; to watch video images from the scopes of fighter-bombers in the Gulf War or to see the documentary *Restrepo* from Afghanistan is to feel even more acutely the power of the Antietam photographs. But the value is more projected than real, and says more about us than the time in which they were first exhibited. We have known since Vietnam and the so-called living room war that images could help stop a conflict. But in the 1860s, images did not yet have that power.

# "Brady and the Lilliputians"

If the photographs did not change the course of the war, neither did the battle itself. McClellan missed the opportunity to destroy Lee's army on September 18, and he failed to pursue him aggressively into Virginia, where, as James McPherson puts it, "the Confederates got clean away into the [Shenandoah] Valley." But McClellan did not detect any hint of failure in what he and his army had done at Antietam. He wrote to his wife on September 20, "Our victory was complete . . . I feel some little pride in having with a beaten and demoralized army defeated Lee so utterly, & saved the North so completely."[1]

President Lincoln did not agree with that assessment of his chief general in the field, but he had been waiting since midsummer for a victory of any description in order to issue his Emancipation Proclamation at a moment that suggested it was something more than an act of desperation. After a Cabinet meeting on September 22, the president released a preliminary proclamation, promising that, if the secessionist states did not return to the Union by January 1, 1863, he would sign it into law on that date, and the slaves in those states "shall be then, thenceforward, and forever free."

On October 1, President Lincoln traveled by rail to Harper's Ferry to see the troops and have extensive discussions with General McClellan, a trip that lasted four days. The next day, the president met soldiers encamped around Harper's Ferry and then went north to McClellan's headquarters, which had been moved to a site on a farm two miles south of Sharpsburg. Lincoln slept there on the nights of October 2 and 3, in a tent beside McClellan's, while spending his days visiting the wounded, looking at the South Mountain and Antietam battlefields, reviewing other units of the Army of the Potomac camped in the Sharpsburg area, and conferring with the fast-aging Young Napoleon.

Alexander Gardner took photographs of the president and his party with the general and his staff on October 3 and 4, and Lincoln returned to Washington via Frederick, apparently buoyed by the idea that the army was now well rested and McClellan had gotten his message to move into Virginia and end the war. Gardner sent a telegram to the Washington office on October 4, assuring his colleagues that he had GOT PREST GENLS . . . WILL SEND NEGATIVES TOMORROW. Gardner had taken seven images of Lincoln, but the two best known are of Lincoln with McClellan at the headquarters of Gen. Fitz-John Porter and his staff and one of Lincoln and McClellan alone seated just inside the latter's tent, Lincoln's famous stovepipe hat resting top down on a table at his side. (In the first of the two photos, Capt. George Armstrong Custer makes one of his Zelig-like appearances, posing to the side of the main group; he was an aide to McClellan at the time.) Given the magnitude of what had happened at Antietam, the continuing concerns in the North about a war that was dragging on due to missed opportunities, and the troubled relationship between the understandably impatient president and the arrogant and overly cautious general, these images had real journalistic value. But their enduring historical power also comes from what would happen between the two men in the future—two years later they would run against each other for the presidency. In addition, these Gardner photographs are the only images of Lincoln on any of his several trips into the field to meet with his generals during the war.[2]

Whatever the relationship between Gardner and Brady at this time, Gardner's two photographic coups, first on the battlefield and then with the president, must have made Brady eager to return to the field himself. Within a week of the *New York Times* article about the Antietam photographs, Brady was on his way to join McClellan's army as it crossed the Potomac from Maryland into Virginia, in slow-motion pursuit of Lee. A photograph taken near the river on October 28 shows Brady in a characteristic pose, his arms clasped behind his back, surrounded by members of his party and their equipment, wagon, horses, and tents. David Woodbury is in the photograph, as are two other

Brady assistants, E. T. Whitney and Silas Holmes, a man identified as "H. Hodges," a cook named Stephen, and the teamster, Jim. Nobody knows who took the image at what was then locally known as Berlin, Maryland, and is now Brunswick, six miles east of Harper's Ferry.[3]

On the back of another photograph taken at about the same time, Woodbury notes that the Brady party "crossed this pontoon bridge with Genls McClellan and Burnside on our way to Warrenton." This print might well be from a photograph that Gardner attributes to himself in his *Sketch Book of the War*, entitled "Pontoon Bridge Across the Potomac, at Berlin," and dated November 1862. A third photograph, at the Chrysler Museum in Norfolk, Virginia, is dated by the museum to October 1862 and attributed to David Woodbury. It shows a man looking very much like Mathew Brady, standing with his arms behind his back, near a rail line at Harper's Ferry.[4]

Besides the photograph in which Brady appears at Berlin, no other image is definitely connected with his trip to Maryland and into Virginia. Did he visit Sharpsburg while he was so close? Did he himself grow restless at McClellan's inactivity and soon return to Washington? We don't know. But if Brady came up empty-handed again after his second foray into Virginia, it could not have made it any easier for him to be in Gardner's presence.

On October 29 the president wrote to McClellan, "I am much pleased with the movement of the Army. When you get entirely across the river let me know." But the army took nine days to cross, and even when he had assembled his troops in Virginia, McClellan failed to cut off Lee as he moved his army from the Shenandoah Valley eastward toward Richmond. A report reached Washington on Election Day, November 4, that elements of Lee's army had beaten McClellan to Culpeper and the Orange & Alexandria line there, and on November 5 a fully exasperated Lincoln issued orders firing McClellan. It would take the general two days to get the official news and the better part of a week to return to Washington.[5]

Pinkerton claims in his memoirs that President Lincoln and war secretary Edwin Stanton asked him to stay on after McClellan's dismissal, perhaps not realizing that Pinkerton's Secret Service was the source of much of the misinformation about Lee on which McClellan had based his failures to attack. But, Pinkerton writes, "I declined to act any further in the capacity in which I had previously served."[6]

President Lincoln and General McClellan at McClellan's
headquarters near Antietam (October 1862). Photograph by
Alexander Gardner. *Library of Congress*

Gardner maintained his own connection with the Army of the
Potomac after McClellan was fired. He was back in the field in November photographing General Burnside, who replaced McClellan,
and Burnside's staff in Warrenton. The split between Gardner and
Brady had not yet taken place, because a Burnside photograph appeared crediting Gardner as the photographer and Brady's studio. But
none of the post-Antietam Gardner photographs give any credit to
Brady in an Anthony catalogue also published in November.

Gardner likely left Brady's employment sometime after his November photographs of Burnside and before the end of 1862. He and
his brother, James, at first opened a studio at 332 Pennsylvania Avenue,
under the name Philp and Solomons Metropolitan Gallery. Philp and
Solomons was a book publishing firm located at 332, which gave the
Gardners space for a gallery. It would also become the publisher of
Gardner's wartime photographs—both gathering them into books,
such as the *Sketch Book*, and printing and mounting them in quantity,
as the Anthony brothers had done and were doing for Brady. But
Gardner soon moved around the corner of Seventh and Pennsylvania

and up one block, to the northwest corner of Seventh and D, above Shepard & Riley's bookstore. Directly across Seventh was the *Washington Daily National Intelligencer*, in whose pages Gardner announced on May 26, 1863, the opening of his new business, Gardner's Gallery, on "premises expressly fitted up as a Photographic Gallery," and "stocked with the newest and most improved apparatus."[7]

When Gardner left Brady's studio he took all the negatives from the year 1862 with him, including O'Sullivan's work from the coastal campaign and Pope's Virginia campaign; Barnard's from Centreville, Bull Run, and Manassas; Gibson's on the Peninsula; and the images from Antietam—more than four hundred negatives in all. But if these were the original negatives, they certainly had been copied, because all these images were published in the Anthony *Catalogue of Card Photographs* in November of 1862 under the heading "Brady's Photographic Views of the War." O'Sullivan, Barnard, and Gibson soon went to work for Gardner in his new gallery.

By the time he left, Gardner had worked for Brady for six years, years that had been successful for both men. Brady had given Gardner his first job in the United States, and a year and a half later had made him manager of his new gallery in Washington. That gallery had prospered under Gardner, and the connections and experience he got working for Brady contributed to his later success with his own gallery. Brady's first wet-plate prints in the months before Gardner went to work for him were not of the same quality as his daguerreotypes and ambrotypes, but soon after Gardner arrived, the quality improved. Although Gardner often gets credit for introducing large-format prints to the Brady operation, Brady had already been working in the larger formats, but presumably these prints, too, improved in quality.[8]

Whether or not Gardner was, as is generally supposed, the better businessman of the two, he clearly ran Brady's Washington studio in a way that Brady found more than acceptable, and no evidence exists to suggest that Brady pushed Gardner into leaving or was happy to see him go. Gardner and other extraordinarily talented photographers such as O'Sullivan had been allowed and even encouraged to spread their wings while working for Brady, and their own reputations were enhanced by their connection with his fame and his ability to translate that fame into publicity and sales. And, as we've seen, the idea that Brady stifled his photographers, or took undue credit for work that was theirs—

undue by the standards of their day, not ours—is based in supposition and not evidence, and seems wrongheaded. Brady allowed his photographers not only to freelance for the army while working for him, but also to copyright the photographs they took while in his employ.

However mutually beneficial that relationship was, it came to an end. People change, and business relationships can end with or without rancor. Gardner had owned his own businesses in Scotland, and might simply have wanted to do that again. The letters that Brady and Gardner would write to the federal government after the war, each claiming to have had the original idea to document the conflict in a comprehensive way, had some justification on each side. But the purpose of these letters was simply to promote their separate business interests, and there is no hint of animosity in them. No direct evidence of any sort exists to explain Gardner's decision to leave.

Still, two facts about the breakup do hint at discontentment. The most obvious has to do with how many Brady employees followed Gardner. Even with his famous name and his willingness to use his resources to put his photographers in the field, Brady could not prevent most of the talent that he had helped develop from deserting him. Although Brady was a presence in the Washington gallery, Gardner had managed the men day in and day out, and they would naturally have been closer to him. And Gardner was, like them, a photographer in the way we think of one today—the man who takes the photographs—which Brady for the most part was not. By the end of 1862, Brady had been in business for two decades, and however much responsibility he had ceded to Gardner, his business was clearly hierarchical, with all that might imply about sharing credit and profits. Gardner the social idealist took a different approach.

Discontentment also seems self-evident in Gardner's decision not to mention Brady at all in his 1865 *Photographic Sketch Book of the War*, even though about a fifth of the one hundred photographs in the book were taken under Brady's aegis. Gardner is often praised for crediting his own photographers by name, in the *Sketch Book*, in his *Catalogue of Photographic Incidents of the War*, and elsewhere, so his failure to credit photographs to which he and Brady at the very least held joint title (in a figurative and perhaps a legal sense) seems to show hard feelings toward his former boss. But even this could be explained away as a business decision, given that Brady was one of his main competitors for Civil War images—and would incorporate images that he did not own, including those indisputably Gardner's, into his collection. Still, the stinginess of spirit seems out of character for Gardner, and is likely to have had some cause.

Brady and what remained of his photographic corps went on hiatus from covering the war during the winter and spring of 1863. But Gardner and his men also mostly missed the disastrous first battle at Fredericksburg, on December 13, 1862, where Burnside proved himself to be utterly unfit to lead the Army of the Potomac. James Gibson and David Woodbury were taking photographs for Gardner at Fredericksburg and Falmouth (just across the Rappahannock River from Fredericksburg) in December and January, but only one photo by each man and one attributed to Gardner himself made it into the *Sketch Book* or Gardner's *Incidents of the War*.

But at his New York gallery, Brady continued to focus on subjects other than the war. His old neighbor P. T. Barnum had been distracting the nation from the sorrows of the conflict by introducing new "midgets" at his American Museum, where Charles Stratton, known as General Tom Thumb, had been an ongoing draw for two decades. Early in 1862, Barnum had brought on another little person, George Washington Morrison Nutt, known as Commodore Nutt and also as "the $30,000 Nutt," which Barnum claimed (more for its publicity value than its veracity) was the amount of Nutt's first contract. Nutt rivaled Tom Thumb in popularity.

Soon Barnum approached Lavinia Warren, an appealing and charming female little person, for his show. She had already caught the interest of the press at a reception at the St. Nicholas Hotel on December 22, 1862. She at first rejected Barnum's offer of a thousand dollars per week to go on display at his museum, explaining that she was planning to tour Europe, as Tom Thumb had once done to international acclaim, meeting Queen Victoria at Buckingham Palace and King Louis Philippe at the Tuileries. But Barnum wore her down, at the same time introducing her to the famous and by-now-wealthy petite general.[9]

On January 10, 1863, according to an advertisement in the *New York Daily Tribune,* Barnum was already exhibiting Warren with Commodore Nutt, and rumors had been floated about a possible infatua-

*Mathew B. Brady*, oil portrait by Charles Loring Elliott (1857). THE METROPOLITAN MUSEUM OF ART/ ART RESOURCE, NY

Juliette Handy Brady, Mathew Brady, and Mrs. Haggerty, possibly his sister-in-law (circa 1851).
NATIONAL PORTRAIT GALLERY/SMITHSONIAN INSTITUTION/ART RESOURCE, NY

British scientist Michael Faraday (circa 1851). LIBRARY OF CONGRESS

Henry James Sr. and Henry James Jr. (August 1854). HOUGHTON LIBRARY, MANUSCRIPT DEPARTMENT, HARVARD UNIVERSITY

Commodore Matthew C. Perry (circa 1857). Carte de visite. LIBRARY OF CONGRESS

Jefferson Davis while a U.S. senator (circa 1860). LIBRARY OF CONGRESS

Colonel Elmer Ellsworth of the New York Fire Zouaves (1861). Carte de visite. LIBRARY OF CONGRESS

Members of the Seventh New York Militia Regiment at Camp Cameron in Washington, D.C. (1861), photograph by George N. Barnard and C. O. Bostwick. LIBRARY OF CONGRESS

Colonel Ambrose Burnside with members of the First Rhode Island Volunteer Regiment at Camp Sprague in Washington, D.C. (1861). LIBRARY OF CONGRESS

A federal encampment at Cumberland Landing on the Virginia Peninsula (May 1862), photograph by James F. Gibson. LIBRARY OF CONGRESS

Wounded soldiers at a field hospital at Savage's Station in Virginia (June 28, 1862), stereograph by James F. Gibson. LIBRARY OF CONGRESS

Quaker guns in the Confederate fortifications at Centreville, Virginia (March 1862), photograph by George N. Barnard and James F. Gibson. LIBRARY OF CONGRESS

Mathew Brady, standing at right, with his photographic team, including David Woodbury, seated beside him, in Berlin, Maryland (October 28, 1862). NATIONAL PORTRAIT GALLERY/SMITHSONIAN INSTITUTION/ART RESOURCE, NY

Charles Stratton (General Tom Thumb) and Lavinia Warren posing prior to their February 10, 1863 wedding day. NATIONAL PORTRAIT GALLERY/SMITHSONIAN INSTITUTION/ ART RESOURCE, NY

Mathew Brady at Gettysburg in a photograph erroneously titled "The Wheat-Field in Which General Reynolds Was Shot" (July 1863). U.S. NATIONAL ARCHIVES

Mathew Brady (right) at Gettysburg in a photograph accurately titled "Woods in Which General John F. Reynolds Was Killed" (July 1863). U.S. NATIONAL ARCHIVES

Stereograph of three Confederate prisoners on Seminary Ridge at Gettysburg (July 1863). LIBRARY OF CONGRESS

After Cold Harbor, General Ambrose Burnside, seated on a bag of oats, reads a Washington newspaper as Mathew Brady, arms crossed, looks on (June 1864). LIBRARY OF CONGRESS

Near the beginning of the siege of Petersburg, Mathew Brady stands (at the middle of this photograph), hands in pockets, with a battery of the First Pennsylvania Light Artillery (June 21, 1864). LIBRARY OF CONGRESS

General Robert E. Lee in Richmond the day after he returned home from Appomattox (April 16, 1865). U.S. National Archives

A sketch of Mathew Brady in pencil by James Edward Kelly, signed by Brady (June 19, 1891).
SMITHSONIAN AMERICAN ART MUSEUM/ART RESOURCE, NY

tion on the latter's part. But by January 13, Barnum's ad in the same newspaper mentioned the planned nuptials between General Thumb and Miss Warren. Soon crowds as large as twenty thousand people a day, paying twenty-five cents apiece, flocked to the American Museum to see her, and others stopped to look at her wedding dress, which Barnum placed in a Fifth Avenue store window for a time to help promote what he was billing as the "Fairy Wedding." Commodore Nutt would be the best man, and Lavinia's even more miniature and fetching little sister, Minnie, would be the bridesmaid. The ceremony took place on February 10, 1863, at Grace Church, across Broadway from Brady's gallery, a street that on the morning of the wedding was densely crowded with mostly female spectators. Barnum, who let it be known that he was paying for the wedding and the reception, led the bridal party up the aisle to the altar.

Brady photographed the couple in their "wedding costumes" sometime before the nuptials. According to Mary Panzer, in *Mathew Brady and the Image of History*, his "many carte-de-visite photographs in preparation for the wedding . . . doubtless profited everyone, including the performers, who sold portraits wherever they appeared." The day after the wedding, the *New York Times* devoted more than three full columns to the ceremony and the reception following it (and it was also covered at length in the *Tribune*, the *Herald*, the *Sun*, and the *Evening Post*), and the day after that, Brady was able to score a notice—in effect an unpaid advertisement—on page two of the same paper, titled BRADY AND THE LILLIPUTIANS. It asked those who had not been invited to either nuptial event to visit Brady's gallery, from which "they can carry copies of the smallest quartette extant home with them in their vest pockets, for a very trifling outlay." One of the wedding pictures was the basis for an engraving on the cover of the February 21 *Harper's Weekly*, which also quoted at length from the *Herald* article about the ceremony.[10]

The images were distributed by the Anthony brothers, who gave the couple a wedding gift, described as a "Beautiful photograph album for 200 pictures, heavy binding, elaborately decorated and gold-mounted; by Messrs. E. and H. T. Anthony, 501 Broadway." Other merchants on Broadway also gave gifts and were presumably among the nearly one thousand guests, led, oddly enough, by the now-disgraced General Burnside, whom Lincoln had replaced with Gen. Joseph Hooker on

January 25. Others in attendance included the wives of John Jacob Astor and William H. Vanderbilt, plus those of James Gordon Bennett Sr. of the *Herald* and Horace Greeley of the *Tribune*.

The reception afterward was held at the Metropolitan Hotel (Mrs. Lincoln's favorite on shopping trips to New York), down Broadway at Prince Street. Although tickets to the reception cost seventy-five dollars per person, Barnum claims in his letters that more than six thousand people who wanted tickets to attend were denied them. The wedding gifts were on display at the hotel during the reception—the many pieces of jewelry and silver exhibited in locked glass cases—and the four tiny members of the wedding party were lifted onto a grand piano, where they could tower over the many guests they received. As the *Observer* mildly put it, the wedding was "the event of a century, if not unparalleled in history."[11]

It's hard to imagine anything short of a serious illness keeping Brady away from this sort of spectacle, but no mention of his attendance exists. Not only was he the official photographer for the event, and a longtime acquaintance of Barnum, but Grace Church was filled with just the sort of New Yorkers Brady most loved to photograph—a universe of those in the city who either were or wished to be wealthy or notorious. Even President and Mrs. Lincoln were drawn in by the hype: the First Lady held a reception for fifty people at the White House on the evening of February 13 to honor the Strattons, who were in Washington on their honeymoon.

The next day, February 14, Brady photographed the four Harper brothers, James, John, Joseph Wesley, and Fletcher, at the Tenth Street gallery. James and John had begun as printers in 1817 but soon evolved into book publishers, and all four joined together in 1833 to form Harper and Brothers, which by the 1850s had become the largest employer in the city of New York and the biggest publisher in the world. In 1850, Fletcher started *Harper's New Monthly Magazine*. *Harper's Weekly* began in 1857 and by 1860 had a circulation of two hundred thousand. All the brothers were strong nativists, and James had been elected mayor of New York in 1844 on an explicitly anti-Catholic, anti-Irish, pro-temperance platform. Any political or temperamental differences between the Harpers and Brady, leaving aside outright prejudice against the Irish, had presumably long since been overcome by their close business relationship. But prejudice against Irish immigrants had been a fact of life in New York City since well before Brady arrived on the scene. Even Samuel Morse, whom Brady claimed as a teacher, had run for mayor of New York City as a nativist in 1836 (losing handily), and had written a number of anti-immigration tracts.[12]

Throughout the rest of the war the Brady studio did a robust business in portrait photography. The registers from his business at the time, which list the sitters, the size and number of photographs ordered, and the charge, are at the New York Public Library, where one Brady biographer counted 5,412 photographs taken between February 1863 and April 1865. He notes that the graduating class from West Point went each year to Brady's studio for portraits, and that the fathers of both Franklin Delano Roosevelt and Theodore Roosevelt had photographs made during this period. One notation in the register reads "Send the bill to Secretary of State [William H.] Seward as soon as possible," referring to a bill of $12.50 for seven photographs of the visiting British statesman Lord Hartington, who would become the Duke of Devonshire. But many of the names on the register were not famous, then or now.[13]

Brady's portrait business in Washington also remained active. Horatio Nelson Taft, who was an examiner for the U.S. Patent Office during the Civil War and kept a regular diary of everyday life there, writes in his entry for March 6, 1863, that after leaving work at the Patent Office, "I went down on the Ave, droped [*sic*] into Bradys Photograph Gallery which is one of the *Institutions* of Washington," and there saw and had a conversation with Maj. Gen. E. V. Sumner, who was also in the gallery. (As it happened, Sumner, who had fought on the Peninsula and at Antietam, and had just taken a leave after the carnage at Fredericksburg, would die of a heart attack two weeks later.) Earlier in the war, Taft had stopped at Brady's and seen Major Anderson, the hero of Fort Sumter. In March of 1864, Taft would take his wife, Julia, there to have her photograph made. He writes that "The Artist who is to *touch them up* with his pencil came to see her last evening." This is a man named Mulvaney or Mulvany, whom Taft had described before in his diary, on January 7, 1863, as someone who boarded with him and who was "on excellent terms with himself, but a great talker and an unsparing critic of other Artists productions." Brady's was still doing a vigorous-enough business to keep at least one artist busy putting what Taft called "the delicate touches to Bradys pictures."[14]

Registers from Brady's postwar years in Washington, now in the Library of Congress, offer instances of his lifelong tendency to make complimentary photographs of those with some sort of reputation—most often a congressman. So even when his business became less than robust after the Civil War he still saw photographing the famous as a business strategy, a way to draw in the less than famous who would provide his steady custom. In the era of the carte de visite, of course, having the right image of the right person—Elmer Ellsworth after he was killed, or the general of the hour, or the unlikely presidential candidate who within a matter of a few years would prove to be the greatest president in the nation's history—was itself a way to increase income. But many of those complimentary daguerreotypes and ambrotypes and large-format wet prints went on the walls of one of his galleries to flatter by association the ordinary sitter, or to appeal to his or her aspirations. Brady was not only enamored of the rich and famous, but in his own increasing role in creating a culture of celebrity saw them as a means to an end.[15]

In the next phase of his coverage of the Civil War, Brady would make explicit use of his own celebrity, which had grown out of his proximity to others of renown but also out of the name recognition he had built through every aspect of his business. From here on, a photograph by Brady could mean that one of any number of his operators, but not Brady himself, had been at the scene depicted in the photograph. It could also mean that Brady had bought or appropriated the rights to a photograph someone not in his employment had taken, and then added the image to the Brady collection. But now a certain number of his photographs would show Brady posing there within the camera's field of vision, authenticating the photograph in the most indisputable way possible. In these photographs, Brady was standing in for the photograph's viewer. It was not just the Brady name, but the man himself who would take you there.

# CHAPTER 13

# *"Rebel Invasion"*

Fairy weddings notwithstanding, the war lumbered on. But it was not until the middle of 1863 that Mathew Brady was drawn back into it. Neither he nor his operators were present in May for the Chancellorsville campaign, including the Second Battle of Fredericksburg, which was covered most notably by the talented military photographer Capt. A. J. Russell. Earlier in the year, Alexander Gardner and his men had taken photographs of the encamped Army of the Potomac, then under General Hooker, but his men apparently were, like Brady's, absent from the big engagements in May. But both Gardner and Brady would appear soon after the war's next great battle, Gettysburg, in which Lee's Army of Northern Virginia faced the Army of the Potomac, newly placed under the command of George G. Meade. The main battle began on July 1 and ended on July 3.

Gardner, James Gibson, and Timothy O'Sullivan, in two photographic wagons, got to the battlefield first, by way of Emmitsburg, Maryland. Gibson took a stereo photograph of the Farmer's Inn and Hotel in Emmitsburg, for which Gardner later wrote a caption, stating that at that inn "our special Artist was captured, July 5, 1863." We don't know which of the three photographers Gardner was referring to, but Gen. J. E. B. Stuart's official report of his actions during the Gettysburg Campaign notes that his cavalry had entered Emmitsburg at dawn on July 5, while defending the Confederate retreat after the battle, and "we captured sixty or seventy prisoners of war, and some valuable hospital stores en route from Frederick to the [Union] army."

Whoever was detained by Stuart's troopers was soon released, because by three P.M. that day all three men were on the road to Gettysburg, ten miles away. Accompanied by Charles H. Keener, a volunteer from Baltimore with the United States Christian Commission (which offered religious and other forms of support to soldiers during the war), they reached the southernmost edge of the battlefield by the Emmitsburg Road late in the afternoon. Then, according to Keener,

> We passed over the battle-field for more than 3 miles, where we had a fresh view of things as they looked two days after the battle. First we saw the smoking ruins of a house and barn; fences were all leveled; breastworks were thrown up on all sides; the road barricaded; dead horses laid about by dozens, and filled the road with a horrible stench. Though our army had held the field but 24 hours, we saw but one dead body on the road, and all the wounded were in houses and barns.[1]

Not visible from the road were far more dead and bloating bodies that had not yet been buried. Given their experience at Antietam, Gardner and Gibson were drawn to the dead, not the many wounded, and O'Sullivan joined in. All but a few of the thirty-one hundred Union soldiers who had been killed were already buried, but small bunches of the forty-seven hundred Confederate fatalities still awaited the Union burial parties, since the retreating Confederates once again left their dead on the field—as well as seven thousand of their wounded. William Frassanito writes in *Gettysburg: A Journey in Time* that three fourths of the sixty images Gardner and his photographers took "contain as their main subject matter bloated corpses, open graves, dead horses, and related details of wholesale carnage."[2]

Photographic historian Bob Zeller attributes Gardner's focus on such scenes almost to the exclusion of all others to his "journalistic soul," and William Frassanito attributes it to Gardner's commercial acumen. But as we have seen, the Antietam photographs, which have so much impact upon us today, made very little journalistic or commercial impact in Gardner's time, and the Gettysburg photographs would have even less. Still, on the morning of July 6, Gardner and his men started their work in the part of the battlefield where the last of the dead remained unburied, and where the scenes they saw were as profoundly dramatic then—as moving in simple human terms—as they seem to us today. Even if Gardner's calculations were not primarily journalistic or commercial, it would be hard for him not to have realized, two years into this great national trauma, that the views of the dead were important historically. Gardner could not ignore the corpses any more than O'Sullivan, who had taken photographs of dead horses at Cedar Mountain the previous August, could ignore those dozens of dead artillery horses still on the battlefield at Gettysburg.[3]

And there is a slightly more banal explanation. The weather was bad on July 6, when they took most of their photographs. It would have been futile in the mist and weak light for Gardner's team to focus on the wounded men huddled in barns or farmhouses, on battlefield panoramas, or on local structures of interest, such as the buildings of the college in the town of Gettysburg, which were also used for the wounded. The next day, when the weather was better, Gardner and O'Sullivan did take a few photographs of structures. But for the most part at Gettysburg, Gardner calculated that the drama of dead soldiers and horses would mostly suffice, and that getting these images back to his Washington studio was more important than doing a more comprehensive survey of the battlefield and the town after the weather had improved.

Gardner evidently left Gettysburg separately from Gibson and O'Sullivan, because he sent an undated telegram to O'Sullivan at HEADQUARTERS ARMY POTOMAC—which had been moved to Frederick, Maryland, by July 7—saying, I HAVE JUST GOT BACK FROM GETTYS-BURG and that WOODBURY AND BERGER WERE THERE. That would have been their former colleagues David Woodbury and Anthony Berger, who were working for Brady. Gardner's telegram to O'Sullivan also says of the two Brady photographers, IF THEY COME YOUR LENGTH I HOPE YOU WILL GIVE THEM EVERY ATTENTION. This somewhat ambiguous request could mean if the two Brady photographers also followed the Army of the Potomac, please be friendly—perhaps because Gardner hoped to recruit them to his new operation. But "give them every attention" might simply mean "Keep an eye on the competition."[4]

Although Brady's men from the Washington gallery were on the scene only a few days after Gardner got there, Brady himself apparently did not arrive from New York for several more days after that. In the meantime, Woodbury and Berger took no photographs themselves. If Brady was bringing the equipment from New York, or if he had given definite orders that he himself would direct all the photographs that were taken by his men on the battlefield, then his intention had almost certainly been to get to town when his men did. Traveling from New York would have been possible but not easy. Trains were running as far as Harrisburg, Pennsylvania, but the tracks from there to Gettysburg had been commandeered by the military, which was trying to get the thousands of wounded to hospitals elsewhere. Probably, then, Brady would have rented a wagon in Harrisburg to travel the remaining forty miles to Gettysburg.

But he might have been delayed in leaving New York. Before and during the battle, New York City felt directly threatened by General Lee's army—more than one newspaper for more than one day in early July led its war coverage with the headline REBEL INVASION. As Edwin G. Burrows and Mike Wallace put it in *Gotham*, "If Lee eluded Meade he could be in Jersey City, and at New York's throat, in a matter of days." Since so many troops from the city had gone to fight with General Meade, New York was not heavily defended against a Rebel attack. Given the unreliability of the first newspaper reports, which often proclaimed victory prematurely, New Yorkers could not really feel assured of Lee's defeat or their own safety from Lee's army until about July 6. Brady might well have been reluctant to leave his gallery at a time when the city could come under siege.[5]

But not all the threats were from the South. The news that many New Yorkers were among the casualties at Gettysburg came just as the federal government held a draft lottery in the city. State and local officials had opposed the lottery on the grounds that the Republican federal government was overburdening the mostly Democratic city, and rumors of resistance were in the air. A protest meeting took place on July 4 at the Academy of Music, only a few blocks from Brady's gallery. The lottery itself began on July 11 in a city that was tense, angry, and still virtually without military reinforcements for its unpopular police department. Many people in the city openly sympathized with the South, and racial hatred would be a deadly component of what was to follow two days later, when the infamous New York City Draft Riot began. By the time it ended on July 16 it was (and still is) the worst incident of civil disobedience in the nation's history—leaving aside the Civil War itself. The riot could have changed Brady's calculation from wanting to protect his property to a concern that he might not be able to leave the city at all, and in any case, the mostly Irish rioters were encouraging shops and factories to close down, so it would have been unwise for Brady to keep his gallery open. Whatever his reasoning, he probably left the city on the thirteenth or fourteenth.[6]

The delay worked to Brady's advantage. Gardner got the scoop, and got the bodies. (The immense job of burying all the Confederate dead was said, in the July 15 *New York Times*, to have been completed by July 10, but more than two weeks after that a visitor to the battlefield reported seeing unburied Rebel bodies.) But Brady's photographs showed a firmer sense of the important sites on the battlefield and of the growing public understanding of what had happened there. They were also far superior to Gardner's as photographs. Woodbury and Berger evidently made good use of their days in Gettysburg, waiting for their boss to arrive, by familiarizing themselves with the town, the battlefield, and the reports of the battle itself. The metaphorical fog of war had begun to lift in the first days after Gardner left, as continuing newspaper accounts of the battle became more detailed and more accurate. By the time Brady set off from New York he had a good understanding of the contours of the battle and of its most important figures, information he could coordinate with the local knowledge Woodbury and Berger had been gathering.[7]

Brady and his men took thirty-six photographs in the time they spent there, estimated to be between three days and a week. Brady himself appears in at least six of the images, but so do his assistants. He and two assistants appear together in the distance in one photograph, a panoramic view of the hills Little Round Top and Big Round Top, which means a third assistant was also on hand, perhaps someone who accompanied Brady from New York.

Two of the subjects his men focused on show Brady's familiarity with the news of the battle. One of the first men who had been killed, late on the morning of the first day, was the highest-ranking officer to die there, Maj. Gen. John F. Reynolds, who commanded the Army of the Potomac's left wing as the battle began. A cavalry division under his command had dismounted and fought the first real engagement at Gettysburg, and Reynolds had brought up and was positioning two infantry corps when he was shot from his horse, possibly by a Confederate sharpshooter, and died on the spot. A Pennsylvanian who had gone to West Point and fought in the Mexican War, Reynolds was thought by many to be the best general in the Union army, and as Henry Steele Commager writes in *The Blue and the Gray* of even Reynolds's limited action at Gettysburg, "the rapidity with which he brought up his scattered forces and the discernment which led him to order the occupation of Cemetery Hill contributed to ultimate Union victory." The first newspaper reports out of Gettysburg, as early as July 3, mentioned General Reynolds's death, and three of Brady's photos, in all of which Brady himself appears, are connected with this signal event.[8]

One photo (actually two plates meant to be joined as one composite photograph) shows a pond in the foreground, beyond which Brady stands alone before a split-rail fence, on the far side of which is what was erroneously called "The Wheat-Field in Which General Reynolds Was Shot." Another photo bears a similar caption. In it, Brady stands to the right side of the image with an assistant who points to woods to the right of them, which is where General Reynolds was in fact shot. The third photo taken by Brady's crew shows, as a woodcut based on it appearing in the August 22 *Harper's Weekly* put it, "the barn to which [General Reynolds] was carried, where he breathed his last moments, etc." (That "etc." seems a little unfeeling to us today.) The barn in the photo was near enough to the place where Reynolds fell to have been a plausible place for him to have been taken—except that Reynolds was killed instantly by a bullet to the head, and his body was transported to a small house south of town on the Emmitsburg Road. (He would be buried on July 4 in his native Lancaster.) In this third Brady photo, as in the other two, Brady stands in the middle distance, wearing a long dark coat and a round light-colored hat with a dark band. In all three photos, his back is to the camera, so that the viewer is in effect looking over his shoulder. The same assistant who appeared in the wheat field with Brady now kneels or sits beside him in this other field, and two more men sit at the opening of the distant barn itself.[9]

Frassanito, who has written two long studies of the photography at Gettysburg, believes that Brady left Gettysburg without knowing the details of Reynolds's death, and so did not mislabel his photographs intentionally to capitalize on Reynolds's fame. By contrast, Gardner's *Catalogue of Photographic Incidents of the War*, published in September of 1863, included a view of a field to which Gardner added the words "where General Reynolds fell" to the original caption, "View in field on right wing." Gardner clearly did this to exploit the general's heroic status.[10]

A second Brady subject at Gettysburg also featured an early hero of the battle, John Lawrence Burns, a sixty-nine-year-old veteran of the War of 1812 who was the only known resident of the town to fight in the battle for either side (although other townspeople were injured, and one was killed). His story became well known. One twelve-year-old apprentice to a Gettysburg photographic firm later remembered watching Burns leave his house on Chambersburg Pike on the morning of July 1 and walk in the direction of the fighting, carrying "his flint lock" musket "and powder horn." Burns was a crotchety old man, a former town constable who was often the victim of practical jokes by the town's boys. When he volunteered for duty with the Pennsylvania 150th Regiment that morning, he was wearing a swallowtail coat and a battered top hat, according to the major to whom Burns reported.[11]

Later that day Burns was wounded three times during the fighting. The wounds were not serious, and two weeks later Brady photographed him seated in a rocking chair outside his house, his left foot still bandaged, his crutches behind him, and his musket at his side. One of Brady's men also took a long shot of the Burns house, with Burns again seated in a rocking chair accompanied by crutches and musket, but this time on a second-floor landing to an outside stairway, with a woman at his side. But what was not noticed until 2004 was that Brady himself, wearing his characteristic hat, is seated with another man on the steps of a side porch, and that a portable developing tent appears beyond Brady at the far right edge of the photograph. The tent, which was set on a tripod, was just large enough for a man to lean into to prepare and develop the glass negatives. Its presence there suggests that neither Brady nor his men took a special photographic wagon to Gettysburg, as Gardner had.[12]

Here, and in at least two other images taken at Gettysburg, there is a "Where's Waldo?" aspect to Brady's appearance in a photograph. His position in the John Burns house photo remained undetected for almost a century and a half. In a photograph taken from Little Round Top looking west, the Brady assistant who posed in the Reynolds photographs appears in the center foreground of the panoramic view wearing a floppy, light-colored hat. But seated amid boulders to the right of the image, and looking north, is Brady himself, who would be almost undetectable except for his own characteristic hat. In a third photo—the one that includes Brady and two assistants—Brady appears in the distance at the extreme left of a panoramic shot of Little Round Top and Big Round Top, across what became known as the Valley of Death. Given where and when these photographs were taken, the intent was clearly not playful. Perhaps at a time so soon after Gardner had made off with negatives taken under Brady's auspices, and after a year or more of eager copyrighting of images, a practice that would soon fall out of favor, Brady saw this as the best way to hold title to a photograph. If he could point to himself, or at least to his hat, appearing however obscurely in an image, then the image was certainly his.

But if this was Brady's reason for putting himself and his men in almost every photograph he took at Gettysburg, then in at least some of the images the effect went well beyond the intention. In those connected with General Reynolds, especially, the photos introduce in an explicit way a human consciousness of the violence that had been played out in these now-serene fields. We see one or two people contemplating the placid landscape, and we know what must be on their minds—the chaos and death that had filled these scenes only days before. Even now, when we know that General Reynolds (whom many of us today would know nothing about anyway) did not fall or die within the scope of the photograph, we feel the drama of the battle that unfolded there, if only in the thoughts of Brady and his colleagues. All photographs imply the presence of a human viewer, of course—the person who points the camera. But more explicitly, perhaps, than had yet been done in this medium, Brady introduced what might be called first-person photography, an assertion that a photograph is not just the doings of a sunbeam, an objective rendering of a scene, but a view created, in effect, by an individual consciousness. Its journalistic equivalent might be William Howard Russell's report from First Bull Run, where we are getting an account not of a battle, but of Russell's whole day, a very personal view of what happened.

Brady the photographer shown contemplating the scene of the fighting reflects and makes explicit the work of the operator standing behind the camera. Even if in his own mind putting himself in front of the camera was only an act of promotion (self-promotion being inseparable from promotion of the Brady brand and business), it is hard not to admire the audacity of what he did. No dead bodies appear in any of Brady's Gettysburg photographs, and only one dead horse, but in their psychological pointedness his photographs are more intense than any of the gruesome pictures Gardner and his men took. These Brady photographs question the main argument photography claimed as an improvement upon painting and drawing—its scientific objectivity. They steal photography from the sun.

Did Brady do anything more than borrow a technique from journalism, and at least indirectly from literature? Does asking, whether implicitly or explicitly, how we can tell the photographer from the photograph make these images works of art? As we have seen, Brady at times wished to be taken seriously as an artist. The three General Reynolds photographs would seem to qualify as works of art in that they have a clear idea behind them and are executed in a way that enhances that idea. In each picture, Brady carefully poses himself close enough to the camera to be a focal point for the image but far enough away to be less than the whole subject of it. We always see his back, which makes him in one sense anonymous, allowing him to stand in for every viewer, and yet his hat and the hat of the assistant who appears in two of the images are so distinctive as to particularize them. This is not "Man Standing in Field"; even if the viewer did not know that this was Brady himself in the images, the viewer would know that this is a distinct individual contemplating the horrible scenes that took place within the camera's view.

One image from Gettysburg that has long been praised for its artistry does not include Brady or any of his assistants. It is a stereo photograph of three Confederate prisoners taken on Seminary Ridge. Since the photograph was likely made two weeks after the battle, it has been speculated that these men were stragglers, three of twenty-five hundred Confederate prisoners who would be transported the next day to prisons in the North. Some writers praise the photo for its detailed documentation of Confederate uniforms. But the three figures in the image do not seem like stragglers and do not seem to be wearing regular uniforms, or uniforms of any sort. They have about them the air of scouts or spies, people who are a little distant from and feel their superiority to the ordinary run of soldier. If their poses do not quite suggest arrogance, they at least suggest self-confidence and self-possession. These three don't carry themselves like members of a defeated army, or like prisoners.[13]

Did they simply strike their poses, so perfect as a composition, or did Brady pose them? Even among the studio photographs, when Brady or his operators were working with willing customers in optimal conditions, few if any exist in which several subjects are so naturally yet thoughtfully posed. The likelihood is that this is how the men arranged themselves, but Brady knew enough to leave them as they were, or to take the image quickly, before they moved. In any case, it is universally recognized as one of the most striking images of the whole war. Nothing that Gardner or his men did with their more dramatic subject matter can compete with this Brady photograph as a work of art.

The widespread misunderstanding of who took which photographs when during the Civil War has allowed one questionable act that occurred after Gettysburg to taint not only all the work of the various photographers there, but, in the minds of many, Civil War photography in general. The act involved moving a single Confederate body some seventy yards to set up an Alexander Gardner photograph that has been known as "Home of a Rebel Sharpshooter." Two photographs were taken of this view, one full plate and one stereo, but the stereo did not turn out well. Gardner attributes the successful photo to Gibson in his 1863 *Incidents of the War* and to himself in his 1865 *Photographic Sketch Book of the War*, whereas William Frassanito attributes both images to O'Sullivan.

Frassanito proved conclusively in his 1975 book on Gettysburg that the body in the photograph is the same as one that appears in four other photographs Gardner and his men took farther down the hill in what was known as the Devil's Den. Nobody knows whose idea it was to move the dead soldier, but probably all three photographers were needed to haul it in a blanket from where it had been, unless Gardner had the audacity to ask members of one of the burial parties working in the vicinity to move it for them. Not only was the corpse moved, but it was arranged for the photo to look as if it had fallen back from a small stone wall erected between two large boulders at the foot of Little Round

Top, and under the dead soldier's head a knapsack was placed. (The blanket used to move the body appears in the stereo image.)[14]

According to the narrative Gardner created for the photo, the rocky scene had been a sharpshooter's position. Gardner wrote a long caption for the *Sketch Book* at least two years later, but the outline of the story he would tell had already been in his mind, because to help establish it, the photographers leaned a rifle against the stone wall. The same rifle also appears in the photos taken of the body in its original position, and it isn't a sharpshooter's rifle, but one that would belong to an ordinary infantryman. Gardner's caption for the *Sketch Book* creates the dead man's story out of whole cloth, suggesting that "The sharpshooter had evidently been wounded in the head by a fragment of shell which had exploded over him, and had laid down upon his blanket to await death. There was no means of judging how long he had lived after receiving his wound, but the disordered clothing shows that his sufferings must have been intense." As if this were not enough, Gardner gins up the pathos even further:

> Was he delirious with agony, or did death come slowly to his relief, while memories of home grew dearer as the field of carnage faded before him? What visions, of loved ones far away, may have hovered above his stony pillow! What familiar voices may he not have heard, like whispers beneath the roar of battle, as his eyes grew heavy in their long, last sleep![15]

Gardner goes on to say that he returned to the scene of the photograph in November 1863, when he was in Gettysburg for the ceremonies that included Lincoln's "Gettysburg Address," and found the musket still in the same place, but "rusted by many storms," and the skeleton of the soldier "undisturbed within the mouldering uniform." He concludes, "some mother may yet be patiently watching for the return of her boy, whose bones lie bleaching, unrecognized and alone, between the rocks at Gettysburg."

This is treacle of the most disheartening sort. Devil's Den was a much-visited site after the battle, so the possibility of the rifle still being there was nonexistent. But if Gardner did return to the site, he might well have seen a body or bodies that had become disinterred, since the ground was so rocky in that area that the burial detail covered some corpses with only gravel and sometimes a big rock, and battlefield visitors did subsequently come across bones and other remains. But this leaves aside Gardner's responsibility for moving the body to a more remote spot, where its chance of a proper burial might well have been reduced. Gardner has managed to avoid historical censure for both his bad judgment in moving the body and his worse judgment in so blatantly exploiting it. Even Frassanito sets up the original decision to move the body to the visually promising setting of the stone wall between the boulders by writing, "In what must have been a flash of creative excitement, the cameramen chose to improvise."[16]

If the effect of Frassanito's exposure of this episode has been to make many people who know a little something about Civil War photography believe that this practice was widespread, the good news is that there is no other conclusive evidence of a body's being moved for a photograph, by Gardner, by Gibson, by O'Sullivan, or by any other Civil War photographer. (O'Sullivan did use another musket as a prop for photographs of the dead at the battle of Spotsylvania Court House the following May.)

Brady himself was guilty of one smaller misstep of a similar nature at Gettysburg. A report appearing in the *New York Herald* on July 9, 1863, described the woods of Culp's Hill, where some intense fighting occurred on July 2 and 3, as the Union army defended its right flank from Confederate assaults. The *Herald* reporter Thomas W. Knox, writing under a dateline of July 6, compared the scene to the Shiloh battlefield, which he had also seen in his reporting: "The traces of the fighting there are but slight compared to those on this ground. I find tree after tree scarred from base to limbs so thickly that it is impossible to place one's hand upon their trunks without covering the marks of a bullet." Perhaps Brady saw this report in New York before he left for the battlefield, and noted this spot as a good subject for a photograph. In any case, Brady would be the only photographer at Gettysburg to photograph Culp's Hill until November of 1863. The scene might also have drawn Brady because five New York regiments were among the hill's defenders.[17]

Brady took four Culp's Hill photographs, in three of which appears a Brady assistant in a white dustcoat. In one he sits on a rock with another assistant as they look across a Union breastwork in the direction from which the Rebels came. A second photo has the man sitting alone, looking in the same downhill direction, but from the opposite side, so that he is facing to the right in this photo, but to the left in the other one. But in the third photo he has lain on his back on the ground amid a copse of trees pockmarked with bullet holes as Thomas Knox described. He has drawn up his knees and spread his arms to his side in a posture of death, and indeed Brady's caption reads, "in the middle ground a dead soldier."

Other photographers at Gettysburg would also pose subjects in places where men died, and neither those photographs nor this one by Brady are terribly convincing, especially compared to those taken of real corpses by Gardner, O'Sullivan, and Gibson. But Brady's intention, both in taking the photograph and in writing the caption for it, was to fictionalize. Having a live man pose as a dead soldier seems far less offensive than moving a dead body to compose a photograph, at least as a matter of simple human decency. But both the photographs, Brady's as well as Gardner's, were deceptions, and thus difficult to defend.

CHAPTER 14

# *"That Memorable Campaign"*

fter Gettysburg, Brady and his men took another break from covering the war. The major armies in the East were staggered by the losses in that great battle, and except for skirmishes and relatively small engagements, the war moved to the West and South, farther away than Brady was willing to send his photographers. But his galleries in New York and Washington remained busy. When a Russian naval fleet made its first visit to the United States, docking in New York in October and November of 1863, Brady photographed its officers and crews. The next spring, the Brady studio took a number of photographs before the start of the great Metropolitan Fair in support of the U.S. Sanitary Commission, which offered relief to sick and wounded Union soldiers. The images included portraits of the president of the fair and the commission, scenes inside and outside its buildings on Fourteenth Street, and a group portrait of the twenty members of the Gentlemen's Executive Committee on Art for the fair, of which Brady was one. In the photograph he is seated squarely in the middle of the group, which also includes such artists as Albert Bierstadt, Thomas Hicks, and Daniel Huntington, the architect Richard Morris Hunt, and Brady's friend and collaborator Edward Anthony. The fair, intended as "an index of the patriotism of the *whole* city of New York" and one of several held in the North in late 1863 and 1864, raised more than $1.3 million by selling not only art and photographs, but a huge variety of donated merchandise and artifacts.[1]

Brady continued to provide portraits of generals, politicians, and other public figures to *Harper's Weekly*. Images taken from his photographs made the cover of *Harper's* three weeks running in late March and early April of 1864, beginning with one of a hatless Brig. Gen. George A. Custer dramatically leading a cavalry charge. Presumably Brady's contribution to this engraving involved only Custer's face, since exposure times were still too long to take any sort of action shot. The next week's cover featured an obituary photograph for another cavalry officer, Col. Ulric Dahlgren, son of the Union admiral John Dahlgren. The colonel died in an ambush on March 2 as part of an audacious but unsuccessful cavalry raid on Richmond designed to free Union prisoners, during which Dahlgren's raiders had come within two miles of the capital. The Confederates, who took Dahlgren's body into Richmond, claimed to have found papers in his possession ordering the assassination of President Jefferson Davis and other ranking officials of the Confederacy, but this has been a matter of lasting historical dispute. The third *Harper's* cover offered head-and-shoulders portraits of two Union generals, one of whom had been Colonel Dahlgren's commander.[2]

Two of the three covers attribute the images not just to "Brady," which was the usual *Harper's* attribution, but to "Mathew Brady." Because he almost always styled himself "M. B. Brady," there are very few contemporary references to his Christian name, which has led a couple of scholars to question whether his name wasn't actually spelled in the more orthodox way as *Matthew*, with two *t*'s, instead of the generally accepted spelling of his name with one. *Harper's* used his first name in a few other instances, and it seems likely that Brady would have corrected them if they were consistently spelling his name wrong on their cover.[3]

On August 9 and again on November 8, 1863, President Lincoln went to sit for Alexander Gardner at his Seventh Street studio, the first portraits made of Lincoln since Gardner's photographs of him in the field after Antietam the previous October. Brady was almost certainly galled by this, given his own relationship with the president, and on Friday, January 8, exactly two months after the latter of Lincoln's sittings for Gardner, the president appeared in Brady's gallery for a series of four photographs credited to Brady himself. Perhaps because it was an election year, Lincoln, who was never shy around a camera, was even more than usually willing to be photographed, and a month later, on February 9, 1864, a Tuesday afternoon, he went once again to Brady's Pennsylvania Avenue gallery, where he had an even longer sitting for Brady photographer Anthony Berger.

According to the painter Francis Bicknell Carpenter, who had just started working in the White House, he himself joined the president and Mrs. Lincoln that day under the front portico of the executive mansion, where a carriage was to take them to a three o'clock appointment at Brady's. But after they had waited for a time and the carriage had not shown up, Lincoln proposed that he and Carpenter walk the mile or so along Pennsylvania Avenue to the gallery, saying, "It won't hurt you and me to walk down." Carpenter said that Lincoln entertained him on the way by telling stories, including one of a long-ago visit by Daniel Webster to Springfield, Illinois. Presumably Mrs. Lincoln followed once the carriage could be rounded up, and was accompanied by their ten-year-old son, Tad, who posed with Lincoln that day.[4]

It's a charming photograph, with Tad standing beside his father, who was seated in the famous Brady posing chair, turning the page of a book that they are both looking down at. Lincoln has on tiny reading glasses; Tad is dressed like his father, in a tie and dark jacket, a watch chain strung across his front. His arm, presumably steadying him on the arm of the chair, makes an intimate visual connection with his father. This is the most informal photograph ever taken of Lincoln, but it is not the most significant of the half-dozen pictures Berger made that day. One, a profile, became the model for Lincoln's head on the U.S. penny.[5]

Lincoln sat for Berger at Brady's one more time that spring, on April 20, but only a single negative from the sitting exists, and that one is broken. The following Tuesday, April 26, Berger and at least one other photographer from Brady's studio went to the White House at the request of Carpenter "to make some stereoscopic studies for me of the President's office." Carpenter was preparing to paint his heroic work, *First Reading of the Emancipation Proclamation by President Lincoln*, which now hangs in the U.S. Capitol, in the Senate wing. Carpenter used Brady photographs of Lincoln and members of his Cabinet for his painting, and when Berger made the April 26 visit, Lincoln posed both seated and standing at the table in his office on which he had signed the historic document.[6]

In his memoir, *The Inner Life of Abraham Lincoln*, Carpenter tells

President Lincoln and his son Tad
(February 1864). Photograph by Anthony Berger.
*Library of Congress*

a story about Tad and his father on that day. Brady's men had requested an interior room at the White House where they could have the darkness necessary to prepare and then develop the stereoscope plates. Carpenter showed them to a room that Tad had been using as a small theater, "with stage, curtains, orchestra, stalls, parquette, and all." Berger and whoever was helping him set up their equipment in this room and, after preparing plates there, took them to the president's office, where they made photos of Lincoln. When one of Brady's men carried an ex-posed plate or two back to the interior room, he found the door locked. Tad had discovered their presence in his theater and thrown a fit, locking the door and going off with the key. The photographers could not get to the chemicals they needed to fix the exposed images and prepare new plates.

They were explaining the problem to Carpenter and the president, who was sitting in his office chair for another photograph, when Tad "burst in, in a fearful passion." Lincoln calmly told Tad to unlock the door. The boy ran off, and when Lincoln learned that he had gone to his mother's room and refused to obey his father, the president rose abruptly from his chair and "strode across the passage with the air of one bent on punishment." Soon he came back with the key and unlocked the door himself, returning to his seat to wait for the next exposure. The presi-dent explained, as Carpenter recounts it, "Tad is a peculiar child. He was violently excited when I went to him. I said, 'Tad, do you know you are making your father a great deal of trouble?' He burst into tears, in-stantly giving me up the key."[7]


"I took Gen. Grant almost at once when he appeared in Washington City from the West," Brady told the reporter George Townsend in 1891, meaning he took Grant's photograph. And, indeed, according to the Washington *Daily National Republican*, Brady was in a crowd of several hundred people who met Grant's train late on the afternoon of March 8, 1864, when "the hero of the Mississippi and Lookout Mountain" ar-rived in Washington to receive the rank of lieutenant general from President Lincoln, followed by an order making him commander of all the armies of the Union. Grant kept the crowd at the station waiting, but when he at last appeared, "a number of gentlemen stepped forward and took him by the hand, the first of whom was M. B. Brady, Esq., the celebrated artist of New York."[8]

Brady said in other articles late in life that he had then asked Grant to come to his gallery for a photograph and had also recommended that the general stay at Willard's Hotel. The general and his fourteen-year-old son, Fred, took Brady's advice and checked in there, drawing cheers when he arrived from army officers who recognized him. The next day, he received his new rank at the White House and promised the president that "it will be my earnest endeavor not to disappoint your expectations," which were to destroy Lee's army and end the war.[9]

It was by now an established tradition that every new Union general of the hour would make a stop at Brady's to be photographed. Although Grant does not mention it in his *Personal Memoirs*, sometime in the busy three days he was in Washington, which included one quick trip to see General Meade at his winter quarters in Virginia at Brandy Station, Grant found time to visit Brady's photographic pantheon, and to join it. It was the first of many photographs Brady or his men would take of him.

Grant spent the rest of March in the West with General Sherman, who had served with him since before Shiloh in the spring of 1862 and was now replacing him as commander of the Military Division of the Mississippi. Grant began to make plans for a coordinated attack on the South by all the armies now under his command and, in late March, established his own headquarters not in political Washington but in the field at Culpeper Court House, Virginia, near General Meade, who remained the commander of the Army of the Potomac. In another month Grant was ready to put his vast plan into effect, and, as he put it in his memoirs:

> Soon after midnight, May 3d–4th, the Army of the Potomac moved out from its position north of the Rapidan, to start upon that memorable campaign, destined to result in the capture of the Confederate capital and the army defending it.[10]

As Grant hastened to admit, achieving his goal would take longer than "a single season," and "losses inflicted, and endured, were destined to be severe," but what had amounted to a stalemate after three years of suffering would now at last be broken, whatever the cost.

One cameraman was there to record this auspicious beginning of the end of the war, and that was Brady's old protégé and now his competitor, Timothy O'Sullivan, still working for Alexander Gardner. Late in the afternoon of May 4, after the bulk of the fifty thousand Union soldiers, complete with cannon, ammunition, and supplies, had crossed the Rapidan River in Virginia on two pontoon bridges assembled overnight, O'Sullivan set up his stereo camera on a rise on the south bank of the river and took three photographs of the long line of Union soldiers still crossing. O'Sullivan could not have known how significant these images would be, since armies on both sides had crossed many a stream before this to not much avail. But the three photographs make up an extraordinary panorama even leaving aside the history being made, or begun.[11]

As so often happened in the photographic coverage of the war, there then was an inexplicable pause. O'Sullivan did not take another photograph for more than two weeks, during which time the battles of the Wilderness and Spotsylvania Court House occurred, with a combined casualty total for the Union of thirty-three thousand men. The usual explanations for this lapse—dense terrain, bad weather, bulky equipment—might explain why no combat photographs were made, but the May 4 photographs of the Rapidan crossing prove that you can take a historic picture during wartime without training your camera on actual fighting. And on May 21, two days after beginning to photograph again, O'Sullivan would reiterate the point with his extraordinary series of images of Generals Grant and Meade and their staffs at Massaponax Church. O'Sullivan took his camera to a second-floor window of the church, where he could shoot down on the officers, seated in pews dragged out and arrayed under the trees in the churchyard. We see them consulting maps and conferring, and we watch as General Grant apparently writes an order. The caption that Gardner would later write for these photographs calls them "A Council of War," and no other such photograph exists from the whole conflict. It's worth noting that when one of these pictures and others O'Sullivan took at the time were used as the basis for a two-page spread in the July 9 *Harper's Weekly*, the credit went not to O'Sullivan but to Gardner.[12]

How many photographs as valuable as these might have been taken if O'Sullivan had not kept his equipment in the wagon during those two weeks of fighting? One possible explanation for O'Sullivan's pause is that as the only photographer with the Army of the Potomac during this part of the war, he may have had commitments to reproduce maps or orders for distribution among the commanders. These commitments would have been more urgent, as men were fighting and dying, as troops were being deployed and redeployed, as messages about how the battle was unfolding prompted new plans and orders. Perhaps O'Sullivan simply did not have time to do anything else.

Toward the end of O'Sullivan's break from making photographs, Brady's men reentered the field, apparently without Brady himself but possibly in the company of Alexander Gardner's brother and partner, James, and the military railroads photographer A. J. Russell. On about May 16 all of them, either individually or together, reached an important Union supply depot at a spot north of Fredericksburg called Belle Plain. Probably they hitched a ride on one of the many supply boats going down the Potomac River from Washington and Alexandria and then up Potomac Creek to the landing. At that point in the war, everything heading from points north to Grant's army in Virginia, including photographers with passes, went through Belle Plain, and many of the wounded from the Wilderness and Spotsylvania battles went through in the other direction, as did numbers of Confederate prisoners.[13]

Brady's men took photographs of the pontoon wharves that had been constructed there, and of prisoners being held on hillsides and in ravines near the landing, awaiting transport to a prison in the north. Then, on about May 18, the photographers made their way to Fredericksburg, where Brady's men took panoramic shots of the battlefields from the 1862 and 1863 battles, and of the small city itself. They also took several photographs of wounded soldiers in the yard of Brompton, the Marye mansion, above the heights that had been made infamous in the earlier Fredericksburg battles. On the next day, or perhaps the day after that, May 20, the Brady men took both stereoscope and full-plate photographs of a burial party at work, photographing one scene simultaneously with two cameras at a ninety-degree angle from each other. In all seven of the images, four bodies and two caskets are laid in a row as a group of black men works on a burial trench beyond the bodies, and various white men stand around watching. Blankets cover the bodies, but in two images they have been turned down to reveal the heads of the deceased. Although there is certainly pathos in the way the dead soldiers' bare feet stick out from beneath the blankets, there is nothing grotesque about the bodies or the images themselves.[14]

O'Sullivan continued to follow the front of Grant's army for the rest of the month and into early June, taking one series of photos of dead Confederate soldiers awaiting burial, but for the most part photographing bridges and mills as Grant crossed stream after stream maneuvering to the south and east as his army got closer to Richmond. Eventually its progress was checked at Cold Harbor, only ten miles to the northeast of the Confederate capital. O'Sullivan again went silent, from May 29 until June 4, the day after the worst day of the Cold Harbor battle, and then took four fairly nondescript photographs of an inn and a hotel within a couple of miles of each other, of the Cold Harbor crossroads, and of a nearby camp in the woods. Gen. Philip Sheridan's cavalry officers were housed at the hotel, and the rumps of a number of horses appear in the middle distance, but it's hard to see what the point of any of these photographs was, other than to prove, perhaps to Gardner, that he was nearby soon after the battle unfolded.

Brady's men, meanwhile, had been consigned to the rear of the army, photographing another staging area down the Rappahannock River from Fredericksburg, at an old river ferry landing and village called Port Royal, through which John Wilkes Booth would pass less than a year later just before he was killed. But sometime in the late spring, General Grant chose Brady as the official photographer for his command, and his name, along with those of Berger and Woodbury, plus one S. T. Denney, appear on the official register of citizens "doing business with the Army of the Potomac." In early June, a week after the bloody debacle at Cold Harbor, Virginia, Brady would join his men in the field. On the morning of June 3 some seven thousand Union troops had been killed or wounded at Cold Harbor in less than an hour, in an assault that Grant said in his memoirs he regretted, because "no advantage whatever was gained to compensate for the heavy loss we sustained."[15]

Before Brady arrived, his men stopped at the supply base at White House Landing in Virginia, about fifteen miles due east of Cold Harbor, which had been established by the Union during the Seven Days battles of the Peninsula Campaign in 1862. Mrs. Robert E. Lee had moved to the estate at White House Plantation after being forced out of Arlington House. Her great-grandmother Martha Custis had lived on the plantation during her first marriage, and had married her second husband, George Washington, there. When Mrs. Lee found herself caught in enemy territory at White House during the Peninsula Campaign, General McClellan permitted her to pass through the Union lines, to move to a house in Richmond.

Brady's men took about a dozen photographs at the landing on June 9 or 10, including a remarkable panoramic view of dozens of Confederate prisoners. Brady arrived at White House himself on June 10, and between then and June 12 took a series of photos of General Grant and his top commanders as their troops recovered from the Cold Harbor battle.[16]

With Brady there, his men began to make the sort of images that were the most characteristic of all Brady's war pictures, and indeed of all the photographs from his whole career: those of people who were making history and would be remembered by it. These were individual and group portraits, subjects that his operators had not been taking before he arrived and that Brady now sought out and even helped to compose. We see so clearly from these images what Brady's values were.

The portrait of a somewhat contemplative Grant leaning on a pine tree, left hand on hip, would undoubtedly have commercial value. But if Brady's chief goal had been making money, why would he have used only a full-plate camera and not also, or perhaps instead, the stereo camera his men had with them, which would have expedited the turning out of large numbers of card photographs? Brady used the stereo camera for other subjects during those two days, but for this portrait of Grant and another of Grant with his staff, he exposed the larger negatives. Doesn't this suggest that he had history in mind for these portraits? He used the same camera for Meade and his staff, and for the always-picturesque Gen. Winfield Scott Hancock and his staff.

Brady photographed no fewer than eight other generals, the commanders of four of Meade's five infantry corps, missing only Gen. Gouverneur K. Warren, whose corps had moved out early on June 11. He also photographed Assistant Secretary of War Charles A. Dana, whom Brady had known and photographed during his days at the *New York Tribune*. Dana had been with Grant and Meade in O'Sullivan's Massaponax churchyard photographs. All these figures posed confidently if

General Ulysses S. Grant at his Cold Harbor headquarters (June 1864).
*National Portrait Gallery, Smithsonian Institution*

not cockily for Brady's cameras, and for history. No sense permeates any of these photographs of the sickening and, as Grant admitted, pointless loss of life that they had so recently caused or witnessed, or both.[17]

As Brady moved quickly among the various field headquarters of the major commanders in the vicinity of Cold Harbor, one general with whom he loitered a bit was Ambrose Burnside. He took four images of Burnside—more than of any other general but Grant—in two of which he himself appeared. Brady's men had photographed Colonel Burnside with his soldiers before the war began, when he was encamped with the First Rhode Island Volunteers in the District of Columbia, and he posed alone for at least two Brady studio photographs, one as a brigadier general and one as a major general. Brady would undoubtedly have seen him at First Bull Run, and again in the weeks after Antietam, and yet again at Tom Thumb's gala wedding in New York, after Burnside had been demoted from the job that General Meade now had.

When Brady photographed him here, after Cold Harbor, Burnside was commander of the Ninth Corps under Meade. In one photograph Burnside stands alone in front of his tent in the Napoleonic pose, right hand inside his tunic, left hand steadying him on a camp chair for the five or ten seconds of the exposure. Brady also photographed the general seated in the chair in a clearing, twenty members of his staff arrayed around him. Evidence exists in the photograph that Brady himself was posing this large group of men. The camera operator began the exposure before Brady could get out of the way, because about two thirds of his body appears at the far left edge of the plate, a half-exposed picture of him facing the camera, clearly an effect that was unintentional. In another photograph, Brady sits, arms crossed, watching in a companionable way as Burnside reads the *Washington Daily Morning Chronicle*. But the general later wrote that after "Mr. Brady had finished with us and I sat down on a sack of oats to read a paper some one had handed me," Brady had "without my knowledge . . . told the operator to take us. He came and sat down in the group." The general's words make it possible to see the photograph in a different way, with Burnside seeming believably oblivious to Brady and the camera's presence. As in so many other photographs in which he puts himself, Brady is not looking at the camera but is turned half away from it, urging the viewer to look over his shoulder and focus on the subject of the photograph, General Burnside at his ease.[18]

Brady's other portraits during these two days were characteristically heroic, none more so than the Napoleonic photo of Burnside alone before his tent. Perhaps Brady was only showing that there were two sides to this by now very famous man, and Brady's own presence was meant to personalize the scene, and humanize the general, who is after all sitting on a sack of oats in the pose of a morning rider on an omnibus rattling down Broadway. Brady was never naïve about any chance to market the Brady brand, but he also genuinely enjoyed his proximity to the famous, and it is possible to imagine him wanting this image for his own private photo album. *Yes, young man,* he might say decades later to a nephew, *I once knew the great Burnside. Here I am with him as he reads the* Daily Chronicle.

CHAPTER 15

# *"The Ball Has Opened"*

G rant covertly withdrew his army from Cold Harbor on June 12,
and once again tried to slip around Lee and take Richmond.
Brady and his men followed the main part of the Army of the
Potomac south and east to Weyanoke Point, where several Union corps
took three days to cross the James River on a pontoon bridge in the
middle of June 1864. On June 15 they took ten photographs of the bridge
and the troops crossing it with their support wagons, shooting from
both sides of the river. Then they followed the army to the outskirts of
Petersburg. Gardner's men Timothy O'Sullivan and James Gardner
took photos at Weyanoke Point on the same day, and all the photographers, who were competitors but also colleagues and even friends, apparently traveled together to Petersburg.

They hauled out their cameras, typically, after the initial Union
assault (June 15 to 18) had ended, a larger Union force once again hesi-
tating to take the advantage, and thus failing to win a decisive battle
that could have ended the war sooner. The Union infantry had managed to push the Confederates back toward Petersburg from a lightly
manned ten-mile line of earthworks, entrenchments, and artillery batteries stretching north to south several miles east and south of the city.
Union artillery occupied this defense, called the Dimmock Line, and
when the infantry did not press their advantage soon enough, General
Lee was able to reinforce his troops at Petersburg, setting up the months-
long trench stalemate that followed.

Brady and his cameramen and O'Sullivan, perhaps assisted by

James Gardner, began taking photographs along the Dimmock Line on the morning of June 20, starting at its northernmost point and working south. Their first pictures were, oddly, of the hanging of a black Union soldier who had been convicted by a military court of attempting to assault a white woman at New Kent Court House earlier in June. When permission to hang him finally came through, Union officers curiously chose to build the gallows at a place in full view of the Confederate lines, and the Confederates shelled the position just before the soldier, William Johnson, was brought to the scene to be hanged. For the first photograph taken of the gallows, a Brady operator set the camera well back, behind a large group of mounted and standing Union witnesses who themselves had been moved out of harm's way. As the prisoner was being readied to meet his fate, the shelling stopped long enough for the Brady men and O'Sullivan to move their cameras closer to record the execution itself. But just as Johnson swung, a Confederate shell crashed in, hitting an observer, Sgt. Maj. George F. Polley of the Tenth Massachusetts Infantry. The Tenth's term of enlistment had ended the day before, and Polley and his men were preparing to go home at the time of the hanging, making this unfortunate soldier— the highest- ranking enlisted man in his unit—the regiment's last wartime death.[1]

The Brady team recorded at least four more photographs in the vicinity of the gallows. One was of Union generals Russell, Martindale, and Neill standing before Neill's tent, probably taken an hour or so before the execution, and the other three were taken immediately afterward, of a Union artillery unit located two hundred yards to the north. The fortified battery where the Union guns were now positioned had been captured from the Rebels five days earlier; it was located about three miles from the city of Petersburg and about a mile behind the established Union line. Brady's men and O'Sullivan each took three photographs of the battery at this time, and Brady himself appears in two of his photographs. The morning's work established a pattern as his cameras moved down the Dimmock Line during the rest of June 20 and the following day: almost all the pictures were of either generals, mostly with their staffs, or of artillery batteries, often with Brady himself unobtrusively standing among the artillerymen in the photograph and gazing in the direction of the enemy lines.[2]

William Frassanito writes in *Grant and Lee* about an image made farther south, at another captured Rebel battery later on June 20, where Brady again poses, hands in pockets, this time with members of the Twelfth New York Artillery Battery. The photograph, he points out, is clearly staged. For one thing, an officer stands heroically in front of the guns, which would have been inadvisable during an actual artillery exchange, and the men loading the cannon are motionless, as they of course would not be under fire. Frassanito makes the same sort of point with each of the photographs in which Brady appears, pointing out how relaxed everyone seems; noting the likelihood that "with such a prestigious guest as Mathew Brady calmly posing next to one of the guns," no photograph would have been allowed during the "heat of action"; and supposing that, for Brady, "a middle-aged civilian" who "was not a combat hero . . . it defies common sense to assume that he would risk his own life to see that any given photograph be taken."[3]

Although the images make evident that Brady was never under fire during this series of photographs, a persistent myth says that he was. This misinformation can be traced to *The Photographic History of the Civil War*, a ten-volume compendium published for the fiftieth anniversary of the war, edited by Francis Trevelyan Miller, with essays by "Special Authorities," as the title page puts it. One story in these volumes, often retold by later writers, is that when Brady set up a certain photograph with a Union artillery battery, it "provoked fire of the Confederates, who supposed that the running forward of the artillerists was with hostile intent," and that "the Confederate guns frightened Brady's horse which ran off with his wagon and his assistant, upsetting and destroying his chemicals." No evidence of this exists.

*The Photographic History* would have the reader believe that Brady's intrepidness in many battles (that he was in reality never near) led to a number of photographs that they attribute to him (and which in reality neither he nor any of his employees took). Several times in the book it refers to him as being under fire during these June 20–21 artillery photos, as in one caption that reads, "Shells were flying about the entrenchments before Petersburg at the time the photograph above was taken . . . but so inured to this war-music have the veterans become that only one or two of them to the right are squatting or lying down. The calmness is shared even by Brady, the indomitable little photographer."[4]

One image, of the Eleventh Massachusetts Battery, taken late in the day on June 21, only a half mile from the Confederate line and a mile from Petersburg itself, suggests a possible exception to the rule that Brady was not under fire or about to be. Here again the artillery-men are clearly posing, but the camera has been taken off its tripod and put on or near the ground, presumably so the photographer could already be prone if shells started to come his way. A hat that looks like Brady's straw boater shows in the left of the photograph, but the person beneath the hat is obscured by an officer standing behind him. If this is Brady, it is as close as the photographer had knowingly put himself in danger since First Bull Run. By the end of the second day, Brady had stood with so many artillery units that he was perhaps used to potential danger, and for this particular photo he was undoubtedly as prepared as his cameraman to get out of the way if the Rebel cannon sounded.[5]

These images do not seem to have a larger artistic intent, or any purpose other than to say *I was there.* Being able to show this had promotional value, certainly, not only suggesting that Brady might deserve the overblown heroic terms that Miller's volumes would years later apply to him, but also saying, as the Gettysburg photographs had, that he was there *for* the viewer, that they could trust this photograph because it is indisputably a Brady. This would distinguish his work at the time from that of Alexander Gardner, with whom he was still competing, because Gardner did not go back into the field after his second trip to Gettysburg, in November 1863, until a few days after Union troops occupied Richmond in April 1865. If Brady was not the figure the Miller work makes him out to be, if *intrepid* is too strong a word to apply to him, still there was a pluckiness about him, a willingness to leave the relative comfort and safety of the city behind, and a need to see for himself. If Brady did feel proud of these qualities, proud enough to put them on display in his own photographs, who can begrudge him that pride?

Perhaps Brady's southward movement along the Dimmock Line had as one of its goals photographing the last of Meade's corps commanders, Maj. Gen. Gouverneur K. Warren, a hero of Gettysburg who now commanded the Fifth Corps, which was positioned at the southernmost end of the line. Warren had moved out earlier than the other corps commanders at Cold Harbor, so photographing him with his staff, as Brady did when he found him on the morning of June 21, completed his documentation of the senior officers of the Army of the

Potomac. The image seems hurriedly posed, with members of the staff looking every which way, but in the afternoon Brady would take one of his most carefully composed photographs, the one of Gen. Robert B. Potter, a division commander in Burnside's Ninth Corps, with his staff. Potter had already been wounded twice while serving under Burnside, at New Bern and Antietam, and he would be wounded again in the last days of the Petersburg campaign. This is the photograph in which Brady positions himself at the extreme right, leaning against a pine tree, his face exposed to the camera as it rarely was.[6]

That same afternoon, President Lincoln and General Grant were inspecting other Union troops facing Petersburg, including African American soldiers who had captured a number of Rebel guns. The president, accompanied by his son Tad among others, had ridden the steamer *Baltimore* for sixteen hours, beginning the evening before in the Washington Navy Yard, arriving at noon at City Point on the James River, where Grant's headquarters had been established. The president admitted to the effects of seasickness from his overnight journey on the Chesapeake Bay, but after wittily declining a well-meant glass of champagne to settle his stomach, he lunched with General Grant and felt well enough to ride on horseback with him the ten miles to the Union line.

Gen. Horace Porter, who wrote an engaging memoir of his years with Grant, rode along, noting that the president "wore a very high silk black hat and black trousers and frockcoat," which by the time he reached the troops had become so dusty that "the black color of his clothes had changed to Confederate gray." Not only that, but "his trousers gradually worked up above his ankles, and gave him the appearance of a country farmer riding into town wearing his Sunday clothes." But the troops apparently ignored Lincoln's hayseed appearance and cheered him as he passed by, and when he reached the black troops, according to Porter, "They crowded about him and fondled his horse; some of them kissed his hands, while others ran off crying in triumph to their comrades that they had touched his clothes." Lincoln passed through these troops with his hat doffed, fighting tears, and "his voice was so broken by emotion that he could scarcely articulate the words of thanks and congratulation which he tried to speak."[7]

It's puzzling that Brady could have missed this scene and the rest of the president's visit, especially since the news of Lincoln's presence was said to have spread rapidly down the line, as did the cheers for the ungainly commander in chief. Lincoln slept on the *Baltimore* that night, as it was docked at City Point, and the next day steamed farther up the James River to inspect the battlements, eventually turning around and arriving back in Washington, "sunburnt and fagged but still refreshed and cheered" from his visit with Grant's Army, according to John Hay. Brady's men would soon be training their cameras on Gen. Grant at City Point, and Brady himself would at almost the same time be heading back to Washington or New York, but there is no evidence, pictorial or otherwise, that the president and the cameraman crossed paths.[8]

Brady did not return to the front again before the fighting stopped in Virginia. But in the last months of the war, Brady's operators and those who had once worked for him were almost everywhere that the pictures we have of those months were being taken. After his men—presumably two or more of Brady's registered assistants, Woodbury, Berger, and Denney—photographed Grant at City Point in late June or early July of 1864, they also made images of two of his commanders, generals whose careers were going in opposite directions. In July they took a number of photos near City Point of the Union cavalry commander Gen. Philip Sheridan, who would soon depart to fight with some success against Gen. Jubal Early in the Shenandoah Valley. At about the same time, just upriver at Bermuda Hundred, they also photographed Gen. Benjamin Butler, who had not performed well under Grant and would be dismissed early in 1865 in spite of his political connections to President Lincoln. Brady's men then continued to photograph scenes along the James River, including military vessels, well into the autumn of 1864, as the Petersburg siege continued, making some seventy-six photographs before leaving the field in late November.

Thomas C. Roche, who was an Anthony man first and last—he had worked for the brothers early in the war and had a decades-long career with them after it ended, during which he took thousands of photographs of the West and was responsible for several photographic inventions—also worked for Brady for a time. But he left Brady in the middle of 1864, and by the spring of 1865, as the final battle of Petersburg took place, he was back working for the Anthonys and for Gen.

Montgomery C. Meigs, now the Union's quartermaster general. According to a spirited 1882 account by A. J. Russell, he and Roche were chatting in Russell's quarters at City Point late one night when "the heavy boom of cannons [was] heard in the direction of Petersburg." Earlier in the evening, according to Russell, Roche had predicted that "the army is sure to move to-night," and was getting his affairs in order so he could cover what he believed could be the last great assault of the war. When the cannons began to fire, Roche "jumped to his feet, and rushing to the door said, 'Cap., the ball has opened; I must be off,'" and within fifteen minutes he and his assistant had packed their wagon and headed for the front lines.[9]

After the federal assault, Lee withdrew from Petersburg on the night of April 2, and the next day, Roche and his assistant took twenty-two photos of dead Confederate soldiers at Fort Mahone in the wet and muddy trenches where they had been killed less than twenty-four hours before. Over the next two days they took nearly thirty more stereographs of the Rebel fort and the Union's Fort Sedgwick. But it is the images of the dead Rebels that are the most memorable. Perhaps because the soldiers were so newly dead and had not been moved in preparation for burial, the Fort Mahone photos are among the most powerful of the war, the bodies sprawled as they could only be in violent death, their wounds and spilled blood all too visible, many of the men dying without shoes or boots, dramatizing just how ill-equipped the Confederate army was at war's end. The fact that Lee's surrender came only a week later makes these deaths among the war's last, adding to the pathos of the images.

George N. Barnard, who had worked for Brady from 1860 to 1862, took a break from covering the war until late in 1863, when he went to work for the topographic branch of the Union Army of the Cumberland. For the next year, Barnard followed William Tecumseh Sherman's campaign from Tennessee to Atlanta and beyond, taking, as the subtitle of an 1866 book of his photographs put it, "Scenes of the Occupation of Nashville, the Great Battles around Chattanooga and Lookout Mountain, the Campaign of Atlanta, March to the Sea, and the Great Raid Through the Carolinas." Of these scenes, his most well known are those taken at Atlanta in the fall of 1864, including many images of Confederate defenses around the city. General Sherman, who was photographed with his staff by Barnard, never mentions him in his *Memoirs*, but Henry Hitchcock, a major on Sherman's staff, did remember Barnard on a particular day in December 1864, when together they visited a stockade that had kept Union prisoners near Millen, Georgia. The prisoners had been moved by the time they arrived, but within the confines of the prison pen were hundreds of graves and no sign of shelter or water anywhere. Hitchcock quotes Barnard that evening as contrasting what he had been seeing on Sherman's march with what he had observed that day: "I used to be very much troubled with the burning of houses, etc., but after what I have seen I shall not be much troubled about it."[10]

General Meigs also employed Jacob Coonley, the colleague of Barnard's who had worked with him for the Anthonys and then in 1861 and 1862 at the Brady Washington studio. In 1864, Meigs hired Coonley to photograph railroads in Tennessee and Alabama, the circumstances of which Coonley remembered in a 1907 article:

> This work called for a negative 9 × 13 inches, and Messrs. Anthony & Co. contracted to take all the stereoscopic negatives I could make on the trip at five dollars each. On arriving at Nashville the military authorities had a box-car equipped for my work, and this, with an engine, was placed at my disposal with authority to go over the territory. The work had many interruptions, owing to the destruction of bridges or being chased by cavalry or similar causes.[11]

Another former Brady man who was making pictures late in the war was William R. Pywell, who took six photographs of Vicksburg in February of 1864. And of course there were other former Brady photographers still working for Alexander Gardner, including his brother, James, and O'Sullivan, who at the end of 1864 photographed the federal attacks on Fort Fisher, near Wilmington, North Carolina. O'Sullivan returned to Virginia soon after the war ended, first to take a handful of photographs of Appomattox more than two weeks after the surrender and then to document the Petersburg area in May, making about two hundred images.[12]

Alexander Gardner himself left his studio as soon as Richmond and Petersburg fell, arriving three days after the Union troops entered the city. A variety of photographers took about three hundred photographs of the Confederate capital in the first two weeks after the fall, and Gardner took about fifty of these. If it's surprising that so much attention was given to the empty city, while no photographer followed Grant in the last few days of the war or was at Appomattox on April 9, Frassanito argues persuasively that "the fallen city of Richmond, the goal of four long years of fighting," was "now a tangible, completely accessible symbol of the Confederacy's death." Still, the burned-out ruins of Richmond were not going anywhere anytime soon, and it is hard not to regret the loss to history of any photograph of Lee and Grant on the day of the formal surrender.[13]

Gardner or his assistant, John Reekie (another former Brady employee), were in Richmond from April 6 to April 15, with Gardner taking photographs during the first half of that period and Reekie taking another fifty or so images during the second. At about the same time, Egbert Guy Fowx, yet another former Brady operator who also worked for Gardner but then for much of the war for A. J. Russell, was also making photographs in Richmond for the Anthonys, as was Thomas C. Roche. The best-known photographs of the city in this period are those of the area near the river where the retreating Confederates set fire to warehouses containing war supplies, a fire spread by the wind and abetted by looting arsonists, which consumed other commercial warehouses and factories nearby and the state armory, leveled by exploding shells and gunpowder. Nearby businesses, hotels, and homes were also destroyed in the inferno. The ruins of these buildings dramatized the price of defeat, and both Gardner and Brady, when he arrived in Richmond on April 12, were drawn to such scenes. But much of Richmond remained intact, and both photographers also took many photographs of the undamaged portions of the city, including the Virginia Capitol.

When he spoke about his career to the journalist George Alfred Townsend more than a quarter of a century after the war's end, perhaps Brady was remembering all these former operators of his when he said, "I had men in all parts of the army, like a rich newspaper." Like so much else in this interview, the implication that he employed all these men at once distorted the truth. But he can be forgiven for thinking of them so many years later as *his* men, and for remembering that, together, he and they *had* covered the war, far and wide.

\* \* \*

The last chapter of Brady's own war coverage feels very much in keeping with his whole career up until that time. As he had at Gettysburg, Brady got to Richmond some days after the main event. Perhaps he had been in New York when the news of Richmond's fall reached him, and perhaps he did not realize its significance until Lee surrendered. Whatever motivated him to go, Brady approached Richmond by way of City Point, which he reached on or before April 12, presumably by boat. Brady's timing could not have been better, because Grant and his staff were also there on the twelfth, having returned from Appomattox "after midnight," according to Grant's *Personal Memoirs*, and "As soon as possible I took a dispatch-boat to Washington City." Brady managed to take two photographs of Grant with members of his staff during these few hours—a general who appeared in one of the photos wrote in his diary that the picture was taken sometime between two and four P.M. A third photograph taken at about the same hour shows Brady himself posing with eleven members of Grant's staff. Although he positions himself to the extreme left of the camera, he is facing it, and wearing a tall, Lincolnesque top hat, which he would be wearing again in Richmond sometime in the next few days.[14]

Brady then went directly to the late Confederate capital, where he and his men took some sixty more photographs, none as important as the ones he made on his final day there, April 16. General Lee had stayed on at Appomattox until April 12, not leaving until the last of his troops had given up their arms and been paroled. Even then, Lee did not race home, but along the way spent one final evening with General Longstreet, at his camp, and another night at his brother's farm in Buckingham County. When Lee finally reached Richmond on the afternoon of April 15, he rode through the streets on his beloved horse, Traveller, while, as Douglas Southall Freeman puts it in his biography, "Along a ride of less than a mile to the residence at 707 East Franklin Street the crowd grew thicker with each block. Cheers broke out, in which the Federals joined heartily."[15]

Brady got wind of Lee's return and asked Col. Robert Ould to appeal to the general to have his photograph taken. Ould, who had been a district attorney in Washington before the war and was the chief Confederate officer in charge of prisoner exchange during it, had, because of this position, been given something like diplomatic immunity by Grant, who excused him from the general surrender and offered him safe passage to Richmond from Appomattox. Brady said in the Townsend interview, "Still Taking Pictures," that both Ould and Mrs. Lee had helped him persuade the general to submit to the camera, although, as Brady put it, "It was supposed that after his defeat it would be preposterous to ask him to sit." But, Brady continued, "I thought that to be the time for the historical picture." Apparently Lee, or perhaps Mrs. Lee, agreed, because it was arranged that Brady could come to the house and make his pictures. The next day, Easter Sunday, Brady took six photographs in all, four of Lee alone and two of him with his aide, Col. Walter Taylor, and his oldest son, Maj. Gen. Custis Lee, who had been captured only three days before the surrender. The photographs were made under the back porch, on the basement level of the house, because the light was better there.

Lee's youngest son, Rob, would write years later of his father that "I believe there were none of the little things in life so irksome to him as having his picture taken in any way." But Lee himself had a fine sense of history. For instance, he donned his best uniform and a dark red silk sash—Grant says in his memoirs that "General Lee was dressed in a full uniform which was entirely new, and was wearing a sword of considerable value"—for the day of his surrender. However much Lee disliked posing, on this Sunday morning he once again donned his best uniform and wore well-shined black shoes, but left aside the sash and the sword and the boots. Lee was also acutely aware of his own power to set an example for the South. Grant wrote in his memoirs that at Appomattox he "suggested to General Lee that there was not a man in the Confederacy whose influence with the soldiery and the whole people was as great as his." In the wake of Lincoln's death the day before, and the charges that the South was responsible, Lee might also have chosen to pose in the domestic setting of his home—a leader still in his uniform, but sans sash, sans sword, sans boots, visibly morphing into a civilian—as a symbol of stability and responsibility in very dangerous and uncertain hours.[16]

Lee was already a beloved figure, and not only in the South, as those applauding Union soldiers on the streets of Richmond attest. But these photographs—in which the physically and morally exhausted general, grizzled at age fifty-eight—summons the strength of his unusual personal dignity for Brady's camera, showing no trace of the humiliation of defeat but only a self-possessed seriousness, gave the

South a hero to cling to in the those dark days after the war, and for decades to come. "The people of Virginia and of the entire South were continually giving evidence of their intense love for General Lee," Rob Lee wrote. "From all nations, even from the Northern States, came to him marks of admiration and respect."[17]

As Brady's photographs of Lee were widely distributed—Brady said later he sold them by the thousands—even Mrs. Lee kept a store on hand for the many people who appealed to her for signed photographs of her husband. Rob Lee quotes a November 1865 letter from his father, then living in Lexington, Virginia, where he had taken up the presidency of Washington College, to his mother, who had not yet joined him there, saying that he had dutifully signed and returned a batch of photographs she had sent to him for that purpose.[18]

Who but Brady could have pulled off this photographic and journalistic coup? He said he had known Lee "since the Mexican war when he was upon Gen. Scott's staff," so "my request was not as from an intruder." Brady had also quite likely met Lee in the 1850s, when the future general was superintendent of West Point. Brady had clearly known Robert Ould in Washington. And of course he had taken portraits of every American general who had mattered at all, including many who had served with Lee in the U.S. Army before the Civil War. Finally there was Brady's own reputation as a portraitist, upon which General Lee could rely. The general chose well, because these images match their subject for dignity and seriousness, for a rich sense of the suffering Lee had overcome to place himself before the camera, and for a firm eye on the historical importance of what showed upside down as Brady or his operator peered through the lens in his last act as a wartime photographer.[19]

# CHAPTER 16

# "A Photographic Pantheon"

Mathew Brady's final journey into the field, when he photographed both Grant and Lee so soon after Appomattox, was also the last high peak of his long career. The descent after April of 1865 would not be precipitate, and there would be lesser peaks in his future—he would again photograph Lee, and Grant as president. And as the years passed, Brady would continue to make portraits of each new president and First Lady, and other important Americans, perhaps most notably Mark Twain and Walt Whitman. He would also photograph many official delegations to Washington, both on assignment for various parts of the federal bureaucracy and in his own gallery. But his fame, and the power of his fame to get him access to the most significant subjects, began to decline after the war.

Men he had hired and helped to train—Alexander Gardner, Timothy O'Sullivan, Thomas C. Roche, and Stanley J. Morrow—covered the next great subject in American photography, the West (as did one other accomplished Civil War photographer, A. J. Russell, who took the famous picture of the trains meeting at Promontory, Utah, at the completion of the transcontinental railroad in 1869). The onetime Brady men were among the West's most important photographic chroniclers. But there's no evidence that Brady himself ever went farther west than Warrenton, Virginia, and although he would work in the photography business for three decades following the Civil War, he would never take or commission a photograph of the Far West. The closest he would come was photographing delegations of visiting American Indians and their leaders, such as the Sioux chief Red Cloud.[1]

The assassination of Lincoln while Brady was in Richmond must have stunned him as much as it did every other American, north and south, and perhaps Brady more than most, given his own connection to the president and his family. In addition to his portraits of Lincoln, Brady's studio had photographed Mrs. Lincoln in her inauguration ball gown in 1861 and in mourning black after the death of Willie in 1862. Two Lincoln sons, Willie and Tad, had also been photographed at the Washington gallery. And at times when he himself was in Washington during the Lincoln administration, Brady attended the New York Avenue Presbyterian Church, where the Lincoln family worshipped, and whose pastor, Phineas D. Gurley, preached in the White House at young Willie's funeral and President Lincoln's.[2]

Lincoln's death led to more work for Brady, both directly and indirectly. As bells tolled and guns fired on April 19, he or someone from his studio took at least two photographs of the procession down Pennsylvania Avenue accompanying Lincoln's body from the funeral in the White House to the Capitol, where it lay in state. On the twenty-fifth, after Lincoln had lain in state again in New York's City Hall, Brady took a photograph as a horse-drawn funeral car bore the casket to the Hudson River Railroad Depot on Thirty-fourth Street. *Harper's Weekly* called the procession "the largest that had ever thronged the streets of the great metropolis." Eleven thousand soldiers and seventy-five thousand civilians marched. The photo was the basis for a woodcut in *Harper's Weekly* that filled a two-page spread on May 13. The cover of the same paper the week before had copied the photograph of Lincoln reading to Tad taken at Brady's the previous year. Brady's men also photographed the interior and presidential box at Ford's Theatre, pictures the Anthonys sold as part of the deluge of Lincoln memorabilia that followed the president's death.[3]

The day Lincoln died, John B. Bachelder, a painter and lithographer who had followed the Army of the Potomac, making sketches for his paintings, went to Washington with the idea of commissioning a work that would commemorate the assassination, which he would then have engraved and offer for sale. His idea was for a fictionalized representation of Lincoln's deathbed scene, including in the picture everyone who had visited the wounded president in the last hours of his life, from the time he was moved across Tenth Street from Ford's Theatre to the Petersen residence at No. 516, until he died there at 7:22 the next morning. Never mind that the actual room in which Lincoln spent his last hours would have held only a fraction of the forty-seven people included in the work, which was about half the total number of visitors that long night.[4]

Bachelder produced a sketch positioning everyone in this crowd and then asked Brady to photograph each person in the pose called for in the sketch. Bachelder also made the initial contact with each of the sitters and scheduled them at Brady's Pennsylvania Avenue studio, asking them to wear the same clothes they had worn when visiting the dying president. The photographic work began soon after Lincoln's funeral train left Washington on April 21. Among those included in the painting was Mrs. Lincoln, shown with her back to the viewer, kneeling in prayer and grief at the bedside. Bachelder undoubtedly sketched her into the composition in this way because she could not have been expected to pose for Brady's camera so soon after the assassination. But Robert Lincoln did pose, standing with head bowed, holding a white handkerchief to his chest, an effect that pushed the legitimate pathos of the young man's grief into bathos. President Andrew Johnson also appeared at Brady's studio to be photographed, as a May 2 letter from his secretary promised he would. The new president was posed sitting, but cabinet secretaries including Welles and Stanton stood for Brady, as did Senator Sumner and Generals Halleck and Meigs. John Hay, who was probably as close to Lincoln as anyone besides members of the family, and who had been at Ford's Theatre when Lincoln was shot, also posed, as did Maj. Henry Rathbone and his fiancée, Clara Harris, who had been in the box with Lincoln when John Wilkes Booth fired.

According to promotional material for the final engraving, those who posed "all cheerfully gave their time for frequent sittings." The promotion did not appear until four years after Lincoln's death, but *cheerfully* nevertheless seems an odd word in this context. Mary Panzer, in *Mathew Brady and the Image of History*, sees the portraits that Brady took "as records of men and women in the act of mourning before a camera. They are also portraits of the nation's leaders performing their public roles." These leaders did their jobs in much the same spirit, then, as Lee did his in posing for Brady—and just as cheerfully.[5]

Bachelder picked Alonzo Chappel, a prolific painter of historical portraits and scenes, to execute the work. Not only were his paintings often made into engravings, but he had also frequently used Brady photographs in the sort of artistic collaboration that Brady had long envisioned for photography. Once Brady's photographs were completed, Bachelder gave the prints and his sketch to Chappel, who took until 1868 to complete two versions of the scene. Panzer writes, justly, that "Today, Chappel's picture of a dying man in a crowded room arouses no emotion," but there is "much to admire in the elaborate documents that Brady helped Bachelder assemble," photographs that "now carry a poignant charge." Eleven of these photographs, which were praised at the time for their accuracy and historical value, were printed for use in subscription books through which the engraving would be sold. But in the end no engravings were ever approved for sale, and the project was a bust, although one print of a rejected engraving survived, and has often been copied since.

Brady also had indirect connections to the assassin. His Broadway location facilitated his interest in photographing the famous actors of his day, and in about 1850 he took a daguerreotype of Junius Brutus Booth, the father of John Wilkes Booth and his two acting brothers, Edwin and Junius Jr. Junius père, who was born in England and became one of the leading actors of his time, began performing Shakespeare in America in 1821, and died in 1852 on a Mississippi riverboat after drinking contaminated water. In 1864, Brady also photographed Edwin, himself a celebrated Shakespearean actor. One of Brady's operators photographed John Wilkes Booth in the Washington studio in 1862. Given the popularity of the Booths in Washington and New York, it seems likely that Brady would have seen all four of them perform, perhaps many times.

Brady's last connection to the assassination was photographing Boston Corbett, the sergeant in the Sixteenth New York Cavalry who shot Booth on April 26, and his lieutenant, Edward P. Doherty, who had led the detachment that found Booth in the barn near Port Royal, Virginia, where he was hiding. Brady took at least five images of Corbett alone, one of Doherty alone, and another of the two standing together. Because Doherty gave Corbett full credit as Lincoln's avenger, reproductions of the photographs sold well. Corbett himself would say some years later that Brady printed thousands of copies of his image but that he himself got only a few of them in payment for posing.[6]

The photographic coverage of the assassination's aftermath suggests the extent to which Brady's preeminence had begun to slip. Both Brady and Gardner took early photographs of President Johnson, but it was Gardner's photo that *Harper's Weekly* used for its cover of May 13. Like Brady, Gardner rushed to get pictures of Ford's Theatre, inside and out, and also images of the livery stable where Booth had kept the horse on which he escaped and the telegraph office where the first word of Lincoln's death went out to the nation. The Secret Service asked Gardner's studio to make copy prints of the three principal uncaptured suspects, including the Brady studio image of Booth, which were then pasted onto wanted posters.[7]

Once Booth was killed, Gardner, with Timothy O'Sullivan assisting, was allowed to witness the assassin's autopsy aboard the ironclad *Montauk*, which was docked at the Navy Yard, and to take a photograph of the body with the stipulation that only one print of it could be made. Many years later a retired policeman in Virginia, who said he had been a detective for the War Department at the time, claimed to have accompanied the two photographers and a black man to the Navy Yard to make the picture and had then gone with O'Sullivan back to the studio and even into the darkroom so that he could be sure that no other prints of the image were made. The detective, James A. Wardell, then claims to have taken both the glass-plate negative and the print to Col. Lafayette C. Baker at the War Department. Neither the negative nor the print was ever seen again, presumably because the War Department believed an image of Booth's body could make him a bigger martyr in the South than he already was. One regional army department even tried to suppress within its jurisdiction "the sale of portraits of any rebel officer or soldier, or of J. Wilkes Booth," but the order was pretty quickly reversed.[8]

After the autopsy photo was made and the negative taken away, Gardner was then permitted to photograph David E. Herold, one of the conspirators on the wanted poster with Booth, who had met up with Booth after the assassination and was captured in the barn where Booth was shot. Herold was being held on the *Montauk*, as was Lewis Powell, known at the time as Lewis Paine or Payne, whom Herold had led on the night of April 14 to William Seward's house on Lafayette Square, where Powell stabbed Secretary of State Seward repeatedly but did not manage to assassinate him. Gardner took a number of photographs of the romantic-looking Powell there and on another monitor docked at the Navy Yard, the *Saugus*. Gardner was also allowed to photograph other conspirators or suspects held on the *Saugus*.[9]

But Gardner's biggest coup was the exclusive commission to photograph the execution on July 7 of Powell, Herold, Mary Surratt, and George Atzerodt in the yard of the Old Penitentiary Building at the Washington Arsenal, now Fort McNair. Gardner also photographed the members of the military commission that tried and convicted the four conspirators, including Maj. Gen. David Hunter, the president of the commission, who issued Gardner a pass on July 5. The day of the hangings was unusually hot. Late that morning, Gardner and Timothy O'Sullivan made their way through a traffic jam on 4½ Street— the *New York Times* reported that by "about 10 o'clock, the streets and avenues were blocked by hundreds of vehicles and perhaps 2,000 lookers-on"—leading to the Arsenal grounds. They set up an eight-by-ten camera in one window and a stereo camera in a second window on the top floor of the old prison workshop building, which had a clear view of the gallows.[10]

There they took a series of photographs, beginning before the conspirators were brought to the scene. Other photos in the series caught the four once they mounted the gallows; after they stepped forward onto the platforms that would drop from under them; as the sentence was read; as the nooses and hoods were placed; just after the bodies had fallen; and several minutes later, once they all had died and, as the *New York Herald* put it, their "bodies hung straight and motionless as plumb lines." One photo even captured a soldier standing below the gallows, where he was about to push aside the post that would release the drop, as he vomited onto the ground, overcome by heat and the emotional stress of the moment. Awaiting her death some eight feet above the soldier was Mrs. Surratt, at whose boarding house the conspiracy had taken place, about to be the first woman ever executed in the United States. The photographs are a remarkable record of a moment of national catharsis, its brutality and finality a punctuation mark not only to the assassination, but also to the long war that preceded it.[11]

The historian in Brady would have jumped at the chance to take these photographs, so it is unimaginable that he could have been offered the job and turned it down. Still, the subject seems more suitable to Gardner and O'Sullivan. They were the ones who had sought out the bodies during the Civil War, who were drawn to the drama of the slaughter, whereas Brady had held back. His interests were generally more commemorative or documentary than journalistic. It's also worth noting that, several years after the hanging, one of the men on the original wanted poster, Mary Surratt's son John Harrison Surratt— who had fled the country after the assassination and, among other things, served as a Papal Zouave in Rome—would appear in Brady's studio to have his photograph made, both in Zouave regalia and in regular dress. Surratt was a controversial figure, much despised in the North, especially by the newspapers; he had been captured in Egypt late in 1866 and brought back to the United States in chains, where he was charged with a number of crimes related to the assassination. He was acquitted at one trial, and a second set of charges against him was dismissed. Surratt, the possible conspirator set free, seems an unlikely person for Brady to photograph, but both Surratts, mother and son, were partly loathed out of anti-Catholic, nativist prejudice, the sting of which would have been familiar to Brady as the son of Irish immigrants.[12]

After the Civil War, Brady's financial situation began to deteriorate. The usual explanations for his money problems begin with his own claim that he had spent more than a hundred thousand dollars covering the war. Then there is the notion that a war-weary public had lost interest in the sort of photographs he had taken, commissioned to be taken, and collected for resale, so that the expense and effort he had put into his massive collection of war images now had little or no value. The decline in his fortunes is often dated to the departure of Alexander Gardner from the Washington studio in late 1862, given Gardner's business acumen and Brady's incompetence or at least growing disinterest in running his business.

But like so much else that has been written about Brady, these explanations of his financial decline are at best simplistic. As we have seen, the Washington gallery continued to function, sending photographers out into the field for the rest of the war. His June 1864 catalogue of photographs and stereographs from the Grant campaign alone included about 165 images, with another 65 or so added later in the year.

Dozens and perhaps hundreds of military men continued to tramp up the stairs of Brady's Pennsylvania Avenue studio to have their photographs made. And the New York studio continued to be busy making portraits. The 1865 register from the Broadway studio lists more than two thousand people whose portraits were taken that year.[13]

Still, on September 7, 1864, Brady made a deal with James F. Gibson, allowing him to buy a 50 percent share of the Washington gallery for ten thousand dollars , half in cash and the rest in promissory notes. Gibson, who like Gardner was a Scot, had worked for Gardner at Brady's at the beginning of the decade, and had begun to be credited as a photographer with his images from around Manassas two years later; he went on to cover the Peninsula Campaign, photographed the crew of the *Monitor* soon after its famous battle with the *Merrimac*, and joined Gardner at Antietam. His last images for Brady's were taken in or near Fredericksburg in November of 1862. Then he left Brady to work for Gardner's new gallery, accompanying him to Gettysburg, and he was working for Gardner as late as February 1864 when he took photographs at Brandy Station in Virginia.[14]

Gibson and Gardner had formed a legal partnership briefly during the Peninsula Campaign, while both of them were still working for Brady. The terms of the partnership would be the subject of a suit that Gibson filed in January 1867 against Gardner and Gardner's publishers, Franklin Philp and Adolphus Solomons. The timing of the suit and the inclusion of the publishers in it suggest that it was predicated on the publication after the war of Gardner's *Sketch Book*, which included among its one hundred photographs thirteen images attributed jointly to Gibson and either George Barnard or John Wood. Although the *Sketch Book* featured three photographs from Antietam and ten from Gettysburg, none of the images attributed to Gibson was among them. Something had gone wrong between Gibson and Gardner, but whether the move to Brady's was itself the problem or whether a rights dispute based on the 1862 partnership caused the move, we simply don't know.[15]

Along with Gibson's half interest in Brady's Pennsylvania Avenue gallery came the responsibility of managing it. Why did Brady enter into this arrangement? Josephine Cobb of the National Archives made a study of the legal actions taken against Brady in both Washington and New York in the decade or so after the Civil War. Her conclusion is that

> Up to this time, the Washington Gallery had yielded about $12,000 annually. Since 1860, there had been an additional income of about $4,000 from the sale of negatives to Anthony and Company. But, between August 1863 and August 1864, the net profits of the Washington Gallery had dropped to $4,860 and the business with Anthony had amounted to no more than $276.[16]

These figures all come from another suit that the litigious Gibson filed, this one against Brady in 1868, and the numbers, widely quoted in subsequent writings about Brady, are merely alleged in this civil action but not proven to be true or confirmed elsewhere. Gibson was asking the court for a financial judgment against Brady, so it was in his interest to suggest that the business had been doing badly in the months before he arrived on the scene. As we know, during the period when the Washington gallery was supposedly doing so poorly, Brady had men almost continuously with Grant's army, which suggests that he could not have been too worried about his finances, and since the Washington gallery continued to operate and to be frequented by soldiers and civilians alike, it seems unlikely that there would have been a dramatic drop-off in revenue. Gardner did for a while have the primary distribution contract with the Anthonys for war photographs, so the small amount of Anthony business seems plausible. A note about Brady in the R. G. Dun & Company report book, dated August 26, 1864, says, "Is under heavy expenses & it is difficult to tell what he is really w[orth]. Had no general cr[edit] & contin[ue]s to buy." But even these reports cannot be taken as gospel, and the point is that we simply don't know what Brady's financial situation was. Another Dun report, dated March 19, 1867, says "some parties believe him wor[th] 30,000 & others do not believe him wor[th] 30 shillings." By July of that year the report says "does gd bus[iness,] credit & stdg [standing] good."[17]

A small suit by a carpenter in 1864 accused Brady of not paying him what he was owed, and as Cobb writes, "There followed a number of suits in which judgments were rendered against Brady, all arising from instances of non-payment of wages due his employees or non-payment of bills for structural alterations to the gallery, for failure to pay his rent, and to pay for photographic supplies." Gibson said in his 1868 suit that the Gardner brothers and Timothy O'Sullivan had liens against Brady for "certain portions of the apparatus and property of great value belonging to [Brady's] gallery." Gibson also said in the suit that he had urged Brady to pay his bills, but Brady had ignored him. But Brady had always been slow to pay his bills, and as manager and part owner of the Washington gallery, the responsibility to keep up with the Washington finances might well have been Gibson's.

In July of 1865, the *New York Times* reported a list of people who were staying in hotels for the whole season at Saratoga Springs, New York, including "M. B. Brady and family," presumably meaning a party bigger than just Brady and Julia, who were childless. Others on the *Times* list included the department store owner "A. T. Stewart, wife and servant," the governors of Pennsylvania and Vermont, and a slew of judges and doctors. If Brady was already on the road to bankruptcy, he was going to arrive there in style.[18]

Before the court could rule on the 1868 Gibson suit, Gibson took out a mortgage on the Washington gallery and, according to a counter-suit by Brady in late June, collected what he could of what the gallery was owed and headed to Kansas. He was never heard from again. Cobb writes that in order to regain sole possession of the gallery, Brady then "consented to proceedings in bankruptcy whereby the gallery was sold at public auction in July. Brady himself was the only bidder and he was allowed by the Court to buy his business back again for $7,600." Clearly Brady was not penniless at this time, and just as clearly the court would have required him to pay off any debts or liens before emerging from bankruptcy and regaining ownership of the Washington gallery.

The Dun report following the lawsuit says of Brady's repurchase of the Washington gallery after the bankruptcy that he "now owns it entire and clear of debt." The report, dated October 31, 1868, for which Brady was probably the principal source, also says that while Brady was in Washington sorting things out, his affairs were badly managed at his Broadway gallery. The Dun report concludes that "There is no doubt but he has been badly swindled by the party he sold out to [Gibson], and his managers here [in New York]." Dun also reported that

Brady was trying to sell a piece of property he owned in New Jersey to settle his new debts from the Broadway gallery. On January 12, 1869, Julia Brady sold a lot in Manhattan at Fifth Avenue and 105th Street for thirty-four thousand dollars, a further effort to square things in New York, however temporarily.[19]

In the years after the war, then, the tides of Brady's finances rose and fell as they do for many small business owners, depending on the season or the strength of the larger economy. But the general trend after the war caused Brady to look for at least one other principal source of revenue. For the rest of his life he would try to capitalize on the photographs of the war he had taken, commissioned, and collected, and those, for a few years after the war ended, he would continue to collect, believing with good cause that they formed a historical record that was valuable to the nation and its culture, and valuable enough that he should be compensated for it. It would take him years of effort to win any sort of compensation at all, but the reasons for the delays, and for the relatively small amount he was eventually paid, had nothing to do with a lack of interest by the general public in Civil War images. And no doubt was ever raised about the historical value of the collection. Outside parties from newspaper writers to a congressional committee to a major museum to General Grant himself were unanimous in attesting to its historical importance.

As soon after the war as December 1865 it was reported at a meeting of the New-York Historical Society that Brady had contacted them about "his collection of historic portraits and views." One of the people with whom Brady had served in 1864 on the Gentlemen's Committee on the Fine Arts for the Metropolitan Fair was Abraham M. Cozzens, who appears in the photograph that Brady took of the committee. An oil merchant and patron of the arts, Cozzens was the chairman of the New-York Historical Society's Committee on the Fine Arts, which in 1862 had produced, over his signature, a remarkable statement of the historical importance of photography. Its conclusion recommended that the historical society commit itself to collecting "Not only the likeness of eminent men & women, but views of streets, houses, landscapes, processions, reviews, battles & sieges and indeed almost every thing which can be photographed."[20]

The statement's emphasis on the historical importance not only of heroes and battles, but also of the minutiae of everyday life, puts it far ahead of its time. Cozzens's report alludes to a small stereograph of Broadway on a rainy day, in which "The street is almost rattling with carriages—the side walks are bustling with people—the stones shine in the wet—the rain drips from the umbrellas," and it speculates on the historical value of the same sort of photo had the medium existed during Roman or biblical times.

The historical society's executive committee responded to Brady's overture by suggesting that a discussion be initiated with him, and as a result Brady wrote the committee a four-page letter (signed by him but not written in his hand). It formally requested that the society accept a collection of his photographs for display and preservation "within the walls of a fire-proof building, under control of so enlightened a body as the New York Historical society." In the letter, Brady alludes to the 1862 Cozzens report, which had already resulted in the historical society's acquisition of some photographs. (Even before the report, the society had begun to collect photographs, and as early as 1857 it was given two Brady images of painted miniatures of George and Martha Washington.) Brady claims in the letter that "Some of my friends, who take an interest in my art, have recently proposed to raise a sufficient sum to compensate me for the large outlay and labor of my undertaking," and so, he continues, "I neither ask or expect a single dollar from the funds of the Society, which is to be put to no expense on account of the Collection, unless it is the trifling one of hanging the important views . . ." The society responded favorably and with alacrity to Brady's offer, even calling a special meeting to consider it.[21]

One proviso in the historical society's resolution, passed on January 23, 1866, promised to "set apart a suitable room for the exclusive and permanent exhibition of the [collection] in the new building to be erected in the Central Park." The historical society was located at that time in a building it had erected on the corner of Second Avenue and Eleventh Street, not far from Brady's Tenth Street gallery, but although a site for the new building in Central Park was approved by the state legislature twice, lack of funds kept it from ever being built. Both sides had agreed that the Brady collection could be taken over by the society before the new building went up, but that did not happen, either. Brady was apparently sufficiently concerned that the delay could be permanent that he solicited testimony about the collection's importance from General Grant and Admiral David Glasgow Farragut, both of whom weighed in with declarations of the importance of the collection, as did the National Academy of Design.

Beginning in February, only days after the historical society agreed to take the photographs, Brady displayed many of them in his Broadway gallery in what he advertised as a "Grand Exhibition of an entirely new and attractive collection of War Views and Portraits of Representative Men. This collection comprises more than 3000 pictures, several hundred specimen copies of which have just been placed on exhibition." The show, presumably part of his campaign to get the society to accept his collection, ran into the month of April. Brady managed to get the *New York Times* to notice the show not once but twice during the period it was up, and the *Times* later advocated in its pages that the historical society should accept Brady's collection. But a year later, on March 29, 1867, the *Times* reported that the transfer had not occurred.[22]

Money was almost certainly the reason the deal fell through. Perhaps Brady balked because the historical society could not raise the funds for the new building. Or perhaps, upon realizing that his friends were not going to be able to raise the money promised him, Brady had turned without luck to the historical society for compensation. Or perhaps there was some realization by the historical society that its commitment had been greater than it could afford to stand behind. In March 1868, Abraham Cozzens and the oil company he ran went broke, "engulfed in the vortex of common disasters," as a court document colorfully put it. Cozzens died a week later. If he had been the force behind the effort to acquire the Brady collection, perhaps his own financial problems and declining health prevented him from pushing it to the conclusion he had envisioned. Brady himself said in an interview two decades later that the society's failure to construct the new building had been the problem.[23]

Brady's wish to see his collection preserved by the New-York Historical Society would in the long run be fulfilled, although he would never see any direct remuneration for his work. As Sandra Markham, a former archivist at the society, wrote of the society's holdings:

> In portraits alone, there are thousands of Brady images,
> from unique and early daguerreotypes and ambrotypes of

the 1840s and 1850s to salted-paper photographs of the late 1850s, and more generic "published" carte de visite and cabinet card portraits from the 1850s, 1860s, and 1870s.

In 2003 the historical society decided to attribute to Brady's New York studio a holding it had of nearly 6,000 portrait prints from the late 1850s to the late 1860s. Of these, 580 were printed from Imperial-size negatives made between 1856 and 1862, and about 5,300 are carte de visite-size prints taken between the years 1861 and 1869. "Fragile and unmounted," Markham writes, "they were 'file photographs' kept by the studio as a visual patron record and were at one time housed in albums." The collection of prints provides a cross-section of New Yorkers and of American and foreign visitors to New York who could afford to be photographed, and, as a whole, is most surprising, perhaps, because there are as many portraits of women as of men. There are also nearly eight hundred portraits of children.[24]

Brady approached Congress sometime in March of 1869, soon after Grant was inaugurated, to ask that it buy a collection of pictures similar to the one he had offered the New-York Historical Society, "but he asked such an exorbitant price that Congress took no action," according to Josephine Cobb. In 1870 he published a 139-page catalogue, *National Photographic Collection of War Views and Portraits of Representative Men*, which recycled the gist of the 1866 letter to the historical society and included the supporting letters from Grant and others, but now proposed that the collection become a permanent exhibition at the Capitol. Brady renewed his petition with Congress, and in 1871 its Joint Committee on the Library recommended the purchase of two thousand of Brady's portraits, calling his collection "the highest perfection to which the photographic art has attained . . . a photographic Pantheon, in which the votive genius of American art has perpetuated," and so forth. But Congress did not act.[25]

Finally, in 1875, at the urging of former Union general and current secretary of war William W. Belknap, and with the help of two other former generals and Brady portrait subjects, Massachusetts representative Benjamin F. Butler and Ohio representative (and future president) James A. Garfield, Congress took up the matter in a serious way. Garfield gave a speech in the House on March 3, 1875, in which he estimated the value of the collection at $150,000, but Butler slipped a paragraph into an appropriations bill authorizing Secretary Belknap to spend not more than $25,000 on the collection, which would total more than 5,700 negatives (in addition to 2,250 negatives, many in poor condition, that the War Department had recently acquired). Brady would claim late in life that Butler had expected and received half of the appropriated amount as a gratuity for his action, and given the flagrant corruption in Washington at the time (indeed, Belknap himself would resign for corruption the next year, in the Trading Post Scandal) and Butler's porcine eagerness to feed at the trough, the allegation is believable if not provable. In any case, the appropriation was, for Brady, too little too late.[26]

# CHAPTER 17

# "Familiar as Household Words"

When Brady reopened the Washington gallery after he got it back through bankruptcy, he was, according to Josephine Cobb, "forced to operate on a reduced scale, confining himself to one-half of the building," the side above Gilman's Drug Store. By 1870 Brady had sent his longtime employee Andrew Burgess to Washington to run the gallery, while he himself continued to deal with his financial problems in New York. An article by a Burgess descendant says that Andrew and his brother, William, began apprenticeships in the Brady gallery in 1855 and, five years later, became "journeymen photographers," who worked in both the New York and Washington galleries during the first years of the Civil War. At about the time that Alexander Gardner set up his own studio, William Burgess became a Mormon and moved out west. Andrew continued to work with Brady until he went to Mexico in 1864, where he operated a photography business in Mexico City until 1867. Then Andrew went back to work for Brady.[1]

Burgess apparently not only ran the Washington studio after 1870 but also invested in it, and described himself in an 1873 ad as "the successor to M. B. Brady," at a time when Brady was fighting to emerge from bankruptcy in New York. Brady closed his Washington gallery on August 27, 1873, and Burgess reopened the business two months later at the same address, still calling it the National Photographic Art Gallery, as Brady had. His business card included the words LATE BRADY & CO. Cobb implies that there was a struggle between Burgess and Brady for control of the studio, as Brady maneuvered to hold on to the business by putting it in Julia's name and then mortgaging it to her brother, Samuel Handy, and her nephew, Levin C. Handy. Levin had been learning the business in the Brady gallery since he was twelve, and was now seventeen or eighteen years old and well on his way to becoming an accomplished photographer himself.[2]

As early as 1870, Burgess had become interested in the manufacture of guns, and would eventually become a major producer and inventor of them. When he died in 1908 he had acquired nearly nine hundred patents on firearms, the first of which was issued in 1871. Sometime in the early 1870s he opened his own gun factory in Owego, New York, while still operating the Brady gallery. By late 1875, after Brady had emerged from bankruptcy and acquired the money to buy back the gallery, Burgess returned it to him and moved to Owego to manufacture guns full time.[3]

Perhaps with an eye to history, or as part of the bargain to transfer the studio to Brady, Burgess took certain things from the gallery to Owego with him, including cameras; daybooks listing the sitters, which included signatures of many famous people who sat for Brady; and three small wooden boxes containing forty-four portraits on glass wrapped in issues of one of two Washington papers, the *Daily National Intelligencer* from the year 1866 or the *Evening Star* from 1874. After Burgess's widow died in 1926, the Brady Collection, as the Burgess family called it, was left to the wife of the executor of Mrs. Burgess's estate, whose son discovered two of the boxes in his barn in 1948. The boxes, which appeared to have never been opened, included portrait negatives of President Grant; his vice president, Henry Wilson; and George Armstrong Custer, among many others. The plates were in perfect condition.[4]

Brady was taken to federal bankruptcy court in New York in 1872 and declared a bankrupt in January 1873. Nearly a hundred individuals or firms made claims against him, a third of which were for $50 or less, and two of which were for more than $1,000. The largest, $4,347.68, was owed to a Washington businessman named John Patch, who had invested in Brady's business. A number of Brady's debts were to "composing firms," or print shops, presumably those who printed both his images and his advertising materials, and to publications in which he had run advertisements. But he also owed money to the photographer A. J. Russell, employees such as Levin Handy and William Pywell, the gas company, and even his druggist, down the steps from his Washington gallery. His debt to the Anthony brothers, his closest business partners and the source of most of his photography materials, was negligible, only $219.04. (Brady had long satisfied his debts to the Anthonys by giving them negatives.) The whole debt was more than $25,000, and his total worth, including the contents of both the New York and Washington galleries, was judged to be only $12,000.[5]

Lists were drawn up of his possessions in both galleries—mostly prints, negatives, or works made from his photographs in oil, ink, or crayon—but before those in the New York gallery were seized to be sold at auction, Brady persuaded the New York City sheriff, Matthew T. Brennan, a Tammany Hall man, to take nineteen loads of them to storage. The intention was apparently to delay matters until Congress could come through with a big payment, and indeed the sale of Brady's New York possessions took place sixteen months after the June 1873 sale of the contents of his Washington gallery. But at some point before the New York auction the operator of a warehouse in New York offered for sale a set of Brady's negatives of Civil War scenes and portraits, and according to Secretary of War Belknap, "was very anxious to dispose of them." Belknap sent an agent to buy them for his department, who paid the warehouseman $2,500, not a penny of which went to Brady or his other debtors. According to a War Department report to Belknap on the condition of the 2,250 negatives, many had been packed carelessly, and by the time they ended up at the War Department about a third of the negatives had been damaged or destroyed.[6]

Belknap wrote a statement on War Department letterhead saying that on September 28, 1874, "I was accosted by Mr. M. B. Brady in the vestibule of the Fifth Avenue Hotel New York," and that Brady said "I had treated him unfairly and unkindly" by buying the negatives, "which were his property and which he intended to redeem, and expected to redeem in a short time." Belknap says in his statement that he told the photographer that he had waited before buying them, but since Brady had not bought them back himself he had asked around and learned that Brady was "utterly unable to do so." When Brady continued to complain, Belknap told him, "Mr. Brady, if you are ready to pay the amount which I paid, you can have them."[7]

Brady apparently then changed the subject, and his attitude, asking Belknap if he could help him convince Congress to buy another set of negatives in his possession, and Belknap said he would if Brady wrote him a letter "stating the facts." In the letter Brady wrote two days later, he makes his usual case for the value of the collection to the nation, but with his bankruptcy clearly in mind he also points out that he had "spent time and money enough, dictated by pride and patriotism, to have made me independently wealthy," but in his efforts to keep the collection together, "I have impoverished myself and broken up my business and although not commissioned by the Government to do the work I did," still, he was encouraged by everyone "from the President down," to do it.[8]

Whether out of punctiliousness or exasperation with Brady, Belknap asked for legal advice from the War Department's judge advocate general before paying Brady once the second collection was in hand. His question was whether Congress had instructed him to pay all $25,000 or just the portion he thought the collection was worth. The reply from the department's top lawyer, one J. Mott, was nobly reasoned. He suggested that whatever the commercial value of the photographs, Belknap should also consider "the value of the articles to the United States." He suggested that Congress must have considered not only that "the pictures were of national interest and importance, but that they were secured in time of war and under circumstances of unusual difficulty and danger." His conclusion was that even if they had very little value "*except* to the United States," that should not decrease their value in the eyes of the secretary of war. Belknap was evidently persuaded, because he paid the full amount authorized.[9]

Josephine Cobb attributes Brady's bankruptcy to the falling fortunes of Boss Tweed and Tammany Hall, which she claims had previously, if indirectly, protected Brady from his creditors. The evidence for this is unclear, but the timing makes it plausible. Still, one of Brady's protectors was also supposed to be Tweed's supporter Jay Gould, and yet Brady sued Gould in April of 1872 for a bill of $469 that had gone

unpaid for more than two years. At the very least Brady's suit proves
how complicated it was to do business in the corrupt world of Boss
Tweed's New York.[10]

One other legal matter emphasizes the fast-and-loose environment
in which Brady had to operate. After Brady was declared a bankrupt in
January 1873, the U.S. District Court judge, Samuel Blatchford, chose
an attorney named Charles Gerding to oversee the sale of Brady's estate, so that creditors could receive at least partial payment of what
they were owed. Gerding seems an odd choice because he had previously worked for Brady and was one of the ninety-four creditors named
in the bankruptcy suit. In October 1875, Brady petitioned the court
to remove Gerding, charging that he had pocketed the proceeds from
the sales of Brady's possessions, had never given an accounting to the
court, and had given away to friends and family members many of
the artworks in Brady's gallery, "treating the guardianship of said estate
not as a trust for the benefit of the creditors, but as a private emolu-
ment." Brady also claimed that in 1872 Gerding had swindled him out
of a property in White Plains, New York, that he had asked the attorney to recover for him after it had been sold for back taxes. Brady had
to swear under oath that the allegations in his petition were true, but
they were only allegations. Gerding told the court in response to
Brady's charges that his sale of Brady's possession in both Washington
and New York had raised only three thousand dollars, and after his own
expenses were subtracted, the net was one hundred dollars. Still, in spite
of Gerding, Brady emerged from bankruptcy on December 17, 1874,
having made, according to the court, "a full discharge of his debts."[11]

Mathew and Julia moved to Washington sometime in 1873 and lived
there for the rest of her life and all but the last year of his. Their proper-
ties in New York had now been sold (or swindled), but they had mostly
lived as hotel dwellers there and would become hotel dwellers in Washington, moving into the National, just a block east of the gallery, for as
long as they could afford to do so. Close to the Capitol, the National
was still a good place to bump into members of Congress, with whom
Brady could rub shoulders, drum up business, and make the case for
further sales to the nation from his collection. Since Andrew Burgess
now controlled the gallery, Brady's main concerns were this lobbying

effort and monitoring the bankruptcy proceedings as best he could, including his maneuvers to keep the ownership of what was left of his Washington business in the hands of members of Julia's family. He was about fifty years old, and for the first time in more than thirty years he did not have an office to go to.

Josephine Cobb writes that at this time "his business troubles and his failing eyesight and his bouts of rheumatism had led him to indulge ever more frequently in spirituous liquors," and that he was "often fretful and quarrelsome." Even leaving aside that remarkable word *spirituous*, it's hard to know how much weight to give to Cobb's conclusion. Although she spent many years studying Brady while she was a photography archivist at the National Archives, her principal work about him was an article she wrote in the early 1950s called "Mathew B. Brady's Photographic Gallery in Washington," which is at times only loosely attributed. In a footnote, she gives as a source an old woman in Washington who had known Brady, and who "has recalled many impressions of M. B. Brady which are reflected in this article."

The woman was Lydia Mantle Fox, the author of *Eighty Plus: 1861 to 1945*, a memoir of her years in Washington. Fox had run an establishment inside the Riggs Hotel that offered stenography and typing services to the public, including a number of congressmen. She makes only one reference to Brady in the book, saying "he would pour his sorrows in my pitying ear," and calling him "a sad little man." But Fox is writing here of Brady twenty years after he and Julia had settled in Washington—and after Julia's death in 1887, his career mostly over, his health declining. It doesn't seem fair to use her later impressions of him to describe the earlier time in his life. Still, the year 1873 was undoubtedly one of Brady's worst, with the business and wealth he had built up across the decades slipping away from him, probably the hardest time until the period after Julia's death.[12]

After Brady got his payment from Congress and regained his gallery in late 1875, on December 18 he ran one of many ads over the coming months in Washington's *National Republican* that read, "Mr. Brady has the pleasure of announcing to his friends and the public that he has returned to Washington and reopened his gallery." He claimed in the ad to have reassembled "a corps of the best artists" and promised he "will give his personal attention to his patrons daily from 9 A.M. to 5 P.M."[13]

Soon Brady was operating again as if nothing had changed. When the emperor of Brazil, Dom Pedro II, visited Washington in June 1876, he asked to visit the nation's portrait gallery, where he could see "the faces of illustrious men," especially those of the Great Triumvirate— Clay, Webster, and Calhoun. Told that there was no public gallery but only Brady's National Portrait Gallery, now back in business, the emperor went there and "under the chaperonage of Mr. Brady, studied the various works of art, pausing long and thoughtfully before the forms of the three men he most desired to see." He then sat for Brady, "who secured a good likeness, which will be on exhibition at the Brady gallery during the week." The quotations come from a report in the *National Republican* of June 5, 1876, but the source for the story, and even the language itself, shows that Brady had not lost his touch for getting good publicity.

In addition to the small paid display ads in the *National Republican*, always headed BRADY'S NATIONAL PORTRAIT GALLERY, which ran throughout 1876 and into 1877, Brady got several favorable notices in the paper's news columns. A month or so after the gallery reopened, the newspaper reminded its readers that "the name of M. B. Brady is 'familiar as household words,'" and asserted that "Mr. Brady is to-day without a superior in his profession." A small notice in the news columns had already commented on how reasonable his prices were. By the spring of 1876 the *National Republican* was calling Brady's return to Washington in his rebuilt studio "one of the pleasantest events of current Washington history." According to the paper, "his gallery is visited daily by ladies and gentlemen eminent for their position in the social and political worlds," and Brady himself was not only a "great master of the art of photography" but "a historic celebrity." Bombast of this sort had long characterized American newspaper writing, but not just everyone could inspire it, and even when the elevated language is taken with a grain of salt, it seems fair to conclude that Brady was back in form. The evidence doesn't match Cobb's characterization of him as a "fretful" drunk at this time.[14]

A few weeks after the Brazilian emperor visited Brady's gallery, a writer for the *National Republican* showed up, attracted by portraits on display of the presidential and vice-presidential candidates in the election of 1876: Rutherford B. Hayes and William A. Wheeler for the

Republicans, Samuel J. Tilden and Thomas A. Hendricks for the Democrats. Brady's walls had been hung as ever with his portraits of the famous, from Webster, Clay, and Calhoun to Hawthorne to Garibaldi to more recent portraits such as Dom Pedro's, but the portraits of the candidates stood out, each drawn in crayon from a Brady photograph and displayed on an easel. The reporter, who after all worked for a Republican newspaper, notes that "Hayes looks frank and hearty, honest and enthusiastic," whereas the Democrat Tilden "has a sphinx face, inscrutable, from the little shrewd eyes, sunken in a bed of wrinkles, to the boyish mouth. All is incompatibility."[15]

Six months later, on February 3, 1877, Brady held a Saturday evening reception at his Pennsylvania Avenue gallery, where, the *National Republican* reports, "the guests included many Senators and members of Congress, representatives of the press and other gentlemen well known in Washington." The purpose of the event was to draw attention to portraits on display at the gallery that had been part of Brady's contribution to the international Centennial Exhibition in Philadelphia, which had celebrated the nation's anniversary. The fair had ended in November, and according to Josephine Cobb, Brady had created "a costly photographic exhibit" for it. Cobb says the judging of the photography entries dealt him "a professional blow," because Brady had been "fully anticipating that he would win first prize," but got only "a belated commendation for the value of his work as an historical record." If this was the case, Brady put the best face on it, claiming repeatedly in advertisements that his collection had gotten *"the highest awarded medal"* at the 1876 Philadelphia fair, and a newspaper report confirms that an official of the fair had traveled to Washington to give Brady the medal.[16]

At the gallery reception, the most noticeable portraits on display were "six large pictures life-size and three quarters length, representing Lincoln, Sumner, Grant, Sherman, Thomas and Farragut." (Thomas is the Union general George Henry Thomas, the "Rock of Chickamauga," whom Brady had captured in a fine photographic portrait.) These pictures were presented under glass in gilt frames. For the reception, Brady expanded his gallery space, displaying in his upstairs posing studio the portraits of press barons from Brady's heyday in New York: the elder James Gordon Bennett of the *Herald*, Horace Greeley

of the *Tribune*, and Henry J. Raymond of the *Times*, as well as Charles
A. Dana, Greeley's longtime right-hand man at the *Tribune*, described,
in the words of the *National Republican* reporter, "as he appeared a
score of years ago, before he developed piratical tendencies to such an
extent as he had of late years." Dana was now the editor of the *New
York Sun*, a Democratic newspaper.

Brady is often acknowledged as the photographer of presidents,
having photographed almost every president alive during his working
life. But the *National Republican* article about the Brady reception also
notes, "Since the days of Mrs. Madison he has taken portraits of the
ladies of every administration, and has gained the title of court photographer."

A month after Brady's reception, President Hayes would be inaugurated, and a month after that the president went to the gallery on a cool
but sunny Sunday, having gone fishing up the Potomac at Great Falls
the day before. Brady took twenty-five photographs of him, and Hayes is
reported to have said he had gone to Brady's because "What is worth
doing should be done well." The same report says that Hayes stayed on at
Brady's gallery for two more hours after the sitting was over, looking at
the portraits and war images hung there and praising Brady for his
work.[17]

If the president seemed at loose ends, perhaps he was still recovering
from the ordeal that had made him president. The election of 1876 was
the most contentious in U.S. history, triggering a greater constitutional
crisis than even the 2000 election and, like it, resolved along political
lines. In this case Congress created a special Election Commission including five senators, five representatives, and five justices of the Supreme
Court, which met in the Court's chambers inside the Capitol to decide
who got Electoral College votes from Florida and several other states
where the outcome was in dispute. Brady photographed the commission
members and the principal attorneys from each side and offered the images for sale on three cards, at the cost of a dollar for the set.[18]

During the summers of 1877 and 1878, Cornelia Adèle Strong
Fassett, an artist whom Brady had also photographed, was allowed to
use the Supreme Court chamber while the court was out of session to
paint a composite portrait of the Electoral Commission in action. A
number of the 256 people portrayed in the resulting oil painting, *The
Florida Case Before the Electoral Commission*, were drawn from Brady

images. Fassett included people on the busy canvas who were not in truth present at the Election Commission hearing, among them herself, Frederick Douglass, and a suffragist named Mary Clemmer Ames. Brady appears in the painting near the back of the room, but he was not a fanciful addition, because a *Harper's Weekly* sketch made at the hearings includes a figure that appears to be Brady among the "attentive listeners" on hand. Fassett's painting, which is five feet high and more than six feet wide, hangs today, as it has for more than a century, on the third floor of the U.S. Senate.[19]

In the fall of 1877, on September 27, Brady set up a camera in the East Room of the White House to photograph President Hayes with a delegation of Native American leaders, led by the Sioux chiefs Red Cloud and Spotted Tail. They joined the president and several Cabinet members in a series of meetings to urge that the government enforce a treaty promising the Sioux and other tribes good lands for their reservations. Brady's photograph was the basis for an image in the October 13 *Harper's Weekly*, which ran an article under the rabble-rousing headline CUSTER'S SLAYERS IN CONFERENCE WITH THE PRESIDENT. Custer, so often photographed in his short life by Brady or his men, had died at Little Bighorn just fifteen months before the White House meetings. Members of the delegation, including the two famous warrior chiefs, also went to Brady's gallery to have photographs made. Red Cloud led four such delegations to Washington, and had been photographed at Brady's at least twice before, in 1870 and 1872. The gallery had become a ritual stop for groups of Native Americans on official visits to the capital.[20]

Prominent politicians also continued to climb the stairs of 625 Pennsylvania Avenue. Just ten days after James A. Garfield received the Republican presidential nomination in Chicago in June of 1880, he went to Brady's gallery and, according to a notice in the *National Republican*, "was photographed at full length, half length, profile, full face and bust." If there was any doubt about who planted the notice, it concluded, "Some very fine pictures were obtained, which Mr. Brady will have on exhibition in a few days." Garfield would be the last in a long line of presidential candidates to be photographed at the Pennsylvania Avenue studio.[21]

By 1880, Brady was back in court in Washington, and the Washington gallery had become run down. Because of financial problems,

A delegation of visiting Sioux and Arapaho, including Red Cloud,
seated at left, and Little Big Man, standing at Red Cloud's left
(September 1877). *Library of Congress*

he and Julia could no longer afford to live in the National Hotel, or in
a boardinghouse, and moved into the same building as the gallery.
Even with this attempt at consolidating their expenses, their landlord,
William Ward, soon sued them for two thousand dollars in back rent
and claimed that they had removed property from the premises in order to avoid paying the debt. As part of the settlement with Ward they
mortgaged much of what was left in the gallery to a prominent Washington attorney and former general named Saul S. Henkle. This property included the oil portraits of the Great Triumvirate, which Brady
would nonetheless sell to Congress the next year for four thousand
dollars. A quit-claim deed giving the rights to these portraits to the
U.S. government was filed in 1911, which suggests that Brady had not
cleared the ownership with Henkle before selling them. But for some
reason Henkle apparently let this slide. Among the items the attorney
also owned title to was the famous Brady posing chair, in which Lincoln and nearly every important American who passed through Washington in the past twenty years had sat.[22]

In April of 1881 the *National Republican* reported that Brady had taken a new photograph of Admiral Farragut, "which should be possessed by every admirer of the great naval hero." But Brady's financial situation continued to deteriorate. The money from Congress for the Clay, Calhoun, and Webster portraits would go to Julia's nephew, Levin Handy, to whom Brady owed that much and probably more, and in November of 1881 the end came for Brady's National Photographic Art Gallery, which had borne his name for almost twenty-four years, the longest of any of his establishments.[23]

Even with the gallery gone, Brady continued to work in the photography business, under his own name or with others. City directories list him at 450 Pennsylvania Avenue in 1882, near the site of his first gallery in Washington in 1849, but by December of the following year he had moved some blocks west, to 1113 Pennsylvania, where according to an ad in the *Evening Critic*, "he has associated himself with Chester & Handy, where they are prepared to make fine work, any size or style." Levin Handy had gone into business with a New Jersey photographer named Samuel C. Chester, and they were partners for about four years, operating a studio in Cape May, New Jersey, as well as the one in Washington.[24]

In March of 1885, a reporter spotted Brady on Pennsylvania Avenue at the inauguration of Grover Cleveland. "The old party leaders are evidently gone for good," Brady told the reporter. "There are hardly a baker's dozen of the prominent men who were at the Buchanan inauguration who are here now. All the faces I see are new." Indeed, his former colleagues were also disappearing. Both Alexander Gardner and Timothy O'Sullivan had died in 1882. Henry T. Anthony, of the Anthony company, had died only months before, in October 1884, and Brady had attended the funeral in New York. Edward Anthony would die in 1888.[25]

Julia was not well. Where they lived during the last years of her life is not clear, but when Brady's name turned up in the Washington papers from time to time because he had attended some sort of evening event, she was never listed as accompanying him. When she died at Providence Hospital in Washington on May 23, 1887, at the age of sixty-five, her occupation was listed on the death certificate as "Lady Housekeeper" and the cause of death was "Valve disease of the Heart." The *Washington Critic* reported her death in a small item on its front page that evening, adding, "She had been an invalid for a long time, afflicted with acute rheumatism." Julia was buried the next day in the Handy family plot at Congressional Cemetery on Capitol Hill in Washington. Although the Handy family was from the Eastern Shore of Maryland, both Julia and her mother were listed on her death certificate as having been natives of Pennsylvania.[26]

# CHAPTER 18

# "The Stings of Poverty"

A little more than five months after Julia's death, Brady met a reporter from the *Washington Critic* at Willard's Hotel one evening to talk about the death on November 2 of Jenny Lind. The writer wanted to know about Brady's photograph of the Swedish Nightingale when she first arrived in New York in 1850. In his article, he offered a description of the old photographer:

> A straight, well-made man of about medium height, he has a face which reminds you much of that of Louis Napoleon. His hair is thick and bushy. It is combed well up from the forehead, and, like his fierce moustache and imperial, it is iron gray. He has bright blue eyes, and these smiled through blue spectacles last night as he told me how he succeeded in getting Jenny Lind's picture.[1]

Brady's retelling of the Jenny Lind story thirty-seven years later, it's worth noting, comports with a newspaper report at the time of her photographic session at his gallery.

By the following year, 1888, Brady and his nephew, Levin Handy, had completed the sort of massive undertaking that had characterized Brady's whole career: an album of the Fiftieth Congress of the United States, which included not only the photograph of every member of both houses but also those of the president and his Cabinet, and all the justices of the Supreme Court. It contained between four hundred and five hundred photographs, each accompanied by a short biographical sketch. One newspaperman wrote of the album, "It is in itself a fine work of art, and being the only thing of its kind in existence, is sure to prove a popular book." How popular the book became is in some doubt; the Library of Congress has a copy, but otherwise it is extremely rare. According to a 1989 report for the Library of Congress, a prototype for the book "was recently advertised for $25,000 by an antiquarian book dealer"—the same price, the report points out, that Brady was paid by the War Department for thousands of his war images. The report states that the book was never published, but the newspaper quote suggests otherwise. Either way, the work was presented jointly under the names of Brady and Levin C. Handy, the latter presumably having done most of the work. But as usual the newspapers gave Brady all the credit.[2]

The Library of Congress also holds an album of forty portraits Brady took in 1889 and 1890 of delegates to the International American Conference in Washington from February to April of 1890. Among those photographed in the United States delegation were Secretary of State James G. Blaine, who organized the conference, and Andrew Carnegie, a delegate. Apparently albums were given to the delegates or at least to the delegations, because on the cover are the words "Presented by the Government of the United States," which presumably contracted with Brady to do the job. Brady's name is also on the cover, and inside the album is the line "Designed and Photographed by M. B. Brady."[3]

At about the same time, on December 30, 1889, Brady took a group portrait of about one hundred members of the American Historical Association, "assembled for the purpose in front of the National Museum." He also photographed individual officers of the association in his studio, including George Bancroft, perhaps America's most esteemed historian at the time, who was himself as old as the century, and had been an old man even three decades before, when he was at Brady's gallery in New York to greet Abraham Lincoln on the day of the Cooper Union speech. The *Washington Post*, which reported on the historical association photographs, described the images, mildly, as "what may well be called the greatest historical achievement of [Brady's] later professional life."[4]

In 1891, Brady sat for his most extensive interview with the press, the much-cited piece by George Alfred Townsend that appeared in the

*World* under the headline STILL TAKING PICTURES: BRADY, THE GRAND OLD MAN OF AMERICAN PHOTOGRAPHY, HARD AT WORK AT SIXTY-SEVEN. Townsend described Brady then as "a person of trim, wiry, square-shouldered figure, with the light of an Irish shower-sun in his smile." He and Brady spoke in detail about how the cameraman had gotten so many famous people to pose for him. Townsend writes, "I could still see the deferential, sincere way Brady had in procuring these men. His manner was much in his conscientious appreciation of their usefulness." From the context it is clear that Townsend does not mean their usefulness to Brady, but to the world at large. Brady tells Townsend that Mark Twain visited his gallery "the other day" and said, "Brady, if I was not so tied up in my enterprises I would join you upon this material, in which there is a fortune." He added, according to Brady, "these large, expressive photographs . . . would make the noblest subscription book of the age."[5]

A short note published in the Washington *Sunday Herald and Weekly National Intelligencer* in late July of 1891, several months after Townsend's article, confirms that Brady was again operating a gallery in Washington. Calling him "the genial venerable veteran," the paper said Brady had returned from "his old stamping-ground," meaning New York, where "he made arrangements by which some important additions will be made to his 'National Portrait Gallery.'" The city directory says he had moved by this time two blocks farther up Pennsylvania Avenue, to Thirteenth Street.[6]

In the interview with Townsend, Brady was at best imprecise about the facts. But just a year later, when he gave an interview to Frank G. Carpenter in the *New York Herald*, he began with what can only be called a long fantasy about once partnering with Samuel Morse in a daguerreotype business on Beekman Street in New York at the same time that Morse was experimenting with the telegraph, avowing that "Prof. Morse and myself did a fair business." He describes their studio as a long room "filled with electrical machines [where] wires were coiled around it passing to the walls, and stretched here and there across the room," and adds, "Everyone thought that Morse was crack-brained." The letter Brady wrote to Morse in the 1850s, however, is not that of a former partner but, rather, suggests that they were not well acquainted.

Brady gives a different version of the story of getting Jenny Lind to sit for him, saying that he visited her a week after she'd come to New York and convinced her himself. He also says in the interview, "The first time I took President Lincoln was just after his election," but this is clearly wrong, and he alters his old story about Lincoln's saying Brady had made him president to "he once told me that I was the man who had introduced him to the United States."[7]

Brady also tells a colorful story, not for the first time, about when he photographed Grant in his gallery just after the general returned to Washington from the Vicksburg Campaign. Grant arrives at the studio with War Secretary Stanton, and because it is late in the day, Brady asks a workman—"a clumsy Dutchman," as Brady told it another time—to go up on the roof to open the skylight fully to get more light. The man stumbles and knocks "an immense pane out of the plate-glass which fell down at the feet of Grant." The heroic Grant does not even flinch, except for "a slight satirical curl which appeared upon his lip." Carpenter recounts the story in another article a couple of years later, quoting Brady as saying that Stanton had gone "white as a sheet" and taken Brady aside to warn him, "Don't say a word of this, or the newspapers will say it was a plot to assassinate Grant."

Late in life, then, as he saw his career and his health slipping away from him, Brady undoubtedly worried about his legacy, and seemed eager to tell stories about the people he had met and the things he had done over the decades. Like all oft-told stories, his got better with the retelling, and like many storytellers, he probably found it harder and harder to separate fiction from truth. The psychology of this is perfectly understandable, especially in a man who had been an exceptional promoter of himself and his business over the years. But Brady was not just another old man telling stories. His legacy would be of interest to history, and the facts of his career would help chart the history of his time. His own tall tales were sometimes the basis for the myths about him created after his death.

Brady's concern about his legacy was not misplaced. As Frank Carpenter wrote in an article in 1894, the vanity of Washington's great men, especially its congressmen, had made Washington "a city of photographers." That had been the case since the earliest days of the daguerreotype; after all, when Brady first opened a studio in the city in 1849, the competition had been fierce enough to drive him back to New York. For years after his return to the capital nearly a decade later, though, the Brady name had stood out, and the Brady gallery had been the place to be photographed, a magnet for all that Washington vanity.

But now Brady's name most often came up in a nostalgic way, and other photographers wore the mantle that had been his.[8]

One of the photographers now described in the newspapers as Washington's best was George Prince. In 1891, Brady got the assignment to photograph the delegates to the Patent Centennial Celebration, which met in Washington April 8–11. Although the first U.S. patent had been granted in 1790, making the centennial a year late, nobody seemed to care, including President Benjamin Harrison, who addressed the assembly on its first day. On the afternoon of the second day, Brady was photographing groups of delegates in front of the Patent Office Building on Seventh Street when a dispute arose between him and Prince, who had decided to take his own photographs and had asked one of his helpers to stand in front of Brady's camera. They "had some hot words," according to the Washington *Critic and Record*, and Brady told the paper that he had sworn out a warrant against Prince. When the case went to court, Prince was fined twenty-five dollars and given a firm rebuke by the judge. Although Brady was in the right, the incident shows where Prince, at least, felt the old man now stood in the pecking order.[9]

Still, important people occasionally found their way to Brady's door. Vice President Adlai Stevenson was to be photographed by Brady on April 17, 1894, but at eight o'clock the night before, Brady was seriously injured in a hit-and-run traffic accident. As he was crossing Fourteenth Street at New York Avenue, a two-seater surrey with four men in it struck him, and the driver "whipped up their horses and drove out Fourteenth street," according to the *Washington Times*. Brady's left ankle was broken, and he was first thought to have internal injuries. Nonetheless, he was taken in a police patrol wagon not to a hospital but to his nephew Levin Handy's house, on Maryland Avenue in southwest Washington, where Brady might already have been living, and was treated there. A policeman and a detective saw the accident happen, and after the men in the surrey took off, the detective "jumped in a cab and gave chase to the offending parties," but the cab could not catch them, "and they made good their escape." Several days later, the *Times* reported that Brady was "slowly improving, but will not be able to attend to business for several weeks."[10]

A story in the *Washington Post* reported that the detective's cab had caught up to the carriage after four blocks, but the detective found that he had been chasing the wrong carriage. The detective, named Lacy in the *Post* story, kept after the case, however, and in July he received a tip that the driver had been a "tinner" named William McCarthy. When arrested, McCarthy named the others in the carriage, two of whom were also arrested, the third having left town. McCarthy's case was heard on July 31, with Brady attending on crutches. According to the *Post*, Brady, "though he took the stand, did not express much animosity against the prisoner who had been the cause of his suffering." After testimony "that there was no malice in the accident; that McCarthy was perfectly sober at the time, and that, owing to the position of the vehicles in the street, he was unable to see Mr. Brady," the judge dismissed the case.[11]

Brady would live with the Handys at 494 Maryland Avenue (today the location of the U.S. Department of Education building just south of the National Mall) until the spring of 1895. But the arrangement at his nephew's house was apparently not satisfactory on either side. By September 1894 a note in the San Francisco *Morning Call* reported that "the famous photographer, who was once the petted favorite of fortune," had now become "crippled in body, with failing eyesight, and harassed almost to the point of madness by the stings of poverty."[12]

Brady had never given up his affection for New York, and often visited friends there during his Washington years. On one of these visits, in about 1884, he had called at the house of the artist and sculptor James Edward Kelly, with whom he shared a mutual friend. Even then, according to Kelly, Brady was "still in the full flush of business success and physical vigor." He was at the time still only slightly gray, wore what Kelly called "delicately tinted violet glasses," and was "exquisitely dressed, trim and wiry, and was a fluent talker." Indeed, Kelly would hear all Brady's best stories in the last dozen years of the old man's life: the Grant story about the broken skylight, the story about the Poe sitting, the one about knocking on James Fenimore Cooper's hotel room door, one about General Sheridan's hat, and more.[13]

On a late June afternoon in 1891, Brady had walked into Kelly's studio at the southeast corner of Washington Square, on the same block and just steps from where Samuel Morse had first experimented with daguerreotype some fifty years before. Kelly had a commission for a sixteen-foot-tall Civil War memorial statue to be named *The Call to Arms*, which, once mounted on its pedestal in Troy, New York, would reach ninety feet into the air. He had rented the studio, which had first been used by the famous sculptor Augustus Saint-Gaudens, because of its high ceilings. The day was warm, and Kelly had just climbed down the ladder on which he had been modeling the statue, exhausted and spattered with clay. Brady came in "looking spruce and spirited," and since Kelly had been promising to sketch him, he decided to go ahead with it. As Kelly began to draw, he writes, "I saw only the great artist photographer," and "the interest he infused into his sitters seemed to work an inspiration to me and all weariness left me." When he finished the sketch, made in profile, he gave it to Brady to sign. Upon handing it back, Brady said to Kelly, "You have beat my boys"—meaning that Kelly had done better than any of Brady's operators could have done.[14]

By the last spring of Brady's life, he had left his nephew's house in Washington and moved back to New York City. Letters to Levin Handy written for Brady from New York begin on April 8, 1895, and more letters went out in May and June. For at least part of this time, Brady was living at 126 East Tenth Street, fewer than three blocks from his last Broadway gallery. Then the correspondence stops until late September, suggesting that Brady had returned to Washington for a time, before going back to New York for good. Kelly writes that he saw Brady regularly in New York that last fall of the old photographer's life. Brady told Kelly how he had managed in his impoverished state to move back to the city. One day he had been "limping along Pennsylvania Avenue" when an old friend spotted him and said, "You look as if you were in trouble." Brady told him he was broke. The friend, retired Union cavalry general Alfred Pleasanton, asked what his plans were, and Brady said he wanted to move back to New York and reestablish his business. Pleasanton asked how much he would need to get started, and when Brady said fifty dollars, Pleasanton immediately wrote him a check for that amount. Brady had photographed Pleasanton more than once, and the general himself had known hard times before inheriting money from his sisters.[15]

Kelly writes that Brady was now "failing fast and walked with a crutch on a broken ankle." Kelly mentions the crutch repeatedly in his memories of this time, so the ankle had not healed properly even a year and a half after the accident. The first time he saw Brady that fall,

Kelly writes, "it was a shock to see him looking wan and careworn; but at the sight of me his face lit up with his characteristic winning smile." Brady told Kelly that upon his return to New York he had visited the well-known Catholic priest Father Thomas J. Ducey, who had built St. Leo's Church on East Twenty-eighth Street, which had a wealthy congregation that had earned him the sobriquet "apostle to the genteel." Having emigrated from Ireland at the age of five, the son of the housekeeper to the celebrated New York lawyer James T. Brady, Father Ducey lived well and died a wealthy man, but he was also known for his good deeds. He took a special interest, according to Kelly, in "easing the burdens of stricken men of brains and culture, to whom his generosity was boundless." Father Ducey told Brady to check into a hotel and send him the twenty-five-dollar-a-week bill. Brady did this for a time, but then felt he could accept only so much charity, and got a room on Astor Place, scene of the riot so many decades ago over Brady's actor friend Edwin Forrest.[16]

On Brady's visits that fall, Kelly writes, he often seemed exhausted, so Kelly would put him on a bed, set up his drawing easel beside it, and the two men would talk while Kelly sketched. Once while Brady was visiting, he told Kelly, "I sometimes dream that I am again in my gallery, under the skylight." Kelly writes that during this period "his frequent changes of rooms and occasional streaks of irritability could not at first be understood by his friends." But Kelly attributes them to what was then called Bright's disease, which covered a range of kidney ailments, one of which would soon kill his elderly friend. Kelly also writes, however, that "during all those days of growing illness and financial troubles, Brady retained much of his old time attractiveness, and continued to dress well." Later in the fall, Kelly remembers, Brady brought along on a visit a volume of *Harper's Weekly* articles from the war years, which included many portraits and scenes rendered from his own images. As he leafed through the book, Brady broke down, saying, "To think of it! Those men were my companions and friends, and by them I was respected; but now I am nothing but a damned old . . ." Kelly writes that Brady left the sentenced unfinished and "was choked with sobs."[17]

But the last year of Brady's life was not only one of sadness and poor health. The first of the letters from the previous April, written for him by the sculptor James Wilson MacDonald, asked Handy to make a list of war views related to the New York Seventh Regiment, which intended to honor Brady with a "Grand Testimonial Benefit" at which the old photographer would show magic lantern slides and comment on the images. Brady himself had written one of his rare letters on April 30, discussing what should go on the list of slides and stressing the importance of getting materials for the slides promptly. A letter three days later by an attorney friend named William Slocum said that Brady is "evidently suffering great pain from his injuries," but showing "pluck and perseverance." Brady wrote again on June 14, explaining that he could not find a magic lantern projector, so was having one made for seventy-five dollars, and added that he was trying to sell an oil painting of himself by Charles Loring Elliott in order to get some cash. According to Kelly, Edmund Clarence Stedman—who had been among the corps of journalists Brady accompanied to First Bull Run, and had gone on to be not only a successful poet and critic but also a banker—along with several friends, bought the portrait, which had been painted in 1857, and gave it to the Metropolitan Museum of Art, which owns it to this day.[18]

Brady also wrote that he hoped if the lecture and magic lantern show were successful, he could take the show on the road, to other cities. Plans for the event, originally intended for the fall of 1895, progressed, and eventually it was scheduled for January 30, 1896, at Carnegie Hall, where it would be introduced by Horace Porter, the general who had written a memoir of his time on Grant's staff during the war.

Brady and Handy ended up choosing 135 images from his collection, and Brady worked on the text to accompany the images, which were recorded in a hand not Brady's in what was called the Lantern Slide Lecture Book. William Riley, a friend of Brady's from New York, wrote to Handy on December 5 that plans for the big event were still moving forward, but that "Brady himself of course can do nothing except to suggest, as he is very weak and unable to leave his bed except for a few minutes at a time."[19]

On December 16, Riley wrote again, telling Handy he had taken Brady that morning to Presbyterian Hospital, on Seventieth Street and what is now Park Avenue, where "he will have the most skillful attention and the very best of care." Riley promised to visit him every day. The next letter from Riley, on January 13, 1896, tells Handy that Brady "has suffered a great deal of pain since the swelling in his neck developed.

He is sinking gradually and surely and . . . is likely to drop off any moment." That moment came at five fifteen P.M. on January 15. His doctor, S. W. Thurber, listed the main cause of death as "chronic diffuse nephritis," nephritis being an inflammation of the kidneys. The contributing cause was "suppurative parotiditis," meaning an infection of a gland between the cheek and ear, which could result from extended hospital stays, and was the reason for the swelling in Brady's neck. William Riley was there with him at the end, and the next day telegraphed the Handys with the news: BRADY WAS CONSCIOUS BUT FOR TWO OR THREE DAYS HE WAS UNABLE TO SPEAK ON ACCOUNT OF THE SWELLING IN HIS THROAT. I DON'T THINK HE REALIZED HE WAS DYING. The death certificate gave his age as seventy-two.[20]

Riley had asked in the January 13 letter who would pay for the funeral arrangements and said that the veterans of the Seventh New York had offered to cover some of the expense. Brady's body was embalmed the day after he died, and put on a train to Washington the following day. He was buried next to Julia on Sunday afternoon, the nineteenth, at Congressional Cemetery on Capitol Hill. Evidently there was no money for a headstone, because when one was eventually made, enough time had passed so that the year carved in for Brady's death was 1895, not 1896.

Riley went to Brady's last room—he had moved back to East Tenth Street, to No. 127—and wrote to Handy that, with one exception, he found nothing "it would pay to send you." Riley gave away the few items left of Brady's wardrobe, threw away his papers, and offered to send only the ring that the Prince of Wales had given Brady. Brady had once shown the ring to Kelly, who remembered it as having "a large red stone like a ruby." Brady told him that when he had been photographed standing at the split-rail fence at Gettysburg, looking at the spot he mistakenly believed to be where the Union general Reynolds was killed, "the stone shot out of the setting into a wheatfield on the other side." Brady let out a cry, and his assistant told him to put his hand back on the fence as it had been, and followed the probable trajectory of the stone right to the spot in the field where it lay hidden by the wheat. "Which I thought was very remarkable," Brady concluded. Levin Handy wanted the ring, and on January 21, Riley sent it to him.[21]

\* \* \*

The newspapers that had done so much for Brady throughout his career did not temper their hyperbole now that he was gone. The *Washington Post* wrote in its obituary that "Every eminent man in public life, and every prominent man and woman in every walk of life sat for their pictures to Mr. Brady here in Washington." The *Evening Star* was more circumspect, offering that he had become known as "an excellent workman," and eventually "his name was a household word all over the United States." The *New York Times* opted for pathos, writing that "the famous war photographer" died "alone and unnoticed. The hospital books state that he died from Bright's disease, but his death was really due to the misfortunes which have befallen him in recent years." The papers could not agree on his age at death. The *Times* gave it as seventy-two; the *Evening Star* said seventy-six. A handful of other New York papers offered perfunctory obituaries, the most remarkable of which came from the *New York Sun*. It ended its story with a paragraph that eagerly violated the proscription against saying ill of the dead.[22]

"Fifteen years ago or more," the paragraph began, "domestic difficulties, added to his disappointment at not selling his war collection entire, affected Brady's habits, and he began to drink. He neglected his business and it began to fall away." Even today this sort of hard assessment in an obituary would be jarring, but at a time when newspaper writing still tended toward gushing overstatement, it must have seemed especially surprising. It continued:

> Four or five years ago his fortunes had fallen so low that some of his friends made an effort to rehabilitate him. They fitted out a new gallery for him, and he opened it up with his famous collection of portraits as the great drawing card. But Brady himself was too far gone. He could not mend his habits, and the business soon went to the wall. After that he became practically dependent on the kindness of his friends. A year or so ago he fell down in the street in Washington and was run over by a street car. His legs were crushed and he was practically helpless.[23]

Leaving aside the appropriateness of putting this sort of detail in an obituary, the tone it takes when doing so, its vagueness about dates, and its outright misinformation, the notice undoubtedly says some true if hard things about the last years of Brady's life. It seems clear that "spirituous liquors" eventually took their toll, that Brady was never able to make a success of his various business attempts in his last years, that at the end he was basically broke and relied on the generous support of his friends, and that at least one of these friends, who had either written the *Sun* piece or was a source for it, had grown frustrated with the man Brady had become.[24]

But that feeling was not universal among those friends. On January 18, the day before the *Sun* notice, one of them, Samuel P. Avery, published a letter in the *New York Tribune*. An art dealer and print collector, Avery had helped found the Metropolitan Museum of Art. His letter concluded that since Brady had returned to New York "he had been tenderly cared for by a few friends," and that "Mr. Brady is still warmly remembered by many of our old residents, as a most talented and enthusiastic artist, and as a modest, gentle, generous man."[25]

The chaos of his later years, and his practice going back to the Civil War days of settling debts with the Anthonys by giving them negatives, tended to fragment and scatter his lifetime's work of making and collecting images of Americans celebrated and not, and of the greatest historical event of his lifetime. Thanks to a combination of the honest dealings of an ultimately dishonest secretary of war, and the quite possibly corrupt assistance of a congressman, both men former Union generals, thousands of Brady's Civil War images went to the War Department, from there to the U.S. Signal Corps, and finally to the National Archives, where they are held today. Thousands more of his negatives stayed with the Anthony Company, and as it evolved into Ansco, were purchased from them by collectors, and eventually ended up in the Library of Congress Prints and Photographs Division or at the Smithsonian museums, principally the National Portrait Gallery.[26]

Levin Handy retained a set of Brady images after his uncle's death, and these, too, made their way into the collection of the Library of Congress. Many of the thousands and thousands of images in these and other collections across the country are duplicate negatives or prints, and many were merely collected or copied by the Brady gallery but not taken by him or his employees. Thousands more were mishandled, badly stored, or thrown away, even after the government received them.[27]

Much work remains to be done to attribute, date, and organize this disarrayed trove, and many images will almost certainly never be accurately dated and attributed. But without Mathew Brady's urgent quest over many decades to make these photographs and acquire them, and without the power of his name to give value even to those he did not take, the vast collection of images that remains, many of them digitized and thus easily accessible, would not exist today. These images enhance our understanding of Mathew Brady's America in an incalculable way. His goal of creating a portrait of the nation succeeded far better than even he could have hoped.

*Acknowledgments*

William Howarth planted the seed for this book in 2005. Because Mathew Brady's able protégé, Timothy O'Sullivan, had played a role in a book I had just finished writing, I had read enough to agree with Will when he suggested that a reliable biography of Brady was long overdue. One of the first people I told of my intention to write the book was my learned friend Richard Nicholls. Within a few days, Rich sent me a long bibliography, each selection accompanied by a thoughtful assessment of why I should read it. All these years later, I could not make a better list than the one Rich made off the top of his head. Heather Ewing introduced me early on to Frank Goodyear, a photography curator at the Smithsonian Institution's National Portrait Gallery, who has been generous with his advice, patient in answering questions, and helpful in his reading of a draft of this book. Frank also introduced me to his colleague Ann Shumard, curator of photography at the Portrait Gallery. Ann asked me if I would like to go through the voluminous files that her predecessor, Mary Panzer, accumulated while organizing a major exhibition on Brady in the 1990s, which also produced Panzer's valuable book, *Mathew Brady and the Image of History*. My answer was an eager yes, and Ann generously provided me space to work and asked curatorial assistant Amy Baskette to assist me by photocopying many pages from the files. Ann saved me months of research time.

David Everett, who runs the writing program in the Krieger School of Arts and Sciences at Johns Hopkins University, has asked me to

teach in his program so often that I rated access to the amazing research resources of the university. I am grateful to him and to staff
members of the Sheridan Libraries at Hopkins and its Washington
branch on Massachusetts Avenue, who located books and articles from
their collections and through interlibrary loan. David has also offered
me years of friendship and encouragement, and made it possible to
teach with a host of wonderful writers, including Alice McDermott,
Dave Smith, Mary Jo Salter, Brad Leithauser, Jill McCorkle, Amy
Hempel, Rachel Hadas, and Ed Perlman.

My thanks to my friend Ralph Eubanks at the Library of Congress and to his colleague Carol Johnson, curator of photography and a
Brady expert. Eleanor Jones Harvey, chief curator at the Smithsonian
American Art Museum, found time to talk even while preparing her
impressive book and show on Civil War art. Thanks, too, to Todd Gustafson, Mark Osterman, and Susan Drexler at the George Eastman
House; Sandra Markham at the Beinecke Library at Yale (who wrote an
excellent article about the New-York Historical Society's Brady holdings); John Warren of the *New York History* blog; Carol B. Greenough of
the Skenesborough Museum in Whitehall, New York; and Kevin Lentz
of the Tioga County Historical Society in Owego, New York. James
M. Burgess Jr., of the Manassas National Battlefield Park, offered his
thoughts on Brady at First Bull Run; and Michele Holder of the National Council of Negro Women led Ann Shumard and me through
the rooms where Brady's Pennsylvania Avenue gallery once was. Merry
A. Foresta and Andy Grundberg offered their encouragement and
insights early on at the table of our mutual friends Anne and Gus
Edwards.

Deborah Marquardt loaned me a hard-to-find catalogue from an
Alexander Gardner exhibit at the Chrysler Museum. Elizabeth High-
tower sent me an equally elusive article. Molly Roberts helped with
photo research and took my photo for the book jacket. Robert Roper
offered encouragement and advice, as did David Grogan. Brad Ed-
mondson and Tania Werbizky were there for me in Ithaca, New York.
Steve Goodwin and Jon Wist have been here for me in Manassas, Virginia. Adam Goodheart, friend and exemplar, helped me to think
about this book in a more focused way.

*The American Scholar* has been an excellent place to work, not only
because I love the magazine itself but also because of the talented and

stimulating people I am able to be around: Jean Stipicevic, Sandra Costich, Margaret Foster (who kindly helped with photographs for the book), Bruce Falconer, David Herbick, Ray Sachs, and Steve Anderson. Special thanks go to my longtime colleagues Allen Freeman and Sudip Bose, who have done so much to enrich my life as an editor. Don Lamm, Cullen Murphy, and Brenda Wineapple, three members of the *Scholar* editorial board, have offered me encouragement and friendship. Ann Hulbert, a friend of many years who also graces our masthead, has talked me through a delicate stage or two of this book. Anne Matthews, another friend and masthead colleague, has offered her steady support. John Churchill, publisher of the *Scholar* and the secretary of Phi Beta Kappa, which pays the magazine's bills, has, like everyone in this paragraph, heard more than he ever expected to hear about Mathew Brady, and has been generous with his ideas and reflections about things I had on my mind.

I am grateful to Allen Oren, Ernest B. Furgurson, and Charles Trueheart for reading the manuscript and offering helpfully honest assessments. (Pat Furgurson's own books have been models for me while writing this one.) Whatever its flaws, my book is much better than it would have been without the effort these three friends put into reading and critiquing it. My thanks, too, go to Caroline Jones and Shannon Welch for help with research and fact checking. And thanks to James Gibney for publishing an article about Brady at Bull Run in *The Atlantic*.

Sarah Chalfant of The Wylie Agency put my proposal through its paces, and Edward Orloff worked hard to find the right publisher. That turned out to be a man I have known and admired for many years, George Gibson of Bloomsbury. George did me the good deed of putting my manuscript in the hands of Jacqueline Johnson, an editor's editor both literally and figuratively. Her tactful tough-mindedness has made for a much sharper and more readable book. Others at Bloomsbury to whom I'm grateful are the jacket designer, Lauren Jantz; the art director, Patti Ratchford; the copy editor, Jenna Dolan; the production editor, Laura Phillips; marketing director, Laura Keefe; and senior publicist Carrie Majer—my thanks for their optimism and enthusiasm.

Close friends whose wisdom and good cheer deserve my thanks include Cheryl Merser, Russ Powell, and Mario Pellicciaro. My sister, Laurie Kelly, and sisters-in-law Charlotte Gatto and Susan Barritt (also known as my marketing team), are always ready to spring into action.

Four other members of my family who offered their support passed away while I was writing this book: Dot Ritchie, Leroy Thompson, Kay Stock, and Jack Hodnett. May they rest in peace. Like my first book, this one is dedicated to my wife, Martha. I also dedicate it to our fine sons, Matt, Cole, and Sam. My profoundest thanks to all four of you for your sustaining love.

# *Notes*

## INTRODUCTION: "PHOTO BY BRADY"

1. Quoted from a September 30, 1839, (New York) *Morning Herald* article in Robert Taft, *Photography and the American Scene*, pp. 16 and 72.
2. Ibid., p. 106; Oliver Wendell Holmes, *Soundings from the Atlantic*, pp. 166, 228.
3. In separate e-mails to the author, Todd Gustafson and Mark Osterman, both of the George Eastman House, in Rochester, New York, expressed their doubts that Brady was operating the camera in this photograph.
4. For the development of the halftone process of photoengraving in the press, see Michael L. Carlebach, *The Origins of Photojournalism in America*, pp. 161–65.

## CHAPTER 1: "A CRAVING FOR LIGHT"

1. Jon Alexander, "Native Son's Birthplace Marked in Johnsburg," *PostStar* (Glens Falls, NY), November 17, 2011, reports that Milda Burns and Glenn Pearsall had recently found the Brady homestead. An e-mail to the author from Pearsall says the two depended for the location on a hand-drawn map by the late Johnsburg town historian, Lewis Waddell. (The spelling of the town's name was "Johnsburgh" in Brady's time.) No source for the map is known beyond oral tradition. The brothers who were said to have lived on a farm next to the Brady family are Andrew and William Burgess, whose history is recounted by their descendant Elmer Burgess, along with Lynn T. Wakeling, in *Gun Collector's Digest* 2 (Northfield, IL, 1977): 168–80. Brady's comment about where he was born is in George Alfred Townsend, "Still Taking Pictures," *The World*, April 12, 1891, p. 26.
2. A. W. Holden, *A History of the Town of Queensbury, in the State of New York*, pp. 501–2. See also H. P. Smith, ed., *History of Warren County*; and "The Glen Tannery," New York State Museum (website), at www.nysm.nysed.gov/research/anthropology/crsp/projects/glenn_tannery.html.
3. "The Glen Tannery," New York State Museum (website), at www.nysm.nysed.gov/research/anthropology/crsp/projects/glenn_tannery.html.

4. "Glens Falls in 1831," Chapman Museum, Glens Falls, NY, at www.chapman museum.org/TheCorners/miscellaneous/glens_falls_1831.html.

5. Brady's memories of his early years are quoted in James Edward Kelly, "Matthew [*sic*] B. Brady, Great Historical and Patriotic Photographer," James Edward Kelly Papers, Archives of American Art, Smithsonian Institution, Washington, D.C.

6. William Page's early life is described by Joshua C. Taylor, *William Page*, pp. 1–7.

7. Ibid., pp. xx and 18.

8. Brady's memories of going to New York are from Kelly, "Matthew B. Brady, Great Historical and Patriotic Photographer."

9. Material about A. T. Stewart from Edwin G. Burrows and Mike Wallace, *Gotham*, pp. 638–39.

10. Brady entries in *Doggett's New York City Directory* for 1843–44 and 1844–45, reproduced in James D. Horan, *Mathew Brady: Historian with a Camera*, p. 9.

11. Beaumont Newhall, *The Daguerreotype in America*, pp. 56, 69–70, and 128.

12. Burrows and Wallace, *Gotham*, pp. 651–53 (gold rush) and 598 (fire).

13. Crossing Broadway, ibid., p. 565; Dickens, *American Notes*, pp. 55–56 and 59.

14. Jane E. Boyd, "Silver and Sunlight: The Science of Early Photography," Chemical Heritage Foundation, www.chemheritage.org/discover/media/magazine/articles /28-2-silver-and-sunlight.aspx?page=2; also Beaumont Newhall, *The History of Photography*, pp. 12 and 32.

15. For a brief history of Daguerre and Niépce's contributions to the invention of daguerreotype, see Newhall, *The Daguerreotype in America*, pp. 15–21, and his *The History of Photography*, pp. 12–19.

16. Arago's presentation and the response to it are described in "The Daguerre Secret," *Literary Gazette* (London), August 24, 1839, pp. 538–39, quoted in Newhall, *The Daguerreotype in America*, p. 20.

17. Samuel I. Prime, *The Life of Samuel F. B. Morse*, p. 365.

18. For information about Morse and Daguerre, see "The Daguerrotipe," letter from Morse in *New-York Observer* 17, no. 16 (April 20, 1839): 62, at daguerre.org/resource /texts/04-20-1839_morse.html. Also, Sarah Catherine Gillespie, "Samuel F. B. Morse and the Daguerreotype," p. 71. See also R. Derek Wood, "Daguerre and His Diorama in the 1830s: Some Financial Announcements," at www.midley.co .uk/diorama/Diorama_Wood_2.html.

19. Kenneth Silverman, *Lightning Man*, pp. 192–97.

## CHAPTER 2: "THIS GREAT NATIONAL MAP"

1. William and Estelle Marder, *Anthony: The Man, the Company, the Cameras*, p. 21; *Spirit of the Times*, July 4, 1846, p. 228.

2. This advertisement ran in the *Daily Tribune* at least fourteen times between October 19 and November 15, 1844.

3. Mary Panzer, *Mathew Brady and the Image of History*, pp. 44–45.

4. *New-York Daily Tribune*, October 18, 1844, p. 4. Brady's reference to "a competent and practical person" ran in more than fifty ads in the *Tribune* through May 30, 1845. Biographical information about James Sidney Brown (1819–1893) in Peter E. Palmquist and Thomas R. Kailbourn, *Pioneer Photographers from the*

*Mississippi to the Continental Divide*, p. 130. In 1852 he would travel as a daguerreotypist on Matthew C. Perry's first expedition to Japan.

5. "Controlling aesthetic intellect": Barbara McCandless, "The Portrait Studio and the Celebrity," in *Photography in Nineteenth-Century America*, p. 54; new camera: *Spirit of the Times*, July 4, 1846, p. 228.

6. *New York Herald*, October 7, 1846.

7. Instructions given: *New-York Daily Tribune*, December 10, 1844, p. 4.

8. See introductory preface and appendix to Marmaduke B. Sampson, *Rationale of Crime*, especially pp. xxxviii and 158.

9. Richard L. Bushman, *The Refinement of America*, p. 360; *Photographic Art-Journal* 1 (March 1851): 138.

10. Horace Traubel, *With Walt Whitman in Camden*, Vol. 3, pp. 552–53.

11. Taft, *Photography and the American Scene*, pp. 464–65; William Welling, *Photography in America*, pp. 48–49.

12. *Daily National Intelligencer* (Washington, D.C.), February 27, 1849, p. 4; Brady sign: Panzer, *Mathew Brady and the Image of History*, p. 11, woodcut from New-York Historical Society.

13. For background on Edward Anthony (1819–1888), see Welling, *Photography in America*, pp. 35–36.

14. Brady's first Washington venture, see Josephine Cobb, "Mathew B. Brady's Photographic Gallery in Washington," *Records of the Columbia Historical Society, 53–56* (Washington, D.C.: Columbia Historical Society, 1953–56): 28–33; *Daily National Intelligencer*, February 27, 1849; Allan Nevins, ed., *Polk: The Diary of a President, 1845–1849*, p. 374.

15. Brady's memories of photographing Calhoun, Webster, and Clay from *New York Herald*, May 15, 1892, p. 27.

16. "Mrs. M. B. Brady," *New York Herald*, June 12, 1887, p. 11. A description of correspondence held by the Beinecke Rare Book Library at Yale University reads, "Letters from Robert Handy, serving aboard the United States Revenue Cutters *Morris* and *Howard*, to his brother Samuel S. Handy in 1850 include mentions of Brady and his wife living on Staten Island, New York, and the aftermath of the sinking of the bark, *Elizabeth*, on July 19, 1850." Mathew B. Brady and Levin Handy Photographic Studio Collection, Series III, folders 2449–60.

17. Webster's theatricality, from *Harper's New Monthly Magazine* 38, no. 228 (May 1869): 787–89.

18. Robert V. Remini, *Henry Clay*, p. 724. The Beinecke attributes a daguerreotype of Clay to Brady and says it was taken on November 28, 1849, in Philadelphia; advertisement in *New-York Daily Tribune*, July 12, 1848, p. 3.

19. "This great National Map": *New-York Daily Tribune*, November 9, 1850, p. 4; the Gallery of Illustrious Americans details from *The Literary World* 182 (July 27, 1850): 80–81; Charles Edwards Lester's introduction from the *Gallery of Illustrious Americans* (New York: Brady, D'Avignon and Co., 1850).

20. Alan Trachtenberg, in *Reading American Photographs*, p. 45, writes "the lithographs are the most faithful representations of daguerrean images yet produced in America." Historian of photography William F. Stapp in "Daguerreotypes onto Stone: The Life and Works of Francis D'Avignon," in Reaves, ed., *American*

*Portrait Prints*, p. 200, writes of Brady and D'Avignon, "the partnership produced one of the great moments in the history of American portrait prints and . . . American photographs."

21. See *New York Herald*, September 16, 1850. Brady interviews with Townsend, "Still Taking Pictures" and in the *New York Evening World*, November 5, 1887, p. 2. On von Schneidau, see Newhall, *The Daguerreotype in America*, pp. 154–55. See also Neil Harris, *Humbug*, pp. 113–41. See also R. Bruce Duncan, "Luther Boswell—Mr. Brady's Cameraman," *Photographica*, October 1974.

22. Newhall, *The Daguerreotype in America*, p. 81; Townsend interview, "Still Taking Pictures"; Kelly, "Matthew B. Brady, Great Historical and Patriotic Photographer."

23. Townsend, "Still Taking Pictures."

## CHAPTER 3: "IN DAGUERREOTYPES . . .
## WE BEAT THE WORLD"

1. Welling, *Photography in America*, p. 67.

2. M. A. Root, *The Camera and the Pencil*, p. 366. *Tribune* quote in the *Photographic Art Journal* (June 1853): 334–41. Newhall, *The Daguerreotype in America*, p. 34.

3. "These Jeremiad times": *Daily National Intelligencer*, February 28, 1843; Burrows and Wallace, *Gotham*, pp. 653 and 659. Growth of Manhattan: www.demo graphia.com/db-nyc-ward1800.htm; Jenkins, *Images and Enterprise*, p. 12.

4. *Photographic Art Journal* (March 1851): 189; Taft, *Photography and the American Scene*, p. 70; Horace Greeley, *Glances at Europe*, p. 26; *Illustrated London News*, Vol. 18, 1851, p. 425. Welling, in *Photography in America*, quotes English photographer John Werge as saying of the Americans at the fair, "All employed the best mechanical means for cleaning and polishing their plates, and it was this that enabled the Americans to produce more brilliant pictures than we did. Many people used to say that it was the climate, but it was nothing of the kind" (p. 81).

5. Taylor, *William Page*, p. 106; Panzer, *Mathew Brady and the Image of History*, p. 72.

6. Advertisement in the *Home Journal*, July 17, 1852. William Page was known as "the American Titian," which Taylor uses as the subtitle of his biography.

7. Taft, *Photography and the American Scene*, p. 466.

8. R. G. Dun & Co. Collection, Baker Library, Harvard University Graduate School of Business Administration, Vol. 368, p. 442; Burrows and Wallace, *Gotham*, p. 668.

9. *Humphrey's Journal* 5 (June 15, 1853): 73.

10. Bushman, *The Refinement of America*, p. 361.

11. *New York Tribune*, April 10, 1854, quoted in Newhall, *The Daguerreotype in America*, p. 63. Cheaper daguerreotype: Taft, *Photography and the American Scene*, p. 85.

12. Brady to Samuel F. B. Morse, February 15, 1855, Morse Papers, Library of Congress, Washington, D.C.

13. Taft, *Photography and the American Scene*, p. 52.

14. *Frank Leslie's Illustrated Journal*, January 10, 1857, p. 86.

15. Henry James, *A Small Boy and Others*, p. 52.

16. From *American Phrenological Journal* (New York) 27, no. 5 (May 1858): 65–67.

## CHAPTER 4: "LARGE COPIES FROM SMALL ORIGINALS"

1. Taft, *Photography and the American Scene*, pp. 114–22; Newhall, *The Daguerreotype in America*, p. 66.
2. Taft, *Photography and the American Scene*, pp. 123–24.
3. Ad in *New-York Daily Tribune*, September 3, 1856, p. 1. The case for the Frémont ambrotype is in the possession of the National Portrait Gallery, Washington, D.C.
4. *The Crayon* (New York), 2, no. 3, July 18, 1855, p. 1.
5. Taft, *Photography and the American Scene*, p. 126.
6. The best information about Alexander Gardner available at this time is from Joseph M. Wilson, "A Eulogy on the Life and Character of Alexander Gardner" (Washington, D.C.: Lebanon Lodge No. 7, 1883); D. Mark Katz, *Witness to an Era*; Josephine Cobb, "Alexander Gardner," *Image* 7 (June 1958): 124–36; and Brooks Johnson, *An Enduring Interest: The Photographs of Alexander Gardner*. A comprehensive new study of Gardner is under way for a future exhibit at the National Portrait Gallery, Washington, D.C.
7. Taft, *Photography and the American Scene*, pp. 130–32.
8. For information on gold toning, see George Eastman House, "Notes on Photographs," at notesonphotographs.org/index.php?title=Gold_Toning.
9. *Harper's Weekly*, October 17, 1857, p. 659. "Prized acquisitions": Taft, *Photography and the American Scene*, p. 130.
10. N. Parker Willis, *The Convalescent*, pp. 281–85.
11. *Photographic and Fine Art Journal* (November 1857): 347. Ad in *New-York Daily Tribune*, September 29, 1857, p. 7.
12. Welling, *Photography in America*, p. 126.
13. Taft, *Photography and the American Scene*, p. 131.
14. *American Journal of Photography* 1 (1858–59): 112; Taft, *Photography and the American Scene*, p. 133; Burrows and Wallace, *Gotham*, p. 676.
15. *New-York Daily Tribune*, September 3, 1856, p. 1, and November 10, 1857, p. 1.
16. Panzer, *Mathew Brady and the Image of History*, p. 76.
17. Cobb, "Alexander Gardner," p. 129. R. G. Dun & Co. Collection, p. 442.

## CHAPTER 5: "STARTLING LIKENESSES OF THE GREAT"

1. Cobb, "Mathew B. Brady's Photographic Gallery in Washington," pp. 34–36. The street numbers were later changed to 625 and 627 Pennsylvania Avenue. Robert A. Warnock, Geier Brown Renfrow Architects, "Sears House: An Historic Preservation and New Design Project in Washington, D.C." (November 2, 1984), pp. 3–4.
2. Ernest B. Furgurson, *Freedom Rising*, p. 12.
3. Henry Adams, *The Education of Henry Adams: An Autobiography* (Boston: Houghton Mifflin Company, 1918), p. 99.
4. Much of the detail about Washington comes from Furgurson, *Freedom Rising*; Cobb, "Mathew B. Brady's Photographic Gallery in Washington"; and Margaret Leech's enduring *Reveille in Washington*.
5. *Photographic and Fine Arts Journal* (April 1858): 128; *National Intelligencer*, June 21, 1858.

6. Cobb, "Alexander Gardner," p. 129.

7. Hirst D. Milhollen, "The Brady-Handy Collection," from *A Century of Photographs, 1846–1946* (Washington, D.C.: Library of Congress, 1980), p. 40.

8. Letter from Charles James Fox to his father about a trip he made to Washington, D.C., written in Toronto September 19, 1858, Rare Book Department, Huntington Library, San Marino, CA.

9. Cobb, "Mathew B. Brady's Photographic Gallery in Washington," p. 36. Cobb misattributes the Webster portrait to "John C. Neagle" of Philadelphia. For current information about all three paintings, see the "Art & History" section of the United States Senate website, www.senate.gov.

10. For details about the Washington gallery, see Cobb, "Mathew B. Brady's Photographic Gallery in Washington," pp. 41–44.

11. Welling, *Photography in America*, p. 103.

12. *Photographic and Fine Arts Journal* (January 1858): 24.

13. "Broadway Valhalla," *New York Times*, October 6, 1860. http://www.nytimes.com /1860/10/06/news/a-broadway-valhalla-opening-of-brady-s-new-gallery.html

14. *New York Herald*, October 5, 1860. "Broadway Valhalla" was the headline of the *Times* article of October 6.

## CHAPTER 6: "WONDERFUL STRANGERS"

1. Harold Holzer, *Lincoln at the Cooper Union*, p. 105; Richard C. McCormick, "Abraham Lincoln's Visit to New York in 1860," *New York Evening Post*, April 29, 1865.

2. Richard C. McCormick, "Abraham Lincoln's Visit to New York in 1860," *New York Evening Post*, April 29, 1865.

3. Townsend, "Still Taking Pictures."

4. Roy P. Basler, ed., *Collected Works of Abraham Lincoln*, Vol. 4 (Springfield, IL: Abraham Lincoln Association, 1953), p. 40.

5. *Harper's Weekly*, November 10, 1860. Holzer, *Lincoln at the Cooper Union*, pp. 95–97. See also Harold Holzer, "The Lincoln Image: Made in New York," *Lincoln and New York* (New York: New-York Historical Society, 2009), pp. 129–39. For information on Lincoln campaign badges, see Karina Kashina Beeman, "1860 Lincoln Political Campaign Buttons—Part of American Political Memorabilia," George Eastman House, "Notes on Photographs."

6. Townsend, "Still Taking Pictures." The "Brady and the Cooper Institute" quote has been irresistible to anyone writing about the Cooper Union portrait, but Brady himself is the only source for it.

7. F. B. Carpenter, *The Inner Life of Abraham Lincoln*, pp. 46–47.

8. Brady's note to Gardner reproduced in Katz, *Witness to an Era*, p. 109. George Henry Story quoted in James Edward Kelly, *Tell Me of Lincoln*, p. 223.

9. *New York Herald*, May 20, 1860; *New York Times*, May 10, 1860.

10. *New York Times*, June 16, 1860.

11. Carolyn Peter, in John Hannavy, ed., *Encyclopedia of Nineteenth-Century Photography*, Vol. 1 (New York: Routledge, 2007), p. 418. See also Newhall, *The History of Photography*, 49–50.

12. Taft, *Photography and the American Scene*, pp. 139–40. As Holzer points out, interest in the carte de visite did not pick up enough steam early enough to have had a large impact on the spread of Brady's February 27 Cooper Union portrait of Lincoln, but the Prince of Wales and his suite had cartes de visite images made when Brady photographed them on October 13, 1860. Given the way the format spread, it would make sense that both the French baron who posed for Rockwood and the English prince who posed for Brady would be slightly ahead of the growing popularity of the cards in the United States.

13. See Taft, "The Tintype," *Photography and the American Scene,* pp. 153–66. Also Beeman, "1860 Lincoln Political Campaign Buttons."

14. Taft, *Photography and the American Scene*, p. 158; *Humphrey's Journal* 12 (September and December 1860).

15. Taft, *Photography and the American Scene*, p. 141.

16. Ibid., pp. 144–45.

17. A comprehensive article on Albert Edward's visit to New York is "Movements of the Prince," *New York Times*, October 15, 1860, p. 1. See also *Harper's Weekly*, November 3, 1860, which also reprints an article on the prince's visit from the *New York Herald*.

18. Burrows and Wallace, *Gotham*, p. 672.

19. *Frank Leslie's Illustrated Newspaper*, January 5, 1861, p. 106.

20. Townsend, "Still Taking Pictures."

21. *New York Times*, October 24, 1860.

### CHAPTER 7: "LAST PLACE . . . TO SEE THE NATION WHOLE"

1. James M. McPherson, *Battle Cry of Freedom*, p. 322. He adds that "by early 1862 more than 700,000 men had joined the Union army." On troops sitting for tintypes, Taft, *Photography and the American Scene*, p. 159.

2. *Humphrey's Journal* 13 (February 1862): 319, via Taft, *Photography and the American Scene*, p. 160.

3. *New York Tribune*, August 20, 1862, via Taft, *Photography and the American Scene*, p. 160.

4. McPherson, *Battle Cry of Freedom*, pp. 285–86; Furgurson, *Freedom Rising*, pp. 77–78 and 81.

5. Furgurson, *Freedom Rising*, pp. 82–83; *Anthony's Photographic Bulletin*, No. 2.

6. Adam Goodheart, *1861*, pp. 188–94, 205, 207–8, and 214–15.

7. Leech, *Reveille in Washington*, p. 73; Furgurson, *Freedom Rising*, p. 86.

8. Furgurson, *Freedom Rising*, pp. 91–94; Goodheart, *1861*, p. 280.

9. *Life of James W. Jackson: The Alexandria Hero, The Slayer of Ellsworth* (Richmond, VA: West and Johnson, 1862), p. 28.

10. Ibid., p. 33; Goodheart, *1861*, pp. 285–86.

11. Leech, *Reveille in Washington*, pp. 81–82.

12. Panzer, *Mathew Brady and the Image of History*, p. 101.

13. Anderson cartes de visite: Taft, *Photography and the American Scene*, p. 478, note 186. Brady-Anthony deal: Cobb, "Mathew B. Brady's Photographic Gallery in Washington," p. 47. Cobb cites a letter to Montgomery C. Meigs signed MB

Brady but written "per Alex Gardner" and in the latter's hand, which states, "I have made an arrangement with Mr. Anthony for the publication of cartes de visite of nearly all of my gallery." Cobb and many writers after her give credit for this lucrative deal solely to Gardner, but Brady had been acquainted with Anthony for at least eighteen years and would more likely have been the one to strike the deal with his fellow New Yorker. Tens of thousands: Dorothy Meserve Kunhardt and Philip B. Kunhardt Jr. write in *Mathew Brady and His World* that "In the early 1860s Brady *cartes de visite* sold by the tens of thousands" (p. 55).

### CHAPTER 8: "ILLUSTRATIONS OF CAMP LIFE"

1. Cobb, "Alexander Gardner," pp. 124–27; Welling, *Photography in America*, p. 150.
2. Geoffrey C. Ward, *The Civil War*, p. 58. "A nursery": Warren Lee Goss, "Going to the Front," in Holzer, *Hearts Touched by Fire*, p. 83. Brady would later be made an honorary member of the Seventh New York, which helped pay his funeral expenses thirty-five years later.
3. Welling, *Photography in America*, p. 145.
4. Edwin Forbes, *Thirty Years After*, p. 258.
5. Ibid., p. 257.
6. "More than 300": Kunhardt and Kunhardt, *Mathew Brady and His World*, p. 56; Stapp, *An Enduring Interest*, p. 118, note 12.
7. William J. Cooper Jr., "Introduction," in Forbes, *Thirty Years After*, p. ix.
8. Panzer, *Mathew Brady and the Image of History*, p. 103.
9. Townsend, "Still Taking Pictures."
10. Ibid.; Kunhardt and Kunhardt, *Mathew Brady and His World*, p. 56.
11. McCandless, "The Portrait Studio and the Celebrity," p. 60.
12. Townsend, "Still Taking Pictures"; Roy Meredith, *Mathew Brady's Portrait of an Era*, p. 102.
13. *New York Herald*, March 16, 1860. Brady also got articles about the Irving portrait in the *New-York Tribune* on March 21 and the *Home Journal* on March 31.
14. The Forrest photographs are in the collection of the National Portrait Gallery, Washington, D.C.
15. For details of the Forrest-Macready feud and the Astor Place Riot, see Burrows and Wallace, *Gotham*, pp. 761–66.
16. Henry A. Beers, *Nathaniel Parker Willis*, pp. 309–14.
17. Davis, "A Terrible Distinctness," p. 137; Furgurson, *Freedom Rising*, p. 38.

### CHAPTER 9: "A CONTINUOUS ROLL OF MUSKETRY"

1. Furgurson, *Freedom Rising*, p. 117.
2. P. G. T. Beauregard, "The First Battle of Bull Run," in Holzer, *Hearts Touched by Fire*, p. 85.
3. Louis M. Starr, *Bohemian Brigade*, p. 35.
4. Bob Zeller, *The Blue and Gray in Black and White*, pp. 52 and 55.
5. Townsend, "Still Taking Pictures."
6. Article signed with the initials "LEO." "Notes of the Rebellion: Personal Observations of the Fighting at Bull's Run," *New York Times*, July, 23, 1861, p. 2; Starr, *Bohe-*

*mian Brigade*, p. 43. For a National Park Service summary of the Blackburn's Ford action, see www.nps.gov/mana/historyculture/the-skirmish-at-blackburns-ford.htm.

7. Charles L. Brace, "From Another Correspondent," *New York Times*, July 23, 1861, p. 2; William Tecumseh Sherman, *Memoirs*, p. 204.

8. *New-York Daily Tribune*, July 21, 1861, p. 1.

9. Furgurson, *Freedom Rising*, p. 119.

10. E. B. Long, *The Civil War Day by Day*, p. 97. A useful book on the battle is David Detzer's *Donnybrook: The Battle of Bull Run, 1861*.

11. Henry Wilson would one day be vice president under President Grant. William A. Croffut, *An American Procession*, p. 50.

12. James Edward Kelly, "Matthew B. Brady, Great Historical and Patriotic Photographer."

13. Jim Burgess, a museum specialist at Manassas National Battlefield Park, who has steeped himself in the accounts of that day, supports this surmise.

14. William Howard Russell, excerpt from *My Diary North and South*, in *The Civil War: The First Year Told by Those Who Lived It*, pp. 464–90; Detzer, *Donnybrook: The Battle of Bull Run*, p. 471.

15. Russell, *My Diary North and South*, pp. 475–76.

16. William T. Sherman, Letter to Ellen Ewing Sherman, July 28, 1861, from *The Civil War: The First Year*, p. 529. Sherman continued, "It was as disgraceful as words can portray . . . ," Russell, *My Diary North and South*, p. 483.

17. Russell, *My Diary North and South*, p. 480.

18. John Sampson, "Photographs from the High Rockies," *Harper's New Monthly Magazine*, September 1869, p. 465.

19. Zeller, *The Blue and Gray in Black and White*, p. 59.

20. "Photographs of War Scenes," *Humphrey's Journal* (August 15, 1861): 133.

21. "Photographs of the War," *New York Times*, August 17, 1861, p. 4. Col. Samuel Heintzelman (who was photographed by Brady in his studio sometime after the battle, his arm in a sling from the wound he received in it) led one of the two divisions that went on the flanking maneuver for McDowell.

22. Zeller, *The Blue and Gray in Black and White*, p. 60.

23. Starr, *Bohemian Brigade*, p. 42.

24. Horan, *Mathew Brady: Historian with a Camera*, p. 39; Russell, *My Diary North and South*, p. 480.

25. "The Advantages of Defeat," *The Atlantic Monthly*, September 1861, p. 360.

26. Townsend, "Still Taking Pictures."

27. Peter Cochran, "Byron and Early Nineteenth-Century French Literature," in *The Reception of Byron in Europe* (London: Continuum, 2004), p. 69.

28. For information about Lewis Morrison, see www.blackpast.org/?q=aah/morris-morris-w-lewis-morrison-1845-1906.

## CHAPTER 10: "MORE ELOQUENT THAN THE STERNEST SPEECH"

1. Stephen W. Sears, *George B. McClellan: The Young Napoleon*, pp. 100–101.

2. Cobb, "Alexander Gardner," p. 132; Katz, *Witness to an Era*, p. 28.

3. Sears, *George B. McClellan*, p. 101; Cobb, "Alexander Gardner," p. 132.

4. James D. Horan, *Timothy O'Sullivan*, p. 35; Francis Trevelyan Miller, *The Photographic History of the Civil War*, Vol. 8, p. 24.

5. William F. Stapp, "Chronology: Timothy H. O'Sullivan," in *Framing the West*, p. 187.

6. Ibid., pp. 188 and 236, note 5.

7. Long, *The Civil War Day by Day*, p. 80.

8. *The Diary of George Templeton Strong*, March 12, 1862; Alexander Gardner, *Gardner's Photographic Sketch Book of the War*, Vol. 1. See image 19 in the Library of Congress scan of the unpaginated book at: memory.loc.gov/phpdata/pageturner .php?type=&agg=ppmsca&item=12834&turnType=byImage&seq=19; Sears, *George B. McClellan*, p. 159.

9. *Gardner's Photographic Sketch Book*, image 27; Bruce Catton, *The New American Heritage Picture History of the Civil War*, p. 122.

10. Zeller, *The Blue and Gray in Black and White*, p. 63; *New York World*, September 15, 1862, p. 5, via Carlebach, *The Origins of Photojournalism in America*, pp. 87–88.

11. Katz, *Witness to an Era*, p. 34; Carlebach, *The Origins of Photojournalism in America*, p. 75.

12. In an appendix, Katz helpfully catalogues all the images in the *Sketch Book* and in Gardner's 1863 catalogue of Civil War photographs and *Catalogue of Photographic Incidents of the War,* including Gardner's brief description of each negative and the name of the photographer or photographers to whom he attributes it. Much of the information about the war itself comes from Long, *The Civil War Day by Day.*

13. Katz, *Witness to an Era*, pp. 38–39.

14. "Rather a jollification": from Robert K. Krick, *The American Civil War: The War in the East, 1863–1865* (Chicago: Fitzroy Dearborn, 2001), p. 85.

15. "Editor's Drawer," *Harper's New Monthly Magazine*, November 1862, p. 853.

16. McPherson, *Battle Cry of Freedom*, p. 468.

17. "Fording a tributary": Gardner, *Catalogue of Photographic Incidents of the War*, via Katz, *Witness to an Era*, p. 284.

## CHAPTER 11: "THE TERRIBLE REALITY AND EARNESTNESS OF WAR"

1. Katz, *Witness to an Era*, p. 45; Zeller, *The Blue and Gray in Black and White*, p. 71.

2. *Anthony's Photographic Bulletin*, New York : E. & H. T. Anthony & Co. September 1882, pp. 311–12

3. McPherson, *Battle Cry of Freedom*, p. 537.

4. For a good general history of the Antietam battle, see Stephen W. Sears, *Landscape Turned Red: The Battle of Antietam.*

5. Historian William Stapp suggests that it was an obvious possibility that Gardner stayed with McClellan, given their year-long relationship. *An Enduring Interest*, 117, note 8.

6. Zeller, *The Blue and Gray in Black and White*, p. 72; Forbes, *Thirty Years After*, p. 258.

7. William Frassanito, *Antietam*, p. 71; Katz, *Witness to an Era*, p. 49. A recent book

by Robert J. Kalasky, *Shadows of Antietam*, concludes that "Gardner and Gibson began their Antietam series of photographs on September 18" (p. 26).

8. Kalasky, *Shadows of Antietam*, pp. 22–23. Frassanito concluded in *Antietam* that the Dunker church images were taken on September 19. But Kalasky writes that Frassanito later found a diary entry persuading him that the Dunker church photographs were taken on September 20. The Gardner telegram is reproduced in Zeller, *The Blue and Gray in Black and White*, p. 71.

9. Zeller, *The Blue and Gray in Black and White*, pp. 75 and 77.

10. Katz, *Witness to an Era*, p. 56.

11. Stapp, *An Enduring Interest*, p. 21.

12. Zeller, *The Blue and Gray in Black and White*, p. 74.

13. George Sullivan, *Mathew Brady: His Life and Photographs*, p. 91.

14. Bob Zeller, "Incidents of the War: Alexander Gardner's Antietam Photographs," Southeast Museum of Photography, 1995, p. 12.

15. "Antietam Reproduced," *New York Times*, October 3, 1862; and "Brady's Photographs: Pictures of the Dead at Antietam," *New York Times*, October 20, 1862, p. 5.

16. Oliver Wendell Holmes, "Doings of the Sunbeam," *Atlantic Monthly*, July, 1863, pp. 11–12.

17. Holmes, "My Hunt After 'The Captain,'" *Atlantic Monthly*, December 1862, p. 738.

18. "Scenes on the Battlefield," *Harper's Weekly*, October 18, 1862, pp. 664–65.

19. Stapp, *An Enduring Interest*, p. 24.

20. William Frassanito, *Grant and Lee*, pp. 342–43; Zeller, *The Blue and Gray in Black and White*, p. 164.

21. Drew Gilpin Faust, *This Republic of Suffering*, pp. 65–66.

## CHAPTER 12: "BRADY AND THE LILLIPUTIANS"

1. McPherson, *Battle Cry of Freedom*, p. 544; *The Civil War Papers of George B. McClellan* (New York: Ticknor and Fields, 1989), p. 473.

2. Katz, *Witness to an Era*, p. 112; Frassanito, *Antietam*, p. 275.

3. Zeller, *The Blue and Gray in Black and White*, p. 78.

4. Ibid., pp. 78 and 80.

5. Long, *The Civil War Day by Day*, p. 282.

6. Pinkerton, *The Spy of the Rebellion*, p. 583.

7. Katz, *Witness to an Era*, p. 51.

8. William Stapp has studied the differences in Brady's printing before and after Gardner's arrival. See *An Enduring Interest*, p. 21.

9. Neil Harris describes Tom Thumb's romance and wedding in *Humbug*, pp. 160–64.

10. Panzer, *Mathew Brady and the Image of History*, p. 187; "The Loving Lilliputians," *New York Times*, February 11, 1863, p. 8; "Brady and the Lilliputians," *New York Times* February 12, 1863, p. 2; *Harper's Weekly*, February 21, 1863, pp. 113–14.

11. Charles S. Stratton, *Sketch of the Life of General Tom Thumb* (New York: Samuel Booth, 1874), p. 23. Stratton's book excerpts several newspaper articles about the wedding.

12. Burrows and Wallace, *Gotham,* pp. 681 and 632.

13. Horan, *Mathew Brady: Historian with a Camera*, pp. 49 and 52.

14. The Horatio Nelson Taft diaries from the years 1861–1865 are available digitally through the Library of Congress American Memory collection, at memory.loc .gov/ammem/tafthtml/tafthome.html.

15. Library of Congress Prints and Photographs Division, Brady-Handy Collection, M. B. Brady's Register, June 1870–December 1875.

### CHAPTER 13: "REBEL INVASION"

1. Gardner had presumably stopped just south of Emmitsburg to check on the safety of his son, Lawrence, who remained a student at the Mount St. Mary's College boarding school, having enrolled the previous September. William Frassanito, *Early Photography at Gettysburg*, p. 408, note 12. Katz, *Witness to an Era*, reproduces the back of a print with the caption on it (p. 62). Stuart's official report is at www.factasy.com/civil_war/report14.shtml. Keener quoted in Zeller, *The Blue and Gray in Black and White*, p. 106.

2. McPherson, *Battle Cry of Freedom*, p. 665; William Frassanito, *Gettysburg: A Journey in Time*, p. 27.

3. Zeller, *The Blue and Gray in Black and White*, p. 107; Frassanito, *Gettysburg: A Journey in Time*, p. 26.

4. Katz, *Witness to an Era*, p. 63.

5. Burrows and Wallace, *Gotham*, p. 887.

6. Ibid., pp. 887–99, gives a good short history of the Draft Riot.

7. Later report of unburied bodies: Frassanito, *Early Photography at Gettysburg*, p. 22.

8. Henry Steele Commager, ed., *The Blue and the Gray*, p. 600.

9. "Reminiscences of Gettysburg," *Harper's Weekly*, August 22, 1863, p. 534.

10. Frassanito, *Early Photography at Gettysburg*, p. 58.

11. Frassanito, *Gettysburg: A Journey in Time*, p. 84.

12. Zeller, *The Blue and Gray in Black and White*, pp. 109–11.

13. Frassanito, *Gettysburg: A Journey in Time*, p. 71.

14. Ibid., pp. 187–92.

15. Gardner's *Sketch Book* is also available online at the Cornell University Library website. The caption for this image is reproduced at rmc.library.cornell.edu/7milVol /plate41.html.

16. Frassanito, *Gettysburg: A Journey in Time*, p. 191.

17. Quoted in Frassanito, *Early Photography at Gettysburg*, p. 202.

### CHAPTER 14: "THAT MEMORABLE CAMPAIGN"

1. *A Record of the Metropolitan Fair in Aid of the United States Sanitary Commission, Held at New York in April, 1864* (New York: Hurd and Houghton, 1867), p. 5.

2. *Harper's Weekly*, March 19, March 26, and April 2, 1864.

3. The two scholars are Katz and Frassanito.

4. Carpenter, *The Inner Life of Abraham Lincoln*, p. 35.

5. An authoritative recent study on Lincoln's photographs is *Lincoln, Life-Size*, by Philip B. Kunhardt III, Peter W. Kunhardt, and Philip W. Kunhardt Jr.

6. Carpenter, *The Inner Life of Abraham Lincoln*, p. 91.

7. Ibid., pp. 91–92.

8. *Daily National Republican* (Washington, D.C.), March 9, 1864, p. 2.

9. Ulysses S. Grant, *Memoirs and Selected Letters*, p. 469.

10. Ibid., p. 512.

11. Frassanito, *Grant and Lee*, p. 45.

12. Ibid., pp. 116–21, for his discussion of these photographs; *Harper's Weekly*, July 9, 1864, p. 442.

13. Frassanito, *Grant and Lee*, p. 51.

14. Ibid., p. 88. Frassanito says that this sort of simultaneous exposure was "virtually unique" in Civil War photography, although it's hard to imagine what the point was, beyond proving that it could be done.

15. "Doing business": Zeller, *The Blue and Gray in Black and White*, pp. 141 and 144. "No advantage": Grant, *Memoirs and Selected Letters*, p. 588.

16. In *Grant and Lee*, Frassanito says the panoramic view is "among the rarest of all Civil War photographs," with only one original version of it known (p. 172). His discussion of the White House Landing photographs: pp. 165–73.

17. Frassanito, *Grant and Lee*, p. 193.

18. Ibid., p. 189. For the half-exposed image of Brady, see www.flickr.com/photos /usnationalarchives/3995293389/in/set-72157622549882756/.

## CHAPTER 15: "THE BALL HAS OPENED"

1. Frassanito, *Grant and Lee*, pp. 216–23.

2. Ibid., pp. 224–26.

3. Ibid., pp. 236 and 247.

4. "Provoked fire": Miller, *The Photographic History of the Civil War*, Vol. 1, p. 19. "Shells were flying": ibid., Vol. 8, p. 14.

5. Frassanito, *Grant and Lee*, pp. 252–54.

6. Ibid., p. 249.

7. Horace Porter, *Campaigning with Grant*, pp. 217–20.

8. John Hay, "With Lincoln at the White House," *Harper's Monthly Magazine*, January 1915, p. 170.

9. Welling, *Photography in America*, p. 295; Davis, "A Terrible Distinctness," *Photography in Nineteenth-Century America*, pp. 164–65; Frassanito, *Grant and Lee*, pp. 336–37.

10. Henry Hitchcock, *Marching with Sherman*, p. 150.

11. Zeller, *The Blue and Gray in Black and White*, p. 160.

12. Ibid., p. 145; Frassanito, *Grant and Lee*, pp. 420–21.

13. Frassanito, *Grant and Lee*, pp. 378–80.

14. Grant, *Personal Memoirs*, p. 750; Frassanito, *Grant and Lee*, p. 412.

15. Douglas Southall Freeman, *Lee*, p. 500.

16. Robert Edward Lee, *Recollections and Letters of General Robert E. Lee* (New York: Doubleday, Page and Company, 1905), p. 198; Grant, *Personal Memoirs*, pp. 735 and 744.

17. Lee, *Recollections and Letters of General Robert E. Lee*, p. 198.

18. Ibid.
19. Townsend, "Still Taking Pictures." Frassanito, *Grant and Lee*, p. 418.

## CHAPTER 16: "A PHOTOGRAPHIC PANTHEON"

1. See Carlebach, "The West as Photo Opportunity," in *The Origins of Photojournalism in America*, pp. 102–49, and for information on Morrow, see pp. 144 and 147; also Paul L. Hedren, *With Crook in the Black Hills: Stanley J. Morrow's 1876 Photographic Legacy*, p. 10.
2. See "New York Avenue Presbyterian Church," at Abraham Lincoln Online, at www.abrahamlincolnonline.org/lincoln/sites/nyave.htm.
3. *Harper's Weekly*, May 6, 1865, p. 278, and May 13, 1865, pp. 296–97.
4. Bachelder later became the first serious historian of the Battle of Gettysburg. Thomas Schwartz, "John Badger Bachelder, Commemoration, Commerce, and the Last Hours of Abraham Lincoln," in *From Out of the Top Hat* (Abraham Lincoln Presidential Library and Museum blog), www.alplm.org/blog/2010/09/john-badger-bachelder-commemoration-commerce-and-the-last-hours-of-lincoln/.
5. Details about how the painting was created appear in an advertisement written by Bachelder in a book he published to accompany the painting: Isaac Newton Arnold, *Sketch of the Life of Abraham Lincoln* (New York: John B. Bachelder, Publisher, 1869), p. 94; Panzer, *Mathew Brady and the Image of History*, p. 91.
6. Ernest B. Furgurson, "The Man Who Shot the Man Who Shot Lincoln," *The American Scholar* (Spring 2009): 42–51.
7. Katz, *Witness to an Era*, pp. 149–52.
8. Wardell statement: ibid., pp. 161–62. "The sale of portraits": ibid., p. 171.
9. Ibid., p. 164. Katz, *Witness to an Era*, reprints a number of these photographs.
10. Katz, *Witness to an Era*, describes in detail the executions and Gardner and O'Sullivan's photographing of them, pp. 177–91; *New York Times*, July 8, 1865.
11. *New York Herald*, July 8, 1865.
12. See Andrew C. A. Jampoler, *The Last Lincoln Conspirator: John Surratt's Flight from the Gallows*.
13. Sandra Markham, "Figments of a Mighty Past: Mathew Brady Portrait Photographs at the New-York Historical Society," *New-York Journal of American History* (March 2003): 100, note 23.
14. Cobb, "Mathew B. Brady's Photographic Gallery in Washington," p. 54. Background of Gibson in Thomas Waldsmith, "James F. Gibson: Out from the Shadows," *Stereo World* (January–February 1976): 1, 5, and 20.
15. Katz, *Witness to an Era*, pp. 208–9.
16. Cobb, "Mathew B. Brady's Photographic Gallery in Washington," p. 54.
17. R. G. Dun & Co. Collection, Vol. 368, pp. 442 and 483.
18. "Another Pleasant Day," *New York Times*, July 22, 1865.
19. Cobb, "Mathew B. Brady's Photographic Gallery in Washington," p. 60; R. G. Dun & Co. Collection, Vol. 368, p. 483.
20. Helena Zinkham, "Pungent Salt: Mathew Brady's 1866 Negotiations with the New-York Historical Society," *History of Photography* (January–March 1986): 6. Most of the information about the negotiations comes from this article.

21. Photos of Washington miniatures: Markham, "Figments of a Mighty Past: Mathew Brady Portrait Photographs at the New-York Historical Society," p. 100, note 3. Brady letter, Zinkham, "Pungent Salt: Mathew Brady's 1866 Negotiations with the New-York Historical Society," p. 3.
22. *New York Times*, March 20, 1866; February 26, 1866; and March 29, 1867.
23. U.S. Supreme Court, *Jones v. New York Guaranty and Indemnity Company*. Townsend, "Still Taking Pictures."
24. Markham, "Figments of a Mighty Past: Mathew Brady Portrait Photographs at the New-York Historical Society," pp. 83 and 86.
25. Cobb, "Mathew B. Brady's Photographic Gallery in Washington," p. 61. "Brady's Collection of Historical Portraits," 41st Congress, 3d Session, House of Representatives, Report No. 46. See Congressional Globe on Library of Congress website: http://memory.loc.gov/ammem/amlaw/lwcglink.html
26. Jeana K. Foley, "Recollecting the Past," in Panzer, *Mathew Brady and the Image of History*, pp. 192–94. Kelly, "Matthew B. Brady, Great Historical and Patriotic Photographer": "One day he told me something that gave me quite a shock, saying that some years before he had sold part of his collection of war negatives to the Government for $25,000, but had to pay half of it to the Honorable Gentleman who put through the Bill. Brady told me his name, which I do not propose to give here, but any person sufficiently interested can look it up."

## CHAPTER 17: "FAMILIAR AS HOUSEHOLD WORDS"

1. Cobb, "Mathew B. Brady's Photographic Gallery in Washington," p. 61; Elmer Burgess, with Lynn T. Wakeling, "Andrew Burgess, Gun Designer," in *Gun Collector's Digest* 2 (August 1968): 168–70. It's worth remembering that through much of the war Brady also employed a cameraman named Anthony Berger, who joined him at Gettysburg and took some of the most famous images of Lincoln. Because of the similarities of the two names, Berger and Burgess are sometimes confused.
2. Cobb, "Mathew B. Brady's Photographic Gallery in Washington," pp. 63–64; Hirst D. Milhollen, "The Brady-Handy Collection," in Renata V. Shaw, comp., *A Century of Photographs* (Washington, D.C.: Library of Congress, 1980), p. 43.
3. Palmquist, *Pioneer Photographers*, p. 138.
4. "Historic Brady Photographs," *The Ansconian* (July–August 1949): 3–5.
5. "In the Matter of Mathew B. Brady, Bankrupt," U.S. District Court, Southern District of New York; Kathleen Collins, *Washingtoniana: Photographs* (Washington, D.C.: Library of Congress, 1989), pp. 24–25. Cobb, "Mathew B. Brady's Photographic Gallery in Washington," pp. 62–63.
6. Cobb, "Mathew B. Brady's Photographic Gallery in Washington," p. 63. Although an R. G. Dun & Co. report for July 1873 says that, in New York, Brady's "stock seized and sold out by Sheriff Some time since," Vol. 368, p. 500. William W. Belknap, Records of the Office of the Adjutant General, April 9, 1875, Record Group (RG) 94, Box 4944, National Archives and Records Administration, Washington, D.C. Damage reported by a Mr. Barnard in a letter to Belknap dated November 5, 1874, in RG 107, Box 168.

7. William W. Belknap, Sept. 28, 1874, Records of the Office of the Adjutant General, RG 107, Box 168, National Archives and Records Administration, Washington, D.C.

8. M. B. Brady, October 30, 1874, Records of the Office of the Adjutant General, RG 94, Box 4944, National Archives and Records Administration, Washington, D.C.

9. J. Mott to Belknap, April 9, 1875, Records of the Office of the Adjutant General, RG 94, Box 4944, National Archives and Records Administration, Washington, D.C.

10. Cobb, "Mathew B. Brady's Photographic Gallery in Washington," pp. 62–63; *Matthew [sic] B. Brady against Jay Gould*, Judgment Roll, April 16, 1872, New York Superior Court.

11. M. B. Brady to Samuel Blatchford, "In the Matter of Mathew B. Brady, Bankrupt," October 21, 1875, U.S. District Court, Southern District of New York.

12. Cobb, "Mathew B. Brady's Photographic Gallery in Washington," pp. 63 and 68. Lydia Mantel Fox, *Eighty Plus: 1861 to 1945* (Boston: Christopher Publishing House, 1950), p. 105.

13. This ad appears again as late as June 5, 1876, on the same page as an article about Dom Pedro II at Brady's. *National Republican*, p. 4.

14. *National Republican*, January 6, 1876, p. 4; December 12, 1875; and March 9, 1876, p. 4.

15. *National Republican*, July 21, 1876, p. 4.

16. *National Republican*, February 5, 1877, p. 4; Cobb, "Mathew B. Brady's Photographic Gallery in Washington," p. 65; *National Republican*, September 19, 1877, p. 4.

17. Roy Meredith, *Mathew B. Brady, Mr. Lincoln's Camera Man*, p. 235; *National Republican*, April, 8, 1877, p. 1. On April 27, ex-President Grant and Mrs. Grant sat for Brady; *National Republican*, April 29, 1877, p. 1.

18. *Harper's Weekly*, February 17, 1877, p. 125; Meredith, *Mathew B. Brady, Mr. Lincoln's Camera Man*, p. 234.

19. A good history of the case and the painting is on the U.S. Senate website, at: www.senate.gov/artandhistory/art/artifact/Painting_33_00006.htm. See also Brandon Conradis, "Senate's 'Florida Case' Tells Story of Major Event with Miniature Details," *The Hill*, at: thehill.com/capital-living/cover-stories/204719-senates-florida-case-tells-story-of-major-event-with-miniature-details. A copy of the *Harper's* sketch is in Meredith, *Mathew B. Brady, Mr. Lincoln's Camera Man*, p. 241.

20. For information on Red Cloud and Brady, see Frank Henry Goodyear, *Red Cloud: Photographs of a Lakota Chief* (Lincoln: University of Nebraska Press, 2003), p. 17. Also: anthropology.si.edu/redcloud/bio_slideshow/.

21. *National Republican*, June 19, 1880, p. 4.

22. Cobb, "Mathew B. Brady's Photographic Gallery in Washington," pp. 66–67 and 36–37, note 23.

23. *National Republican*, April 26, 1881, p. 4.

24. Cobb, "Mathew B. Brady's Photographic Gallery in Washington," p. 67; *Evening Critic* (Washington, D.C.), December 21, 1882, p. 2.

25. *National Republican*, March 5, 1885, p. 5. Like Brady himself a few years later, Henry Anthony was hit by a vehicle while trying to cross the street. He died within a few days of the accident. Welling, *Photography in America*, p. 296.

26. *Washington Critic*, May 23, 1887, p. 1.

## CHAPTER 18: "THE STINGS OF POVERTY"

1. *Washington Critic*, November 5, 1887, p. 2.

2. *Washington Critic*, October 9, 1888, p. 3; "Career of a Famous Photographer," *New York Tribune*, October 8, 1888; Collins, *Washingtoniana: Photographs*, p. 25.

3. See www.loc.gov/pictures/item/2004667041/.

4. "Mr. Brady's Historic Groups," *Washington Post*, December 31, 1889, p. 4.

5. Townsend, "Still Taking Pictures."

6. "Town Talk," *Sunday Herald and Weekly National Intelligencer* (Washington, D.C.), July 26, 1891, p. 5. Cobb, "Mathew B. Brady's Photographic Gallery in Washington," pp. 67–68.

7. Frank G. Carpenter, "Men Whose Names Are Household Words," *New York Herald*, May 15, 1892, p. 27.

8. *Morning Call* (San Francisco), March 11, 1894, p. 11.

9. "Photographers Disagree," (Washington) *Critic and Record*, April 9, 1891; Meredith, *Mathew B. Brady, Mr. Lincoln's Camera Man*, p. 237.

10. *Washington Times*, April 17, 18, and 20, 1894.

11. "Could Not Keep Their Secret," *Washington Post*, July 23, 1894, p. 8; and "Driver M'Carthy Exonerated," *Washington Post*, August 1, 1894, p. 8.

12. *Morning Call*, September 18, 1894.

13. Kelly, "Matthew B. Brady, Great Historical and Patriotic Photographer."

14. Kelly, *Tell Me of Lincoln*, pp. 167–68.

15. Letters to and from Brady in the last two years of his life are in the collection of the National Portrait Gallery; Pleasanton story, in Kelly, "Matthew B. Brady, Great Historical and Patriotic Photographer."

16. Kelly, "Matthew B. Brady, Great Historical and Patriotic Photographer"; "Apostle to the genteel": Lately Thomas, *Delmonico's: A Century of Splendor* (Boston: Houghton Mifflin, 1967), p. 220.

17. Kelly, "Matthew B. Brady, Great Historical and Patriotic Photographer."

18. Ibid.

19. All 135 photos are reproduced with a transcription of the text in Meredith, *Mathew B. Brady, Mr. Lincoln's Camera Man*, pp. 263–363.

20. The death certificate is reproduced in Horan, *Mathew Brady: Historian with a Camera*, p. 88.

21. Kelly, "Matthew B. Brady, Great Historical and Patriotic Photographer."

22. "Photographer Brady Dead," *Washington Post*, January 18, 1896, p. 2; "Death of M. B. Brady," *Evening Star*, January 18, 1896, p. 9; "Death of Matthew [*sic*] B. Brady," *New York Times*, January 19, 1896.

23. *New York Sun*, January 19, 1896.

24. The obituary in the *Evening Star* also said that late in life Brady became "desultory and uncertain in his business methods, and neglected rather than utilized his splendid accumulation of valuable work."

25. *New York Tribune*, January 18, 1896. The obituary in the *Washington Post* concluded that "He left behind him a very pleasant memory of his genial and benevolent character, which will be long remembered by a host of friends." The *Evening Star* wrote, "In person and manner Mr. Brady was a most congenial gentleman. His friends were legion, and he preferred for years to give them his time and company rather than confine himself to the demands of his calling."

26. The *Evening Star* obituary had reported that "Last July the last of the negatives in his control was sold under forced sale to a leading photographer on F street." For a brief history of Brady's photographs after his death, see Foley, "Recollecting the Past," *Mathew Brady and the Image of History*, pp. 189–205.

27. A. W. Greely, "Subject Catalogue No. 5, List of the Photographic Negatives Relating to the War for the Union, Now in the War Department Library" (Washington, D.C.: Government Printing Office, 1897), pp. 5–11.

# Selected Bibliography

Barnard, George N. *Photographic Views of the Sherman Campaign.* New York: Press of Wynkoop & Hallenbeck, 1866.

Bauer, K. Jack. *The Mexican War, 1846–1848.* New York: Macmillan, 1974.

Beers, Henry A. *Nathaniel Parker Willis.* Boston: Houghton Mifflin, 1896.

Braudy, Leo. *The Frenzy of Renown: Fame and Its History.* New York: Oxford University Press, 1986.

Burrows, Edwin G., and Mike Wallace. *Gotham: A History of New York City to 1898.* New York: Oxford University Press, 1999.

Bushman, Richard L. *The Refinement of America: Persons, Houses, Cities.* New York: Alfred A. Knopf, 1992.

Carlebach, Michael L. *The Origins of Photojournalism in America.* Washington, D.C.: Smithsonian Institution Press, 1992.

Carpenter, F. B. *The Inner Life of Abraham Lincoln: Six Months at the White House.* New York: Hurd and Houghton, 1872.

Catton, Bruce. *Grant Takes Command.* Boston: Little, Brown and Company, 1968.

———. *The American Heritage New Picture History of the Civil War.* New York: Metro-Books, 2001.

Coffin, Charles Carleton. *The Boys of '61.* Boston: Estes and Lauriat, 1881.

Commager, Henry Steele, ed. *The Blue and the Gray: The Story of the Civil War as Told by Participants.* Indianapolis, IN: The Bobbs-Merrill Company, 1950.

Croffut, William A. *An American Procession, 1855–1914: A Personal Chronicle of Famous Men.* Boston: Little, Brown and Company, 1931.

Detzer, David. *Donnybrook: The Battle of Bull Run, 1861.* New York: Harcourt, 2004.

Dickens, Charles. *American Notes for General Circulation.* London: Lea and Blanchard, 1842.

Donald, David, Hirst D. Milhollen, and Milton Kaplan. *Divided We Fought: A Pictorial History of the War, 1861–1865.* New York: Macmillan, 1952.

Faust, Drew Gilpin. *This Republic of Suffering: Death and the American Civil War.* New York: Alfred A. Knopf, 2008.

Forbes, Edwin. *Thirty Years After: An Artist's Memoir of the Civil War.* Baton Rouge: Louisiana University Press, 1993.

Foresta, Merry A. *American Photographs: The First Century.* Washington, D.C.: Smithsonian Institution Press, 1996.

Foresta, Merry A., and John Wood. *Secrets of the Dark Chamber: The Art of the American Daguerreotype.* Washington, D.C.: Smithsonian Institution Press, 1995.

Frassanito, William A. *Antietam: The Photographic Legacy of America's Bloodiest Day.* New York: Charles Scribner's Sons, 1978.

————. *Early Photography at Gettysburg.* Gettysburg, PA: Thomas Publications, 1995.

————. *Gettysburg: A Journey in Time.* New York: Charles Scribner's Sons, 1975.

————. *Grant and Lee: The Virginia Campaigns, 1864–1865.* New York: Charles Scribner's Sons, 1983.

Freeman, Douglas Southall. *Lee: An Abridgment in One Volume by Richard Harwell of the Four-Volume R. E. Lee.* New York: Charles Scribner's Sons, 1991.

Furgurson, Ernest B. *Freedom Rising: Washington in the Civil War.* New York: Alfred A. Knopf, 2004.

Gardner, Alexander. *Gardner's Photographic Sketch Book of the War.* Washington, D.C.: Philp and Solomons, 1865–66.

Garrison, Webb. *Brady's Civil War.* New York: Salamander Books/The Lyons Press, 2000.

Gillespie, Sarah Catherine. "Samuel F. B. Morse and the Daguerreotype: Art and Science in American Culture, 1835–55" (doctoral dissertation). City University of New York, 2006.

Goodheart, Adam. *1861: The Civil War Awakening.* New York: Alfred A. Knopf, 2011.

Goodwin, Doris Kearns. *Team of Rivals: The Political Genius of Abraham Lincoln.* New York: Simon and Schuster, 2005.

Grant, Ulysses S. *Memoirs and Selected Letters: Personal Memoirs of U. S. Grant.* New York: The Library of America, 1990.

Greeley, Horace. *Glances at Europe in a Series of Letters from Great Britain, France, Italy, Switzerland, &c. During the Summer of 1851, Including Notices of the Great Exhibition, or World's Fair.* New York: Dewitt and Davenport, 1851.

Harris, Neil. *Humbug: The Art of P. T. Barnum.* Boston: Little, Brown and Company, 1973.

Hedren, Paul L. *With Crook in the Black Hills: Stanley J. Morrow's 1876 Photographic Legacy.* Boulder, CO: Pruett Publishing Company, 1985.

Hitchcock, Henry. *Marching with Sherman: Passages from the Letters and Campaign Diaries of Henry Hitchcock, November 1864–May 1865.* New Haven, CT: Yale University Press, 1927.

Holden, A. W. *A History of the Town of Queensbury, in the State of New York.* Albany, NY: J. Munsell, 1874.

Holmes, Oliver Wendell. *Soundings from The Atlantic.* Boston: Ticknor and Fields, 1864.

Holzer, Harold, ed. *Hearts Touched by Fire: The Best of Battles and Leaders of the Civil War.* New York: Modern Library, 2011.

————, ed. *Lincoln and New York.* New York: New-York Historical Society/Philip Wilson Publishers, 2009.

————. *Lincoln at the Cooper Union: The Speech That Made Abraham Lincoln President.* New York: Simon and Schuster, 2004.

Horan, James D. *Mathew Brady: Historian with a Camera.* New York: Bonanza Books, 1955.

————. *Timothy O'Sullivan: America's Forgotten Photographer.* New York: Bonanza Books, 1966.

Howe, Daniel Walker. *What Hath God Wrought: The Transformation of America, 1815–1848.* New York: Oxford University Press, 2007.

James, Henry. *A Small Boy and Others.* New York: Charles Scribner's Sons, 1913.

Jampoler, Andrew C. A. *The Last Lincoln Conspirator: John Surratt's Flight from the Gallows.* Annapolis, MD: Naval Institute Press, 2008.

Jenkins, Reese V. *Images and Enterprise: Technology and the American Photographic Industry, 1839 to 1925.* Baltimore, MD: Johns Hopkins University Press, 1975.

Johnson, Brooks. *An Enduring Interest: The Photographs of Alexander Gardner.* Norfolk, VA: The Chrysler Museum, 1991.

Jurovics, Toby, Carol M. Johnson, Glenn Willumson, and William F. Stapp, *Framing the West: The Survey Photographs of Timothy H. O'Sullivan.* New Haven, CT: Yale University Press, 2010.

Kalasky, Robert J. *Shadows of Antietam.* Kent, OH: Kent State University Press, 2012.

Katz, D. Mark. *Witness to an Era: The Life and Photographs of Alexander Gardner.* New York: Viking, 1991.

Kelly, James Edward. Edited by William B. Styple. *Tell Me of Lincoln: Memories of Abraham Lincoln, the Civil War, and Life in Old New York.* Kearny, NJ: Belle Grove Publishing Co., 2009.

Kunhardt, Dorothy Meserve, Philip B. Kunhardt Jr., and the Editors of Time-Life Books. *Mathew Brady and His World.* Alexandria, VA: Time-Life Books, 1977.

Kunhardt, Philip B. Jr., Philip B. Kunhardt III, and Peter W. Kunhardt. *Lincoln: An Illustrated Biography.* New York: Alfred A. Knopf, 1992.

Kunhardt, Philip B. III, Peter W. Kunhardt, and Philip B. Kunhardt Jr. *Lincoln, Life-Size.* New York: Alfred A. Knopf, 2009.

Leech, Margaret. *Reveille in Washington.* New York: Harper and Row, 1941.

Long, E. B., with Barbara Long. *The Civil War Day by Day: An Almanac, 1861–1865.* Garden City, NY: Doubleday, 1971.

McPherson, James M. *Battle Cry of Freedom: The Civil War Era.* New York: Oxford University Press, 1988.

Marder, William, and Estelle Marder. *Anthony: The Man, the Company, the Cameras.* Plantation, FL: Pine Ridge Publishing Co., 1982.

Meredith, Roy. *Mathew B. Brady, Mr. Lincoln's Camera Man.* New York: Charles Scribner's Sons, 1946.

————. *Mathew Brady's Portrait of an Era.* New York: W. W. Norton, 1982.

Miller, Francis Trevelyan, ed. *The Photographic History of the Civil War in Ten Volumes.* New York: The Review of Reviews, 1912.

Nevins, Allan, ed. *Polk: The Diary of a President, 1845–1849.* London: Longmans, Green and Co., 1952.

Nevins, Allan, and Milton Halsey Thomas, eds., *The Diary of George Templeton Strong: The Civil War, 1860-1865.* New York: Macmillan, 1952.

Newhall, Beaumont. *The Daguerreotype in America.* New York: Dover Publications, 1976.

———. *The History of Photography from 1839 to the Present Day.* Revised and enlarged edition. New York: The Museum of Modern Art, 1964.

Palmquist, Peter E., and Thomas R. Kailbourn. *Pioneer Photographers from the Mississippi to the Continental Divide: A Biographical Dictionary, 1839–1865.* Stanford, CA: Stanford University Press, 2005.

Panzer, Mary. *Mathew Brady and the Image of History.* Washington, D.C.: Smithsonian Books for the National Portrait Gallery, 1997.

Pfister, Harold Francis. *Facing the Light: Historic American Portrait Daguerreotypes.* Washington, D.C.: National Portrait Gallery/Smithsonian Institution Press, 1978.

Pinkerton, Allan. *The Spy of the Rebellion.* Hartford, CT: M. A. Winter and Hatch, 1885.

Poore, Ben Perley. *Perley's Reminiscences of Sixty Years in the National Metropolis.* Tecumseh, MI: A. W. Mills, Publisher, 1886.

Porter, Horace. *Campaigning with Grant.* New York: The Century Co., 1907.

Prime, Samuel Irenaeus. *The Life of Samuel F. B. Morse: Inventor of the Electro-Magnetic Recording Telegraph.* New York: Appleton and Company, 1875

Remini, Robert V. *Henry Clay: Statesman for the Union.* New York: W. W. Norton, 1991.

Reynolds, David S. *Waking Giant: America in the Age of Jackson.* New York: Harper, 2008.

Root, M. A. *The Camera and the Pencil.* Philadelphia: J. B. Lippincott and Co., 1864.

Sandburg, Carl. *Abraham Lincoln: The Prairie Years and the War Years.* One-volume edition. New York: Harcourt, Brace and World, 1954.

Sandweiss, Martha A., ed. *Photography in Nineteenth-Century America.* Fort Worth, TX: Amon Carter Museum/Harry N. Abrams, 1991.

Sears, Stephen W. *Chancellorsville.* Boston: Houghton Mifflin, 1996.

———. *George B. McClellan: The Young Napoleon.* New York: Ticknor and Fields, 1988.

———. *Landscape Turned Red: The Battle of Antietam.* Boston: Houghton Mifflin, 1983.

Sherman, William Tecumseh. *Memoirs of General W. T. Sherman.* New York: The Library of America, 1990.

Silverman, Kenneth. *Lightning Man: The Accursed Life of Samuel F. B. Morse.* New York: Alfred A. Knopf, 2003.

Simpson, Brooks D., Stephen W. Sears, and Aaron Sheehan-Dean, ed. *The Civil War: The First Year Told by Those Who Lived It.* New York: The Library of America, 2011.

Smalley, George W. *Anglo-American Memories.* New York: G. P. Putnam's Sons, 1912.

Smith, Gene. *Lee and Grant: A Dual Biography.* New York: McGraw-Hill, 1984.

Smith, H. P., ed. *History of Warren County.* Syracuse, NY: D. Mason and Co., 1885.

Starr, Louis M. *Bohemian Brigade: Civil War Newsmen in Action.* New York: Alfred A. Knopf, 1954.

Sullivan, George. *In the Wake of Battle: The Civil War Images of Mathew Brady.* Munich: Prestel, 2004.

————. *Mathew Brady: His Life and Photographs.* New York: Cobblehill Books/Dutton, 1994.

Taft, Robert. *Photography and the American Scene: A Social History, 1839–1889.* New York: Macmillan, 1938.

Taylor, Joshua C. *William Page: The American Titian.* Chicago: University of Chicago Press, 1957.

Thumb, Tom. *Sketch of the Life: Personal Appearance, Character and Manners of Charles S. Stratton.* New York: Samuel Booth, 1874.

Trachtenberg, Alan. *Lincoln's Smile and Other Enigmas.* New York: Hill and Wang, 2007.

————. *Reading American Photographs: Images as History, Mathew Brady to Walker Evans.* New York: Hill and Wang, 1989.

Traubel, Horace. *With Walt Whitman in Camden, Volume 3.* New York: Rowman and Littlefield, 1914.

Villard, Henry. *Memoirs of Henry Villard, Journalist and Financier, 1835–1900.* Boston: Houghton, Mifflin and Company, 1904.

Ward, Geoffrey C. *The Civil War: An Illustrated History.* New York: Alfred A. Knopf, 1990.

Welling, William. *Photography in America: The Formative Years, 1839–1900.* New York: Thomas Y. Crowell, 1978.

Wilentz, Sean. *Chants Democratic: New York City and the Rise of the American Working Class, 1788–1850.* New York: Oxford University Press, 1984.

Williams, Robert C. *Horace Greeley: Champion of American Freedom.* New York: New York University Press, 2006.

Willis, N. Parker. *The Convalescent.* New York: Charles Scribner, 1859.

Wills, Garry. *Lincoln at Gettysburg: The Words That Remade America.* New York: Simon and Schuster, 1992.

Wilson, Robert. *The Explorer King: Adventure, Science, and the Great Diamond Hoax— Clarence King in the Old West.* New York: Scribner, 2006.

Wood, John, ed. *America and the Daguerreotype.* Iowa City: University of Iowa Press, 1991.

Youngblood, Wayne, and Ray Bonds. *Mathew B. Brady: America's First Great Photographer.* New York: Chartwell Books, 2010.

Zeller, Bob. *The Blue and Gray in Black and White: A History of Civil War Photography.* Westport, CT.: Praeger, 2005.

# Index

Italic page numbers indicate photographs.

## A Note on the Author

**Robert Wilson** is the editor of *The American Scholar* and a former editor of *Preservation*. His work has appeared in many publications, including *The Atlantic, Smithsonian, Discover, The New Republic, The Wilson Quarterly, The New York Times, The Washington Post*, and *USA Today*, where he was the books editor and columnist for eleven years. He is the author of *The Explorer King*, a biography of Clarence King, and the editor of *A Certain Somewhere: Writers on the Places They Remember*. He lives in Manassas, Virginia.